Fiscal Zoning and Land Use Controls

Fiscal Zoning and Land Use Controls,

The Economic Issues

Edited by
Edwin S. Mills
Wallace E. Oates
Princeton University

Lexington Books
D.C. Heath and Company
Lexington, Massachusetts
Toronto   London

Library of Congress Cataloging in Publication Data

Main entry under title:
Fiscal zoning and land use controls.

Includes bibliographies.
1. Local finance—Addresses, essays, lectures. 2. Municipal services—Addresses, essays, lectures. 3. Property tax—Addresses, essays, lectures. 4. Industries, Location of—Addresses, essays, lectures. I. Mills, Edwin S. II. Oates, Wallace E.
HJ9105.F57   336'.014   74-21877
ISBN 0-669-96685-1

Published simultaneously in Canada

Printed in the United States of America

International Standard Book Number: 0-669-96685-1

Library of Congress Catalog Card Number: 74-21877

To the memory of
Neil David Sosnow

Contents

List of Figures

List of Tables

Preface

Until a few years ago, economists had only a normative theory of government. The paradigm went as follows: "Here is a resource allocation problem that markets cannot handle well, because of monopoly, externalities, public goods or whatever. On the assumption that government is there to improve social welfare, here is what it can do to improve the situation." Sections on "policy implications" at the ends of applied research papers typically followed this format.

All this has changed in recent years with the development of positive theories of government. In a democracy, elected officials compete for the support of voters and interest groups, and executive agencies respond to elected officials, interest groups and the structure of government institutions. These obvious facts have increasingly led economists, as well as other social scientists, to analyze the likely behavior of government institutions as a function of the political environment. The result has been, not to replace the normative theory, but to develop a much stronger sense of what governments can and cannot do, are likely or unlikely to do, in specific situations.

Nowhere has the new positive theory of government been more productive of insights than in the study of local government finance. The U.S. constitution permits great flexibility in the organization of local government. Charles Tiebout provided the first systematic analysis of the notion that this flexibility provides residents the opportunity and incentive to organize local governments in ways that further their parochial interests. In the years since Tiebout wrote, his analysis has been the subject of much comment. Yet it is remarkable how little careful formulation, analysis, estimation and testing have been done. The purpose of the studies in this volume is to help fill this gap. The ways in which the instruments of local government are used to further residents' interests are indeed varied and subtle.

The notion that government is endogenous rather than exogenous to an enlarged economic system goes back at least to Marx. Marx lacked, among other things, a careful distinction between positive and normative economics. The essays in this volume are almost entirely positive. Understanding how a system works is of course logically prior to evaluating its performance. Within the limits imposed by human fallibility, we have stuck to the former issue.

1

The Theory of Local Public Services and Finance: Its Relevance to Urban Fiscal and Zoning Behavior

Edwin S. Mills and
Wallace E. Oates

Almost twenty years ago, Charles Tiebout published a theoretical model of local finance, a model which is now a familiar classic to all students of the subject [12]. The Tiebout model has come to serve as the point of departure for a now lengthy series of theoretical and empirical investigations into local fiscal behavior, particularly studies of metropolitan areas. Although questions remain as to the extent to which Tiebout forces operate in the local public sector, the "sorting-out" process envisioned in the model does seem to possess both considerable descriptive power and important, if controversial, prescriptive implications. On rereading the paper, particularly in light of recent work in local finance and urban economics, we are struck both by the insights and the unresolved problems inherent in the Tiebout treatment. It is quite remarkable, for example, that current studies of urban fiscal problems reach back to a model that contains no mention of a central city and no explicit treatment of local taxation!

For these reasons, we begin this essay with an interpretive review of the original Tiebout model. In the second half of the paper, we consider the application of this structure (including later embellishments) to our understanding of urban fiscal and land-use control policies. It should be noted that it is not our intent to present here a comprehensive survey of the expanding literature on these subjects; rather, we provide background and perspective for the detailed studies that make up this volume.

The Tiebout Model

The Tiebout model of local finance is a static model in which mobile consumers select a community of residence in accordance with their preferences for outputs of local public services; by "voting with their feet," individuals reveal their preferences for local public services and promote an allocation of resources patterned on individual tastes.[a]

---

[a]We stress at the outset that by "local public services" we do not mean pure Samuelsonian public goods which exhibit zero congestion costs; on the contrary, costs of congestion are at the heart of the Tiebout formulation. In addition, there is no presumption that these jointly consumed services need be provided through the public budget. More on all this shortly.

1

The central idea of the Tiebout model is hardly new. The literature in both politics and economics reaching back many decades contains numerous references to this important property of decentralized decision making: it allows individuals with similar demands to provide public services to their liking. Alexis de Tocqueville, in observing the American political system, pointed this out and noted that, "In great centralized nations the legislator is obliged to give a character of uniformity to the laws, which does not always suit the diversity of customs and of districts"[4]. Whereas the basic idea is thus an old one, it was Tiebout's contribution to place it in the corpus of economic theory by constructing a formal model which clarified the implications of the decentralized provision of public services for economic efficiency.

Tiebout's paper served a second purpose. Samuelson had recently published his famous papers on the theory of public expenditure which, along with Musgrave's earlier work, showed that, although there exists a conceptual solution to the problem of the determination of the efficient level of output of a public service, there is in general no way to attain this solution under a system of decentralized decision making because of the incentive for individuals to understate their true preferences [11,9]. Tiebout showed, however, that there exists an important class of public services, namely those whose consumption is limited to a group of individuals in a specific geographic area, for which such a solution is at least conceptually possible. Individuals reveal their preferences for local public services by their choice of a community in which to reside and, in so doing, promote an efficient use of resources in the public sector.

It is instructive to look in more detail at the structure of the model. Tiebout assumed a world of perfectly mobile consumers, each with perfect knowledge of the public expenditure and revenue programs available in a large number of possible communities of residence. Each community offers a *given* level of output of the public service which is provided at minimum cost, and the household selects the municipality that provides the level of the public service that best approximates its demand. If there is a wide range of choice available, a household can find a community which offers a level of the public service close to its desired level.

So far it seems simple enough. Ambiguities arise, however, as to the characteristics of the public services provided by localities. Tiebout assumed that each community provides a "bundle" of outputs of n local public services. For this bundle, there exists an optimum community size.

This optimum is defined in terms of the number of residents for which this bundle of services can be produced at the lowest average cost. This, of course, is closely analogous to the low point of a firm's average cost curve [12, p. 419].

The reason that Tiebout assumed a U-shaped unit cost curve is clear. If unit cost declined at every output level, ''there would be no logical reason to limit community size, given preference patterns,'' (p. 419). Thus, the basic distinction between local and higher levels of government would become blurred.

Of course, Tiebout wrote before publication of the many papers that have attempted to clarify the public-good notion in recent years. But it is clear that Tiebout's local public services are not pure Samuelsonian public goods. The unit cost function for providing more or less of a pure public good *for a given population* may indeed be U-shaped. But the defining characteristic of a pure public good is that no additional inputs are required to extend the existing per capita consumption to additional citizens. The marginal cost of providing a given per capita output to additional citizens is thus zero for a pure public good, neither a realistic description of most services provided by local, or other, governments nor what Tiebout had in mind. He was clearly thinking of public services with the property that the cost of providing a given service level to additional citizens rose, at least beyond a modest number of citizens served.

What is the explanation for the U-shape of the average cost curve for a local public service? Tiebout suggested the presence of some fixed factor, perhaps the amount of land available to the community. What he had in mind is made clear by his example of a beach of a given size in a community. Community members' utility levels depend on the amount of beach available per person; more people mean a more crowded beach. The public service is thus subject to costs of congestion. In fact, we really cannot even determine the level of consumption of the public good apart from the size of the group.

Tiebout apparently envisioned a formulation similar to that of Buchanan [3]. In his theory of clubs, Buchanan postulated that the level of output provided to the members of the club is jointly dependent on the inputs and the size of the membership; in Buchanan's example of a swimming club, the level of ''swimming services'' provided depends on both the size of the pool and the number of swimmers. The optimization problem is to find the combination of pool size and membership for which a given level of swimming services can be provided most cheaply. This, in our view, is identical with the Tiebout solution, although it is admittedly not fully explicit in Tiebout's analysis.

Even if we are able to define conceptually the optimum size community, there remains the further issue of the process of group formation which will realize and sustain this outcome. How do people sort themselves out and, once they are sorted, is the solution a stable one? On this matter, Tiebout offers only a few informal remarks: ''Clearly, communities below the optimum size, through chambers of commerce or other agencies, seek to attract new residents'' (page 419), and ''Again, proper zoning laws, implicit agreements among realtors, and the like are sufficient to keep the population stable'' (page 420).

This is not very satisfactory. If we introduce explicitly a local revenue system, important and difficult problems arise concerning the stability of the Tiebout system. Consider, for example, the realistic case in which public services are financed by a local property tax. Then it would be in the interest of an individual household to locate in a community with property of relatively high value in order to consume public services at a comparatively low "tax price" per unit. It is not hard to visualize an unstable process in which wealthy households locate together to consume high levels of public services only to find their jurisdiction "invaded" by poorer households seeking to take advantage of the large tax base (and hence low tax price) that the concentration of wealth permits.[b] In Chapter 2 of this volume, Hamilton demonstrates that order can be brought to this world by the introduction of a particular form of local zoning policy; this results not only in a stable solution, but also a solution in which the property tax becomes a perfect benefit tax, generating no deadweight losses, and in which the efficiency properties of the Tiebout solution are reestablished.

At any rate, Tiebout assumed that, through mechanisms such as programs to attract new residents or, alternatively, restrictive zoning laws and realty practices, communities attain optimum size. Such a pattern of location promotes an efficient allocation of resources, since individuals consume levels of output which approximate their true demand for these services.[c]

The parallel between this outcome and that generated by the market mechanism in the private sector can be illustrated as follows. Consider a man who wishes to purchase three shirts. Under the market system, he goes to a store that sells shirts and buys three. The analogy to the Tiebout model is a system of shirt stores each of which sells packages containing a specified number of shirts; we have one-shirt stores, two-shirt stores, etc. In this system, our individual (along with others with the same demand) goes to a three-shirt store. Note that under both systems, the individual is able to buy the number of shirts he desires. Tiebout sums up these similarities:

Just as the consumer may be visualized as walking to a private market place to buy his goods, the prices of which are set, we place him in the position of walking to a community where the prices (taxes) of community services are set. Both trips take the consumer to market. There is no way in which the consumer can avoid revealing his preferences in a spatial economy. Spatial mobility provides the local public-goods counterpart to the private market's shopping trip [12, p. 422].

---

[b]Tiebout noted this possibility in a later paper; see [13].

[c]Tiebout assumed earlier an absence of intercommunity externalities so that we need not worry about this source of inefficiencies.

Although he makes references to local taxes, at no point in his model does Tiebout specify the revenue system used by communities. A consumer presumably selects his community of residence by weighing the benefits of available public services against the prospective tax bill. Efficiency requires that there be enough communities to offer a sufficient range of combinations of local public services and that each citizen in a given community pay the marginal cost of its service bundle. A head tax would be the simplest perfect benefit tax. In contrast, efficient finance of local government through real estate taxes requires that there by enough local governments so that a citizen can find a community that provides not only the service bundle he wants, but also a tax rate such that the house he wants will yield tax revenues equal to marginal public service costs. Finance by taxes on income or sales requires other cross-classifications and may lead to inefficiencies.[d] We can only infer from his comparison between his model and the operation of private markets that Tiebout had in mind an efficient benefit tax to finance local governments. Otherwise, the optimality properties of his model would not obtain.

Before proceeding to specifically urban issues, we want to clarify one further aspect of the Tiebout analysis. It should be stressed that Tiebout's concern was solely with efficient resource use: the model describes an organization of the local public sector in which service levels are matched with individual tastes. It is clear, however, that the Tiebout model has some extremely important distributional implications. Once we recognize that the demand for public services is systematically related to income, we see that the Tiebout model implies powerful tendencies toward segregation by income level. In a Tiebout world of a large number of small fiscal jurisdictions, we would expect to find high-income households locating together in communities with high levels of public services, and conversely. In Chapter 4, Hamilton, Mills, and Puryear examine and document the extent of this income segregation in U.S. metropolitan areas.

This implies that a fragmented local fiscal structure of the Tiebout sort blunts the potential for redistribution of income through the local public sector. To take the polar case, consider a Tiebout system in which the demand for public services is perfectly correlated with income; then the sorting-out process leads to the formation of communities perfectly homogeneous in income so that there are no redistributive effects emanating from the local fiscal system. In contrast, if we envision a world of larger fiscal jurisdictions (involving perhaps metropolitan governments) with a reliance on income-related sources of revenues, we can see possibilities for achieving some equalizing effects through the local fiscal structure.[e]

---

[d]This point is explored in more depth in [10, ch. 4].

[e]For an examination of this issue including some quantitative estimates of potential redistributive effects, see [2].

Finally, we note that Tiebout analyzes only one mechanism for satisfying household tastes for public services: consumer mobility. He assumes that moving costs are zero and that locational preferences depend only on local public service and tax provisions, and not on locations of work, friends, or relatives. Neither assumption is, of course, true. If the demand for local public services rises to the same extent for every resident of a community, (e.g., because their incomes increase), they can continue to provide an optimum level of local public services without moving by simply voting for the desired increases in service levels and the corresponding rise in taxes. Realistically, demands for local public services change in more complex ways, as incomes change and people move through the life cycle. Then, at least some people must move to different communities in order to obtain the desired bundle of public services. Such moves are expensive, although the needed frequency of moves is unclear. In fact, there are conflicts about the local public service bundle even within small communities. In addition, residents sometimes resort to private purchase of a service, such as schooling, if the public sector does not satisfy their demands. Moving is only one of several options available to the household to achieve its desired consumption of local public services; it can also try to induce changes in the local budget through the community's process of collective choice or it can seek to provide the service through private activity. These facts suggest, incidentally, that the mechanisms for adjusting local public-service supplies and demands are far from perfect. Moreover, they are presumably more imperfect in large communities, such as central cities, than in small suburban communities.

Analysis of Urban Zoning and Fiscal Behavior

We turn now to the application of this body of theory to urban land-use and fiscal patterns. We noted earlier the problems inherent in the formation of Tiebout-type communities in the presence of income-related forms of local taxes. In particular, there exists the incentive for households with relatively low housing consumption to enter wealthier communities where they can consume public services at a relatively low tax price. This establishes the rationale for "fiscal zoning" to exclude such entrants. White, in Chapter 3, explores such fiscal zoning strategies and their implications for resource use and the distribution of income. The precise form of the regulation and its effects depend in large measure on which groups within the community are able to enforce their interests and what they perceive to be their objectives. As White points out, there are a number of different strategies that fiscal zoning may embody.

There is a second source of exclusionary practices. It is important to emphasize that the Tiebout model involves the consumption of service bundles with differing mixes of *outputs*. Some observers are inclined to regard the model of limited relevance, because it seems likely that individuals do not give much consideration to the budget of the police force or the number of fire engines in selecting their jurisdiction of residence. The conclusion is that, for most local services (public education perhaps being an exception), local public budgets are likely to have little influence on individual location decisions. This line of reasoning is, however, misleading because it focuses on inputs rather than on the associated service levels that presumably enter the individual's utility function. Individuals care about the level of safety afforded by each jurisdiction, which depends upon a number of local "environmental" variables as well as inputs purchased through the public budget.[f] There is almost certainly a good deal more variation among jurisdictions within metropolitan areas in levels of services that matter to households than a tabulation of public service inputs would suggest. This is reinforced by the fact that many of the local "services" consumed collectively may have little to do with the public budget, but may depend for example, on the local terrain. It is interesting that Tiebout in his classic paper chose to illustrate his model by a local beach. The point here is that, in a Tiebout world, individuals congregate in communities according to their similarity in preferences for a range of community "characteristics" that they enjoy in common.

This distinction raises the important question of the extent to which public budgetary actions influence the *outputs* of local services. It may be the case for some services (as suggested by the Coleman Report and certain studies of crime rates) that community characteristics are far more important in determining the levels of collectively consumed services than are budgetary inputs. We need further evidence in this matter, but if the conjecture is true, it carries important implications for local policy.[g]

Suppose, for instance, that the primary determinants of the quality of local schools and the level of personal safety are characteristics such as income levels and attitudes of the residents of the community; regardless of the local school budget or police expenditure, children get a good education if they attend schools populated by bright highly motivated pupils, and the streets are safe if the community is populated by responsible, law-abiding people. Then, a local jurisdiction can exert a much greater influence over the levels of public *outputs* through policy variables that control the make-up of the community than through the local budget. This suggests the

---

[f]For a systematic treatment of the relationship between inputs and public-service outputs, see [1].

[g]It is likely, for example, that crime rates depend much more on characteristics of the local population (poverty, racial antagonisms, etc.) than on the level and allocation of police resources.

critical importance to a locality of various zoning and land-use regulations by which residents can regulate, to some extent at least, entry into the community. These policy variables may dwarf in importance local fiscal variables for purposes of determining output levels of some local services.

Note that we have established a second rationale for local zoning activity. We will term this "public-goods zoning." Under fiscal zoning, residents of a community set admission requirements such that new entrants to the jurisdiction pay at least their share of the public budget. Under public-goods zoning, existing residents try to control characteristics of newcomers that result in higher levels of particularly important local services.

It may be difficult to distinguish between these two forms of zoning. For example, a regulation requiring large lot sizes may be motivated by the desire both to generate substantial inflows into the local treasury and to limit entry to well-to-do and, hopefully, responsible residents. There is little doubt, however, that both elements have been influential in the determination of zoning practices.

In other instances, the objectives of fiscal zoning and public-goods zoning may be in conflict. In Chapter 5, Fischel adopts a conceptual framework of this general sort to explain the location of firms in metropolitan areas. He views the members of a community as consuming jointly a public good called "environmental quality" the level of which varies inversely with the number of firms in the community. The locality must decide how much of its environmental quality it wishes to trade in exchange for the fiscal benefits (lower taxes or, more accurately, lower tax prices) that firms bring to the jurisdiction. Here, a mechanism to control the entry of firms becomes critical in determining the level of environmental quality in the community.[h] Fischel finds, moreover, that his model helps to explain locations of firms and fiscal patterns in northeastern New Jersey. This would seem to be a case where there is a tradeoff between the incentives for fiscal zoning and those for public-goods zoning.

It should be noted that Fischel's model assumes that environmental deterioration depends only on the number of firms admitted to the community. At least some kinds of firms may impart an inevitably inferior ambience to the community. But it is not the appropriate assumption regarding discharges of polluting substances. Pollution depends not only on numbers of firms but also on the details of resource use, e.g., whether and how wastes are treated before discharge. The appropriate place of land use controls in a menu of government environmental policies remains an open issue.

All the studies in this volume focus on metropolitan fiscal and land-use

---

[h]Fischel also allows for effects on environmental quality operating through the local budget.

policies, for it seems clear that the Tiebout model is more likely to have descriptive and prescriptive value in metropolitan areas than elsewhere. Only in metropolitan areas is there sufficient spatial concentration of population and employment to permit choice among even a modest range of local public service bundles. Yet we are struck by the absence of specific spatial considerations in discussions of the Tiebout model. Spatial models of private markets in metropolitan areas are by comparison highly developed.[i] Yet these spatial models contain almost nothing recognizable as a public sector.

There is great variability in local government systems among U.S. metropolitan areas. But the average metropolitan area consists of a central city, containing about half the population and a somewhat larger fraction of the jobs in the metropolitan area, and several contiguous suburban jurisdictions. Most of the specifically spatial issues of the Tiebout model, as well as many of our most serious social problems, are concerned with the relationships between central-city and suburban governments.

Whatever efficiency-promoting properties a Tiebout world may have for suburban governments, it is hard to imagine that they carry over to central-city governments.[j] Most central cities are almost certainly too large and too diverse to be able to provide public service bundles tailored to the needs of particular segments of their populations, and constitutional considerations greatly limit their legal ability to do so. Indeed, the diversity of public service demands between black and white, rich and poor, in central cities accounts for the prevalence of conflict and confrontation in their politics.

In a Tiebout-like metropolitan area, central-city residents get the short end of the stick regarding not only efficiency, but also in the equity aspects of the provision of local public services. We noted earlier the incentives for high-income households to form exclusionary suburban communities in which to consume levels of public services well suited to their tastes while preventing the intrusion of those with lower incomes whose fiscal contributions would be disproportionately small. One consequence of this is that many poorer (particularly black) households find themselves virtually stranded as a residual population of the central city. This means that the change from the typical prewar situation, in which most metropolitan residents lived in central cities, to the postwar situation, in which many high-income residents live in exclusionary suburbs, has tended to deprive the poor of most of the redistributive benefits accruing to the poor, while conferring benefits on upper-income households both in terms of reduced transfers through the local public sector and an enhanced efficiency in the

[i]For a survey, see [8].

[j]This point is developed in [2].

local services they consume. No one knows how much income redistribution resulted from prewar activity of city governments. It is easy to interpret the historical record as saying that it was not large. What is certain is that the present organization of governments in metropolitan areas makes it virtually impossible for them to redistribute income. That is a fact, but it is not necessarily a great loss, since a case can be made that income redistribution is best carried out at the national level.

The above discussion of equity and efficiency is independent of whether the search for exclusionary suburbs has distorted the spatial structure of urban areas. There is much misunderstanding on this issue. Some popular authors write as though the search for exclusionary suburbs were the main reason that postwar metropolitan growth has spilled across central-city boundaries. But it is clear that the expansion has resulted mainly from metropolitan growth, high income, cheap urban transportation, etc. Other authors believe that the availability of exclusionary suburbs is the sole reason that the high-income residents are more suburbanized than the low-income residents of metropolitan areas. But work in urban economics indicates that the relationship between housing demand and commuting cost can account for the propensity of high-income residents to live further from metropolitan centers than do low-income residents, even in the absence of a public sector.[k] Nevertheless, the Tiebout-like organization of suburban governments imposes a constraint on housing location in addition to those imposed by work locations, commuting costs, the availability of different types of housing, etc. This must mean that some people live, and probably work, in places other than those in which they would live and work if there were, for example, a metropolitan area-wide government. The result is undoubtedly more commuting than there would otherwise be.[l] There is also lively debate as to whether the continuing suburbanization of jobs has generated higher unemployment rates in the central cities. This outmigration of upper-income households and employment opportunities has, many people believe, left in central-city ghettos a concentration of poor blacks that exacerbates the dysfunctional characteristics, such as crime and drug abuse, that plague central cities.[m]

Let us return to the basic mechanism of the Tiebout model: consumer mobility in accord with demand for local public services. Some critics have argued that the mobility envisioned by the Tiebout model does not exist because of the information and moving costs of the relocation process. But it is not clear that the Tiebout model intends many moves. For example, accessibility and quality of public schools become important as children

---

[k]See [7, ch. 5] and the references cited therein.

[l]This notion has been formalized in [6].

[m]For a perceptive discussion of these issues, see [5].

approach school age. But that is often a time when families want to make a move anyway, just because increasing numbers and sizes of children make a larger dwelling desirable. Then all that is involved is the addition of new considerations in a move that would be made because of changing family composition. In addition, moves are frequently necessitated by a change in job location. When a household is forced to relocate, either in another metropolitan area or in another section of the same area, there typically exists considerable scope for choice among residental communities. At such a juncture "shopping" takes place. Individuals seek to determine the collective-good characteristics (including the quality of schools, tax rates, aesthetic qualities, etc.) of the alternative communities within a reasonable commuting range of their place of employment. "Mobility" may thus not require that each household stand ready to move immediately when a more attractive consumption bundle becomes available elsewhere. "Normal" moves may provide a reasonably adequate mechanism for the expression of tastes for local public goods. Thus, common sense and casual empiricism do not lead us to doubt that there is sufficient mobility in the U.S. to create and maintain many Tiebout-like metropolitan suburbs. But hard facts have the loudest voice on this issue, and some are presented in this volume.

Even with a substantial degree of consumer mobility in U.S. urban areas, outcomes depend on the structures for local choice, including budgetary systems and land-use controls. We noted earlier some serious omissions in the Tiebout formulation: unresolved issues concerning the process of community formation and its stability, and the absence of explicit treatment of local tax systems. For reasons we have discussed, it seems clear that local decision variables concerning admission to the community and land-use activities are of crucial importance both in the formation of a "stable" community and in the determination of levels of jointly consumed public services. In this volume we seek to explore these relationships. In particular, we attempt to develop a more integrated and comprehensive description of institutions for decentralized public decisions.

References

[1] Bradford, David, R. Malt, and W. Oates, "The Rising Cost of Local Public Services: Some Evidence and Reflections," *National Tax Journal,* 22 (June 1969): 185-202.
[2] Bradford, David, and Wallace Oates, "Suburban Exploitation of Central Cities and Government Structure," in Harold Hochman and George Peterson, eds., *Redistribution through Public Choice* (New York: Columbia University Press, 1974), pp. 43-90.

[3] Buchanan, James, "An Economic Theory of Clubs," *Economica* 32 (February 1965): 1-14.

[4] de Tocqueville, Alexis, *Democracy in America* (New York: Vintage Books, 1945), vol. I, p. 169.

[5] Downs, Anthony, *Opening up the Suburbs* (New Haven: Yale University Press, 1973).

[6] Goetz, Charles, and James Buchanan, "Efficiency Limits of Fiscal Mobility: An Assessment of the Tiebout Model," *Journal of Public Economics* 1 (April 1972): 25-44.

[7] Mills, Edwin, *Urban Economics* (Glenview, Ill.: Scott, Foresman, 1972).

[8] Mills, Edwin, and James MacKinnon, "Notes on the New Urban Economics," *Bell Journal of Economics and Management Science* 4, no. 2 (Autumn 1973): 593-601.

[9] Musgrave, Richard, "The Voluntary Exchange Theory of Public Economy," *Quarterly Journal of Economics* 52 (February 1939): 213-237.

[10] Oates, Wallace, *Fiscal Federalism* (New York: Harcourt Brace Jovanovich, 1972).

[11] Samuelson, Paul, "The Pure Theory of Public Expenditures," *Review of Economics and Statistics* 36 (November 1954): 387-389.

[12] Reprinted from "A Pure Theory of Local Expenditure," Tiebout, Charles, *Journal of Political Economy* 64, by permission of the University of Chicago (October 1956): 416-424. Copyright 1956 by the University of Chicago.

[13] Tiebout, Charles, "An Economic Theory of Fiscal Decentralization," in *Public Finance: Needs, Sources and Utilization* (Princeton: Princeton University Press, 1961).

2 Property Taxes and the Tiebout Hypothesis: Some Empirical Evidence

Bruce W. Hamilton

Tiebout's basic argument is that the existence of choice among communities (that is, choice among public-service offerings) transforms the local public economy into a quasi market, complete with market-like efficiency properties. Yet choice among consumption bundles is not sufficient to obtain Pareto efficiency. We need prices in order to ensure that consumption decisions are made with proper regard for scarcity. Tiebout himself made almost no mention of the price problem, and subsequent research has also tended to focus on other questions. The most important recent strand of research in local public finance is based upon Buchanan's theory of clubs [1], which is that context is concerned with the relationship between the cost (as distinct from the price) of providing a given level of the service and the number of members of the sharing "club" or community. Thus, Buchanan and Goetz [2] assume that (by some unspecified mechanism) it is possible to charge marginal-cost prices to all club members, and then ask whether such a system would be efficient. They are concerned, therefore, with the nature of the goods provided by local governments, and with the ability of an idealized quasi market to provide the good efficiently. Here, on the other hand, we settle for gross oversimplification with regard to the nature of goods provided by local governments, and deal explicitly with the mechanism whereby people pay for the local public services they consume. For if the mechanism for financing local public goods does not have the characteristics of a price, then it is impossible to make the case that the local public economy is an efficient market analogue. As the major revenue instrument of local governments in the United States is the property tax, the public sector can approximate a market only to the extent that the property tax does efficiently ration public-service consumption.

Using the model described in the next section, we have shown [4] that, in an urban area with a large number of independent jurisdictions, judicious use of zoning can convert the residential property tax into an efficient price for local public services. But, it should be emphasized that the empirical work discussed below is a test of a much more general version of the Tiebout hypothesis.

If consumers treat the local property tax as a price for public services, then this price should not distort the housing market any more than the price of eggs should distort the housing market. This statement is true

13

whether or not the details of the model discussed in the next section are an adequate description of reality. Any "tax" which is regarded by consumers as a price need not impose a deadweight loss in the market for the commodity that is nominally being taxed; whether or not the price tax *efficiently* rations the good provided by the taxing authority.

Following discussion of the model, we will offer the argument that the Tiebout mechanism does not function in the central cities of most American urban areas, and that property taxes are not, at the margin, a *quid pro quo* for the receipt of public services. From this it follows that the property tax in the central city does inhibit housing consumption in exactly the manner that an excise tax on any commodity inhibits its consumption. This leads to the prediction that the property tax will depress central-city residential property consumption relative to suburban consumption. If the property tax rate and the demand function for housing are known, it is possible to calculate the amount by which central-city housing consumption falls short of suburban consumption. In the discussion of our results, this predicted differential is calculated and empirical evidence is presented to show that, other arguments of the demand function being equal, central-city housing consumption is less than suburban consumption by an amount consistent with the prediction.

A Model with Zoning

The major weakness of the Tiebout mechanism appears to be that, whereas Tiebout has specified a device (namely migration), whereby consumers "shop" for local public services, he has failed to endow his mechanism with a system of prices for the local public services.[a] In the absence of constraints on the consumption of these services, they will be oversupplied or rationed by some inefficient method such as queueing.[b] Also, in the absence of the constraints that we built into the following model, the

[a]The model and much of the discussion in this section are taken from [4] and are reproduced here with the permission of *Urban Studies*.

[b]Actually, there are restraints on consumer behavior in the Tiebout model, but these restraints are not directed at the problem addressed here. Tiebout's Assumption 6 states in part, "there is an optimal community size . . . defined in terms of the number of residents for which this bundle of services can be produced at the lowest average cost" [7, p. 419]. He goes on to say that, in order to achieve this optimal size, it may be necessary to impose land-use restrictions, agreement among realtors, or something of the sort. However, he further states that, if a community is faced with the necessity of restricting entry, a second identical community can be formed to accommodate the overflow. So, except for the case of something like beachfront, which cannot be reproduced, there is no restriction in the Tiebout model on the number of people consuming any particular bundle of public services. And, there is no hint of a restriction on the *kinds* of people consuming a given bundle. (By different "kinds" of people, is meant people with different income, family size, and so on; in other words, people with different demands for public services.)

Tiebout hypothesis seems to be a formula for "musical suburbs," with the poor following the rich in a never-ending quest for a tax base. It may be that property values will be bid up in those jurisdictions with unusually favorable tax bases, and that entry is regulated by these inflated property values. But, if this is true, and if there is vacant land in the favorably endowed communities, the construction of all types of housing, including low-income housing, would be encouraged there. This process, if not prevented by some force such as zoning, would eliminate any land-price differential due to the favorable tax base. So we are forced back to the conclusion that zoning is necessary to exclude free riders if local services are financed with a property tax.

Casual empiricism suggests that the constraints missing from the Tiebout model are provided in the real world by various forms of land use restrictions classified here under the heading of zoning. We shall therefore construct a model containing the basic Tiebout assumptions, and containing as well the following two assumptions: (i) Local governments finance their operations solely with a proportional property tax (the tax rate may vary among communities); and (ii) each community is authorized to enact a "zoning ordinance" which states, "No household may reside in this community unless it consumes at least some minimum amount of housing."

With this model, it will be possible to derive the following results: (i) The local public service is distributed Pareto optimally, as suggested by Tiebout. (ii) The property tax acts as an efficient price for the public service, and carried no deadweight loss; that is, it does not inhibit property consumption as would a normal excise tax. (iii) All communities are perfectly homogeneous with respect to house value. (iv) Local governments are unable to engage in income redistribution. (v) In equilibrium, tax rates and levels of public-service provision are not capitalized into property values.

Consider an urban area in which there are three goods; x_1, consumption of housing per family; x_2, the local public services (again, per-family consumption); and x_3, a composite commodity consisting of the remainder of the household's consumption bundle. Each household has a utility function of the general from $U = U(x_1, x_2, x_3)$. Households have no locational preference per se; they locate so as to maximize U. There are many communities in the urban area, each of which provides its residents with some amount of x_2, financed by a proportional tax on x_1 (i.e., the local property tax). A community must provide the same amount of x_2 to each of its residents, but the provision can vary among communities, as can the property tax rate.

The zoning ordinance is now specified as follows: No household may live in community i unless its consumption of x_1 is greater than or equal to x'_{1i}, which should be a function of household size (that is, households with more members are required to consume more housing—the reason for this will become apparent).

Now we assume for the moment that x_2 is offered on the private market[c] at a price, p_2, equal to the marginal cost of producing x_2. If production is perfectly competitive, p_2 is also equal to the average cost in the long run. The consumer maximizes his utility function subject to the constraint $Y = p_1x_1 + p_2x_2 + p_3x_3$, deciding to consume some bundle (x_1^*, x_2^*, x_3^*). This (Pareto optimum) allocation will now be compared with the outcome under the system of specified local governments.

We now return this household to the world in which x_2 is provided by local governments. The household looks for a community that will yield the highest attainable level of utility. It can be shown that this search will lead the household to reside in a community whose minimum housing requirement x_1' is just equal to the household's actual x_1 consumption. A household that lives in a community whose x_1' is less than its housing consumption (it cannot legally reside in a community where x_1' exceeds its housing consumption), it can increase its utility by moving to a community with a more restrictive zoning ordinance. (Recall that the zoning ordinance in the old community was not binding on him.) This new community will have a higher tax *base* than the old one. It is thus in a position to provide a higher level of public service or a lower tax rate, or both. Thus, for any household that is consuming more x_1 than is required by the zoning ordinance of its community, there exists a move that will increase its utility. But, this means that in equilibrium no household in any community consumes more than that community's x_1'.

We have now shown that every household in a given community consumes the same amount of housing, pays the same amount in property taxes, and consumes the same amount of x_2. This implies that every household pays the average cost of the x_2 he consumes. Invoking the assumption that, for x_2, average cost = marginal cost = p_2, the household consumption possibilities are restricted to the set $Y = p_1x_1 + p_2x_2 + p_3x_3$. A community is defined in this space by the vector (x_1, x_2), the housing requirement and the public service provision.[d] A consumption bundle is feasible for the household if and only if it satisfies the budget constraint and the x_1 and x_2 arguments define a community that exists. In particular, the utility-maximizing bundle under the free market regime, (x_1^*, x_2^*, x_3^*), is feasible if there is some community for which $x_1^* = x_1'$ and $x_2^* = x_2'$. To the extent that there exist (or can be established) communities of sufficient

[c]To the extent that x_2 is a public good it cannot in fact be offered on the private market, since the nonexclusion character of public goods prevents the market mechanism from working. What is involved here, however, is simply a conceptual experiment where households reveal information contained in their utility functions.

[d]At this point, the definition of a community does not include a spatial component. (The issue of space is addressed in [4].)

diversity in an urban area, the budget constraint faced by the household when x_2 is provided by local governments is identical with the constraint it would face if x_2 were provided (competitively) by the private market. The model is seen to yield a Pareto optimum allocation of resources, since the consumption bundle is identical with the private market result.[e] A somewhat surprising corollary is that the local property tax carries no deadweight loss, since deadweight loss always involves a departure from the Pareto optimality. Note that it is not required that all residents of a community have the same income or the same utility function; it is only required that they all have the same x_1^*, x_2^*. And, this is not an assumption of the model, but a result derived from the assumptions.

The property tax in this model carries no deadweight loss because the tax payment bears no relationship to anything *except* the public services received from the local government. It is possible (by migration) to vary housing consumption without varying the total property tax bill, and vice versa. That is, for any given level of property tax payment (not rate), and its implied level of public-service provision, housing consumption can be varied as freely, and at the same cost to the consumer, as if there were no property tax.[f] This simply means that the property tax is not considered a part of the price of housing, which in turn means it cannot impose a deadweight loss on the housing market. The property tax is seen to be a price for the public services received by the household. This price performs all the rationing functions that the price mechanism performs in the private sector.

Oates [6] pointed out that if local governments finance their operations with a head tax, there will be efficiency in both the public and private sectors:

This scheme [a head tax] would tend to receive excellent marks on . . . efficiency criteria . . . since the tax price paid by the consumer reflects accurately the cost of the public goods he consumes, this system of finance introduces no incentives for inefficient behavior [6].

Oates further states that any other taxation scheme, such as a property tax, leads to deadweight loss and distortion of location preferences. The deadweight loss issue has already been discussed; location is dealt with in [4]. The reason for the discrepancy between these results and the Oates conclusion is that, through a system of specified zoning ordinances the property

---

[e]It is assumed here (along with Tiebout) that community formation is costless. However, it is not necessary to assume that urban land is free. The scarcity of urban land and the assumption that community formation is free will be examined presently.

[f]The mechanism of adjustment, i.e., migration, is undoubtedly quite costly. However, this is a discussion in comparative statics. The point I wish to make is that there is no necessary relationship between the property tax bill and real property consumption.

tax is here essentially transformed into a head tax (with a different tax per head in each community).[g]

All that has been established so far is the existence of a solution to the constrained maximization problem which yields Pareto optimality. No demonstration has been offered that the system has any tendency whatsoever to approach such a point. Some light can be shed on this subject by asking what the system would look like in a state of disequilibrium. Assume that there are fewer dwelling units of a given (x_1, x_2) specification than are demanded by the population of an urban area. The dwelling units that do possess these desirable (i.e., demanded) characteristics will be sought after by an excessive number of households, and will earn a rent. In other words, the value of such property will be bid up. Landlords will have missed an opportunity to maximize the value of their property if they do not devote more land to the relatively scarce activity. Only when all (x_1, x_2) demand sets have been satisfied will all the potential gains have been realized. At this point, property values are completely uncorrelated with levels of public-service provision, zoning restrictions, and property tax rates. That is, property tax rates and expenditure levels are not capitalized into property values. If such correlation exists—that is, if certain (x_1, x_2) vectors earn rent—there is an incentive on the part of landlords to transfer land into those activities which yield relatively high rents. The disequilibrium situation (i.e., a scarcity of some particular type of community) can be characterized by either a positive or a negative correlation between land values and such explanatory variables as tax rates and public-service expenditure. The direction of the correlation is determined by the types of communities that are in short supply.[h]

The Model in American Urban Areas

The model is one of small homogeneous suburbs. But many households in our urban areas do not live in such communities; they live in large heterogeneous central cities.[i] Central cities in general do not exclude

[g]In reality the true head tax would be more efficient, since this system would not require communities to be homogeneous with respect to house value, but only with respect to public service demand.

[h]The empirical work by Oates [5] indicates that property value is significantly correlated with public-service provision and tax rates in his sample. As indicated here and discussed at length in [4], it seems probable that Oates observed this result because his sample was in a state of disequilibrium.

[i]The contention that suburbs differ significantly from their central-cities in terms of homogeneity is supported by evidence reported by Mills, Puryear, and myself in Chapter 4. For a sample of 19 SMSAs, the mean central-city census tract Gini coefficient of income was found to exceed that for suburban tracts by 0.023, or about 9 percent. For only 3 of the 19 SMSAs did the surburban census tract average exceed that of the central city.

residents from their boundaries on the basis of housing consumption (although some residents may be excluded from some sections of cities). And it would appear to be impossible for a central-city resident to vary his housing consumption and his tax burden independently. It seems, then, that the property tax in the typical central city is a standard excise tax which drives a wedge between marginal rates of substitution and transformation. Thus housing consumption should be less, *ceteris paribus,* in the central city than in the suburbs by an amount to be calculated below.[j]

There are important reasons for doubting that the sharp city-suburb dichotomy described here actually exists. In the first place, it has been argued that central cities offer different levels of public services in different neighborhoods, and that they assess property at different rates as well. If this is the case the central city is really a collection of "communities," in the sense the term is used here, all within a single jurisdiction. While there is reason to believe that this is true to some extent, it is difficult to imagine what prevents those in control of the political machinery of a city from exploiting those out of control, at least by an amount equal to the cost of moving to the suburbs.

At the same time, the suburban public economy is undoubtedly not a perfect analogue to a market. For either or both of these reasons, the sharp city-suburb dichotomy postulated here may not exist. Whether such a dichotomy does exist is the subject of the empirical section below.

Empirical Results

A typical central-city property tax rate is on the order of 2 percent per annum of true market value, which translates into a tax of approximately 20 percent of annual gross rental value. This conversion is necessary in order to describe the tax as a percentage of the good which is purchased every time the tax is paid, namely a year's worth of housing services. The tax thus has the effect of raising the price of housing by about 20 percent (ignoring *for the moment* possible capitalization of tax liabilities into land values). In general such a tax would reduce housing consumption by

$$\Delta q = \alpha^{tq} \tag{2.1}$$

where Δq is the amount by which housing consumption is reduced, α is the price elasticity of demand for housing, t is the tax rate expressed as a

[j]As is explained more fully later on, it is not necessary to assume that the price of housing, aside from the way the tax is treated, is the same in city and suburb. Or rather, such an assumption is not necessary if the price elasticity of demand for housing is on the order of -1. In such a case (assuming the same demand function for city and suburb) and deviation of city from suburban prices (due, say, to the failure of the city to approximate a market) will be roughly offset by city-suburb differences in quantity demanded, leaving our dependent variable, house value, unchanged.

fraction of the price of housing, and q is the amount of housing that would be purchased in the absence of the tax. The percentage reduction in housing consumption, $\Delta q/q$, is equal to αt. If α is on the order of -1, the reduction in housing consumption due to a 2 percent annual property tax should thus be about 20 percent. An attempt will be made below to determine whether this housing consumption difference is observable between central city and suburb.

The hypothesis to be tested is that central-city residents regard the property tax as part of the price of housing, whereas suburban residents do not. Let p be the opportunity cost of the resources used in producing housing (including land), and let t be the tax rate as a fraction of p. According to the hypothesis, central-city residents face a housing price of $p(1 + t)$, whereas suburbanites face a housing price equal to p. The suburbanites treat their taxes as a price for pbulic services. The general expression for the price of housing faced by consumers is $p(1 + tD)$, where D is a dummy variable which takes on a value of 1 in the city and 0 in the suburbs. This expression is the "price" argument in the demand function for housing.

The demand function for housing is assumed to take the following form:

$$q_d = C Y^\beta F^\gamma [p(1 + tD)]^\alpha \qquad (2.2)$$

where

$\quad q_d = $ quantity of housing demanded

$\quad C = $ a constant

$\quad Y = $ family income

$\quad \beta = $ income elasticity of demand for housing

$\quad F = $ family size

$\quad \gamma = $ family size elasticity of demand for housing

$\quad p(1 + tD) = $ price of housing as defined above

$\quad \alpha = $ price elasticity of demand for housing

After some transformations to be described below, this equation will be estimated using 1960 Census data for 15 different SMSAs in the United States. A separate regression is run for each SMSA. Observations are the median values of the variables for census tracts, with 12 tracts each drawn from the central city and the suburban sections of the SMSAs.

Before estimation, equation (2.2) is manipulated as follows: First, both sides are multiplied by p. This transforms the dependent variable from quantity to house value, which has the obvious advantage of being observable. Then logs are taken of both sides of the equation:

$$\log(\text{val}) = \log(C) + \beta \log(Y) + \gamma \log(F)$$
$$+ (\alpha + 1) \log(p) + \alpha \log(1 + tD) \qquad (2.2a)$$

Two further transformations are required before this equation is ready for estimation. In addition to not being observable, p is jointly determined with q_d. It is replaced in the equation by u, a proxy for the price of housing which is defined as the distance of the census tract from the SMSAs central business district. The coefficient of $\log(u)$ cannot be interpreted as $(\alpha + 1)$, since the functional relationship between u and p has not been specified. This means that α is not identified in the equation to be estimated. However, all is not lost. If the coefficient (hereafter c_u) is not significantly different from zero, we can infer that α is not significantly different from -1 (the implication being that expenditure is invariant with respect to price).[k] Similarly, if c_u is positive, the demand for housing is elastic (note that u and p are inversely correlated with one another). And, of course vice versa if c_u is negative.[l]

Since the dummy, D, takes on values of zero and unity only, it can be removed from the log operator without changing the value of the term. Thus the final term in equation (2.2a) is

$$[\alpha \log(1 + t)]D$$

where D is the variable and the expression inside the square brackets is the coefficient to be estimated. Note that t is a part of a parameter to be estimated, and is not a set of observations on the central-city tax rate. The coefficient of D, when divided by α, is an estimate of the percentage by which the suburban price of housing differs from that in the central city, as inferred from observed city-suburb differences in pq_d.

The predicted value of t, as was described earlier, is about 0.2, which implies that the predicted value of $\log(1 + t)$ is about 0.18. Unfortunately, in order to compare the estimated coefficient (hereafter, c_D) with the predicted value of $\log(1 + t)$, we need to know, or assume, something about α. But α is not identified. This problem will be mitigated if we can make a case that α is on the order of -1, in which case $c_D = -\log(1 + t)$ and has a predicted value of -0.18.

The SMSAs in the sample, along with the SMSA population and number of school districts, are listed in Table 2-1. Four of the SMSAs were selected because it was thought that the Tiebout mechanism should *not* be operative in those areas. These are Decatur, Honolulu, Lexington, and

---

[k]The result does not strictly follow. A zero coefficient of $\log(u)$ could also imply either a lack of relationship or a highly nonlinear relationship between u and p.

[l]Note that, if α is near -1, a misspecification of the price term (the relationship between u and p) will have little effect on the other coefficients.

Table 2-1
SMSAs in the Sample and Their Characteristics

SMSA	Number of School Districts	Population
Akron	18	513,569
Ann Arbor	21	172,440
Binghamton	26	212,661
Boston	76	2,589,301
Buffalo	46	1,306,957
Columbus, O.	17	682,962
Decatur, Ill.	3	118,257
Evansville, Ind.	7	199,313
Honolulu	1	500,409
Lexington, Ky.	2	131,906
Milwaukee, Wis.	86	1,194,290
Muncie, Ind.	12	110,938
Peoria, Ill.	82	288,833
Richmond, Va.	3	408,494
Rochester, N.Y.	22	586,387

Richmond. Each of these SMSAs has three or fewer school districts, and it was assumed that this number is insufficient to allow efficient shopping among communities.[m] For these, the predicted value of c_D is zero, since t, the percentage price difference should be zero. In the other 11 SMSAs, the predicted coefficient is $\alpha(0.18)$.

The estimated form of equation (2.2a) is

$$\log(val) = \log(C) + \beta \log(Y) + \gamma \log(F) + c_u \log(u) + c_D D \quad (2.2b)$$

The results are presented in Table 2-2.

The c_u coefficient is discussed first, since the interpretation of c_D depends upon the value of this coefficient. The coefficient is negative in seven cases and positive in the other eight. Eight of the t statistics are numerically less than unity and only one is greater than 2.0. So there seems to be some justification for believing that α is on the order of -1, a value which is not inconsistent with other estimates.[n] Too much should not be made of the interpretation of c_u. As α is not identified (that is, no relationship is specified between p and u), it is not possible to perform a statistical test which, for example, establishes that α is, or is not, significantly different from any particular number. The variable was included to account for the possibility of some systematic relationship between distance and housing

[m]We can offer no firm statistical justification for the assumption that three jurisdictions do not make a market, whereas seven do. The number of SMSAs with so few jurisdictions precludes an appropriate test. However, the considerable improvement in the statistical results of Hamilton, Mills, and Puryear (Chapter 4 of this volume) when they considered only SMSAs with more than three jurisdictions lend some weak credibility to this assumption.

[n]The recent important studies of the demand for housing are described and analyzed in [3].

Table 2-2
Estimated Coefficients and *t* Statistics for Equation (2.2b)
Dependent Variable Is log(*val*)

	log(*C*)	β	c_u	γ	c_D	R^2
Akron	−7.85	1.39	0.040	0.331	−0.017	.905
	7.2	10.95	0.657	0.970	−0.229	
Ann Arbor	−4.99	1.19	−0.102	−0.381	−0.190	.755
	−3.28	6.67	−1.51	−1.84	−1.33	
Binghamton	−5.94	1.32	−0.030	−0.623	−0.075	.845
	−5.44	9.77	−0.758	−3.10	−0.885	
Boston	−0.623	1.41	0.137	−1.32	−0.045	.882
	−2.59	4.64	1.64	−3.80	−0.305	
Buffalo	−0.861	0.713	−0.06	−0.513	−0.331	.649
	−0.503	3.55	−0.752	−1.72	−2.20	
Columbus	−4.76	1.14	0.039	−0.298	0.081	.912
	−4.31	11.0	0.527	−0.381	0.919	
Decatur	−4.79	1.15	0.097	−0.426	0.095	.837
	−4.39	9.03	1.64	−1.85	0.942	
Evansville	−3.81	1.06	0.031	−0.727	−0.1441	.835
	−4.27	9.70	0.513	−3.05	−1.29	
Honolulu	−4.05	1.09	0.156	−0.318	+0.165	.535
	−1.84	4.03	1.36	−0.840	0.820	
Lexington	−3.57	1.05	0.196	−0.686	0.098	.828
	−2.34	7.39	1.97	−1.23	0.784	
Milwaukee	−3.86	1.07	0.014	−0.580	−0.107	.823
	−3.17	7.63	0.273	−3.58	−1.15	
Muncie	−0.009	0.631	−0.018	−0.767	−0.215	.992
	−0.291	29.4	−0.652	−4.75	−3.90	
Peoria	−6.92	1.41	−0.084	−0.584	−0.132	.846
	−5.42	9.87	−2.33	−1.98	−1.66	
Richmond	−4.23	1.05	−0.116	−0.108	−0.061	.805
	−2.78	6.64	−1.93	−0.417	−0.657	
Rochester	−5.27	1.17	−0.004	−0.299	−0.231	.874
	−2.89	6.25	−0.078	−0.781	−1.67	

expenditure, and all that can be said for the results is that they fail to demonstrate a deviation of the price elasticity from unity. Interpretation of the other coefficients in this chapter rests upon other researchers' evidence cited above.

On the assumption that $\alpha = -1$, the predicted value of c_D in 11 of the SMSAs is −0.18. Of these 11 SMSAs, 10 of the coefficients were negative as predicted, and the median value was −0.132.[o] Seven of the *t* statistics were greater than unity, and of these two were greater than 2.0. Among the four SMSAs for which a zero coefficient was predicted, three of the

---

[o]I wish to thank E. S. Mills for pointing out that, since local property taxes are deductible from the Federal income tax, the effective local property tax rate is about 75 percent of the nominal rate. Fortuitously, this reduces the predicted value of c_D from −0.18 to −0.135.

estimated coefficients were positive (recall that a negative coefficient was predicted for the other 11 SMSAs), and none had a t statistic greater than 0.94. The difference between the two subsamples is striking.

The results are clearly consistent with the hypothesis that, if there are sufficient school districts, the property tax is regarded by suburbanites as a price rather than an excise tax. The median value of the estimated coefficient is well within the predicted range. Also, the difference between the two subsamples indicates that a large number of suburban school districts is a necessary component of a Tiebout model. There are, however, several alternative explanations for these results; they fall into two general categories.

Alternative Explanations

First, it has been suggested that suburbanites are somehow "different" from central-city dwellers. The argument seems to be that suburbanites have a different demand function for housing—that they demand more housing than their city counterparts. If there are two distinct groups, one of which has a higher demand function for housing, it is reasonable to expect the high-demand group to be located in the suburbs, where land prices are lower. But, this line of reasoning does not lead us to expect that households with a relatively strong demand for housing would make a specific effort to live on the suburban side of the central-city boundary. Rather, such people should be attracted to the more remote regions of the urban area without reference to the central-city boundary, an effect which should be captured in the distance variable. It is possible, of course, that the equation is misspecified, and that the true relationship between $\log(u)$ and $\log(\text{val})$ is not linear. To test for this possibility, the regressions were rerun with an added quadratic term in distance. The coefficient was uniformly insignificant, and the effect on the other coefficients was negligible.

It is also possible that the income elasticity of demand for housing is not constant as assumed, but that it increases with income. If this is the case, the generally higher level of income in the suburban tracts would lead to a spurious correlation between the dependent variable and the dummy. To test for this, a quadratic term in income was added, with no significant change in the results.

Finally, given the striking differences between the two sets of SMSAs, it seems implausible that the dummy coefficient is picking up geographic segregation of population subgroups. The observed correlation between the dependent variable and the dummy appears to be due to the political fact of the central-city boundary, and not to some other variable which is related to distance from the central business district.

But it remains possible that the results are due not to differences in the property tax deadweight loss but rather to city-suburb differences in the capital value of residential property (presumably attributable to differences in the capitalized value of taxes and public service benefits). It should be emphasized that this work is not an attempt to measure the capitalized value of the joys of suburban living. A study of capitalization effects, such as the one by Oates [5], measures the effects of such variables as tax rates and expenditure levels on the *price* of a given parcel of real estate. This work, on the other hand, is an attempt to measure the effect of the city-suburb dummy on the *quantity* of housing consumed by a household with a given set of demand characteristics. The capitalization study takes as its point of departure the identity

$$\text{House value} = (\text{price}) \times (\text{quantity}) \qquad (2.3)$$

By holding constant quantity and other determinants of price through the use of other explanatory variables, the Oates capitalization study measures the effect of tax rates and expenditure levels on the price of housing. The point of departure for this study is the demand function for housing, equation (2.2). The quantity demanded, according to the hypothesis, ought to be influenced by the city-suburb difference in attitude toward the property tax. And this fact should be reflected in a city-suburb difference in house value, after correcting for other arguments in the demand function, including price. But the only proxy for the price argument is distance from the CBD. What if, due to capitalization of tax and expenditure variables, the price of housing is higher in the suburbs than in the central city? This would seem to indicate that the dummy could be regarded as a proxy for price, just like the distance variable. In order to evaluate this possibility, we must ask what would be a reasonable predicted value for the dummy coefficient, assuming it is picking up solely capitalization effects. Consider the equation

$$\frac{d(pq)}{pq} = \frac{(\alpha + 1)dp}{p} \qquad (2.4)$$

which is a simple transformation of the definition of elasticity. The equation gives the percentage change in total expenditure (value) as a function of the price elasticity and the percentage change in price. We wish to know what combinations of α and dp/p are consistent with the observed city-suburb house-value differential which averages 13.2 percent.

Equation (2.4) is graphed in Figure 2-1 with $d(pq)/pq$ set equal to the observed median value of 0.132. Any point on the graph represents a combination of α (price elasticity of demand for housing) and dp/p (city-suburb price-of-housing differential), which would explain the observed city-suburb total expenditure differential of 13.2 percent. First, note that

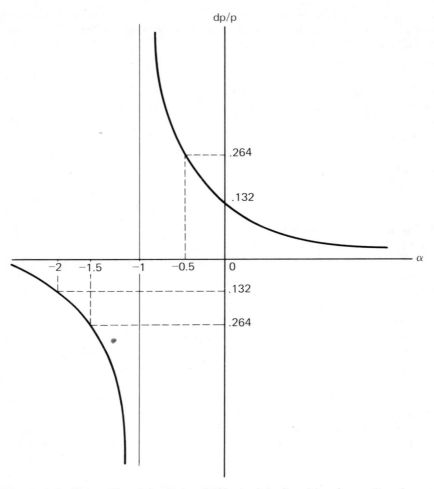

Figure 2-1. Price-Elasticity/Price-Differential Combinations Consistent with 13.2 Percent Total Expenditure Differential

the southwest arm of the hyperbola represents a negative price differential—that is, a higher price of housing in the central city than in the suburbs (having already corrected for distance from the CBD). It seems implausible that our observed city-suburb dummy coefficient is explained by an (α, dp/p) combination represented by this portion of the graph. Similarly, that portion of the upper arm which lies to the right of the origin can be ruled out on the grounds that these points represent a positive price elasticity of demand. So the only combinations of α and dp/p that would explain the dummy coefficient are those which lie between $\alpha = -1$ and $\alpha - 0$.

As discussed above, there seems to be a concensus that the price elasticity of demand for housing is on the order of -1; certainly a value smaller (numerically) than about -0.6 would be regarded as highly improbable. Yet if $\alpha = -0.6$, suburban housing prices must be 34 percent higher than central-city prices in order to explain the observed differential in house values. And as α approaches -1 from this value, the corresponding dp/p approaches infinity.

There is a rather confusing issue here: If the price elasticity of demand for housing is unity, a change in the price will not change total expenditure; and, therefore capitalization cannot account for observed expenditure differences. And yet the dummy is a representation of a city-suburb price difference (due to a difference in perception of the property tax) and the author predicts that it *will* give rise to a change in house value consumed. Apparently a misspecification of the price term in the regression equation will have little effect on the results, yet at the same time what we are trying to isolate is a price effect.

It can readily be shown that the hypothesized city-suburb difference in the perception of the local property tax is a special kind of price effect that can be isolated by looking at differences in house value. Assume that $\alpha = -1$. Total expenditure on housing is invariant with respect to price. Price, recall, is $p(1 + tD)$, and total expenditure on housing is $qp(1 + tD)$. So house value, our dependent variable, is equal to total expenditure only when $D = 0$; in other words, only in the suburbs. Assume now that the central-city property tax is considered as part of the price of housing, and that housing consumption is commensurately reduced according to the unit-elastic demand schedule. We have the following relationship:

$$qp(1 + t)_{\text{city}} = qp_{\text{suburb}}$$

But, if this is correct, qp_{city} is less than qp_{suburb} by qpt_{city}. Since qp (house value), and not $qp(1 + tD)$, is our dependent variable, a city-suburb difference in house value (which is not identical to total expenditure) is predicted. We are able to make this prediction because the central-city tax is part of total expenditure on housing, but is not a part of house value. But with other price effects, the reverse quantity effect tends to make the net impact on house value near zero.

The distinction arises because it is total expenditure on housing (not house value) which is invariant with respect to price if $\alpha = -1$. More generally, it is total expenditure which bears the relationship to price, which is indicated in equation (2.3). While the central-city tax liability is a component of total expenditure, it is not a component of house value. Removal of the property tax as a component of housing expenditure (postulated to occur when one crosses the central-city boundary) leaves total expenditure unchanged. But, this can occur only through a rise in house value equal to the present value of the tax liability which is no longer part of the cost of housing.

In summary, capitalization effects can explain the observed city-suburb house-value differentials only by postulating an implausibly low value for the price elasticity of demand or an implausibly high value for suburb price differential. The argument here is, not that capitalization of taxes and benefits into property values does not take place, but that such capitalization cannot explain the results presented in Table 2-2.

Conclusion

This chapter has offered a test of the Tiebout hypothesis, based on the assumption that the Tiebout model is a model of behavior in suburban sections of urban areas, not in central cities. It is further argued that if the suburban public economy resembles a market, the local tax instrument must be regarded by consumers as *quid pro quo* for local public services. This being the case, suburbanites do not regard the property tax as a tax on housing; and, unlike the central-city tax, it does not drive a wedge between the supply and demand price of housing.

The foregoing leads to the prediction that, after correcting for other arguments in the demand function for housing, suburbanites consume more housing than their central-city counterparts. The magnitude of the difference can be predicted if one has prior knowledge of the price elasticity of demand for housing and the central-city property tax rate. The observed city-suburb house-value differential is, on average, in close agreement with the predicted value. Other possible explanations for the observed city-suburb house-value differential are explored and rejected.

The results lend fairly strong support to the hypothesis that suburban households of American urban areas regard their property taxes as a direct payment for public services, whereas central-city households regard their property taxes as a standard excise tax on residential property.

References

[1] Buchanan, J. M., "An Economic Theory of Clubs," *Economica* 32 (February 1965): 1-14.
[2] Buchanan, J. M., and C. J. Goetz, "Efficiency Limits of Fiscal Mobility: An Assessment of the Tiebout Model," *Journal of Public Economics* 1, no. 1 (February 1972): 25-44.

[3] deLeeuw, Frank, "The Demand for Housing: A Review of Cross-section Evidence," *Review of Economics and Statistics* 53, (February 1971): 1-10.

[4] Hamilton, Bruce, "Zoning and Property Taxation in a System of Local Governments," *Urban Studies* (June 1975).

[5] Oates, Wallace E., "The Effects of Property Taxes and Local Public Spending on Property Values: An Empirical Study of Tax Capitalization and the Tiebout Hypothesis," *Journal of Political Economy* 77 (November/December 1969): 957-970.

[6] Oates, Wallace E., *Fiscal Federalism* (New York: Harcourt Brace Jovanovich, 1972).

[7] Tiebout, Charles, "A Pure Theory of Local Public Expenditure," *Journal of Political Economy* 64 (The University of Chicago Press, October 1956): 416-424.

3

Fiscal Zoning in Fragmented Metropolitan Areas

Michelle J. White

This chapter examines the impact of fiscal zoning by independent suburban communities on the structure of large American urban areas. It is particularly concerned with the impact of an especially chauvinistic type of local zoning policy under which a community tries to make its own residents better off at the expense of newcomers and outsiders. Communities have the power to do this, because the development of zoning laws over the last half century has given them an extraordinary degree of control over land use within their boundaries.

An example of a chauvinistic local zoning policy would be a local community that required payment of a toll to the community at large by anyone who wished to build a new house or new firm within its boundaries.[a] The toll monies would be distributed among all or some of the previous residents, depending on the social choice process as used for decision making within the community. At a basic level, such tolls transfer income and utility from new entrants to existing residents of the zoned community. Indirectly this "beggar-thy-neighbor" localism can also have important allocation and distribution effects on residents of the metropolitan area as a whole.

This zoning policy can be contrasted with an alternative policy which would regulate entry to a community in order to insure that the previous residents remain at the same level of wellbeing before and after the entry occurs. The Tiebout-Hamilton zoning system [6, 18] is of this type. In this case, if the new resident consumes local public services such as education which cost $1000 per year to produce, then he is required to pay $1000 per year in property taxes, but no more. The community ensures this payment by requiring him to buy a house of at least a certain minimum value.

Both of these zoning policies can be said to have fiscal objectives. They regulate the community's land-use pattern so as to insure that the local public sector either breaks even or makes a profit supplying services to new residents. They will be referred to as fiscal zoning policies. The particular policy under which newcomers pay exactly the marginal cost of their public services will be called *neutral zoning*. The policy under which they pay more than their costs will be called *fiscal-squeeze zoning*. The reasons communities might adopt these or other policies are discussed below.

---

[a]In a strict sense, the toll requirement is not a zoning policy. However, such toll payments are usually enforced by requiring residents to buy properties of a certain minimum value.

Another objective toward which communities might direct their zoning efforts is the reduction of negative externalities and loss of property value incurred by land owners because some incompatible land use is located nearby. Since this objective and the objectives of fiscal zoning are often confused, it is worthwhile to define them carefully.

Externalities zoning refers to zoning which deals with the external effects—positive or negative—that one resident's use of land in a community may have on neighboring uses of land. The action of the private land market may not lead to an economically efficient outcome under these conditions and standard Pigovian pricing of the externality may be difficult. Coase [3] has suggested one way in which the private market can deal with externalities: private transfer payments between the conflicting land users can induce one or the other party to modify his economic behavior so that production (or utility) is increased. However, if the transactions cost of private market agreements is too high, then communities might use zoning as a way of creating a more efficient pattern of land use through regulation. Externalities zoning normally segregates land uses by broad categories of users, on the assumption that similar land uses have no (or only small) external effects on each other whereas dissimilar land uses may have large effects.

For example, if a class of users such as industrial firms produces negative externalities which affect another class of users (residential), then externalities zoning could restrict industrial users to a contiguous land area reserved exclusively for them. Factories generate fewer externalities if they are segregated in one area than if they are scattered among residences. In this case, zoning reduces the undesirable externalities of industrial uses because the strength of the externality varies according to the length of the boundary between conflicting uses.

Fiscal zoning refers to zoning motivated by fiscal rather than efficiency conditions. Two fiscal zoning policies have been mentioned. Under either, a community might decide to zone all its vacant land for large-lot, high-value, single-family homes because it believes that only expensive homes pay as much or more in property taxes than the cost of providing their occupants with public services. In such circumstances, the possibility that the community's vacant land might be more efficiently developed in another use would make no difference to the community. As will be seen in later sections, fiscal zoning policies do not in general lead to the same pattern of land use as externalities zoning policies.

Background and History

The history of zoning presents a curious picture of the intertwining of fiscal and externalities considerations. The motives for zoning have from the beginning been primarily fiscal, but the legal justification of zoning as a limitation on the rights of private property has always been couched in externalities terms.

The earliest comprehensive zoning ordinance in this country was enacted in New York City in 1916.[b] The impetus for it was provided not by residents, but by a business group of luxury retail garment sellers, the Fifth Avenue Association. Garment factories tended to locate in lofts above the retail shops in order to save transportation costs. At noon garment workers emerged onto Fifth Avenue, congesting the sidewalk, driving away shoppers, and causing financial loss, so the merchants claimed. A move by the Fifth Avenue shops from the twenties north to the thirties and forties did not solve the problem as the garment factories soon followed. The Association then appealed to the City for help and the form agreed on was a height limitation for new buildings in the area, which would make lofts uneconomic but would not affect retailing operations.

A search ensued for a legal justification for height limitations, which was found in the police power of the state to limit property rights for the protection of "health and welfare." It was claimed that tall buildings caused loss of light and air, dangers to health, and increased risks of fire. However a contrary legal view held that zoning constituted a "taking of property" rather than merely a reasonable regulation of property rights. Under this latter view, zoning would be unlawful unless compensation were paid for the loss of property rights.[c] To strengthen the health and welfare justification for zoning, it was decided to formulate a zoning plan for all of New York City, rather than just for the Fifth Avenue area.

The zoning ordinance of 1916 divided the city into districts of three types and set different height limitations for each. The districts were residential, business, and unrestricted (industrial). Under a concept which became known as "cumulative districting," residential districts were considered the "highest use," businesses the next highest, and unrestricted districts the lowest.[d] Any lower use was considered to have a "nuisance" effect on all higher uses if located nearby, but not vice versa. Thus all lower uses were banned from higher use districts. Districts intended for industry were made unrestricted since there was nothing from which industry needed protecting. If a higher use owner wished to locate in a lower use district and was not concerned about the "nuisance" he incurred, the zoning ordinance did not forbid him from doing so.

These regulations mirror the externalities framework in which the first

---

[b]See [8] for a more detailed discussion.

[c]See [2, pp. 26-27].

[d]See [2].

zoning planners worked. It is interesting to note that the first New York ordinance had no separate single-family and apartment districts. The planners used only one type of residential district because they did not feel they could defend in court the assertion that apartment buildings constituted a "public nuisance" when located in single-family districts.

The Supreme Court ruled on the constitutionality of comprehensive zoning ordinances in 1926. The court accepted the police power argument that justified limiting property rights for the protection of health and welfare. Going beyond the New York plan, the Court also accepted the argument that apartments located in single-family zones constitute a public nuisance. The Court concluded, "Under these circumstances, apartment houses, which in a different environment would be not only entirely unobjectionable but highly desirable, come very near to being nuisances."[e] Thus the foundation for suburban exclusionary zoning was laid.

In the half century since 1926 the legal situation with respect to zoning has not changed in substance. But the "nuisance" justification for zoning has been stretched beyond recognition. Suburbs have adopted zoning wholeheartedly and have become increasingly skillful in their use of it as an exclusionary tool. Exclusion of apartments is no longer the sole concern. Suburbs since World War II have refined zoning to the point where it can be used to exclude all but specific uses that communities wish to admit, usually expensive single-family houses of a specified character. They can now exclude non-nuisance as well as nuisance uses. They can ban motels, trailers, discount stores, and modern architecture. They can demand two-acre lots for single-family houses and can require that apartments be too small to house families with school age children.

Thus communities have won almost complete power over land use within their boundaries. The only limit to their power seems to be that when challenged, they must clothe their motives—whatever they are—with an externalities justification. Reflecting the legal base on which zoning rests, the minimum lot sizes, bulk requirements, architectural controls, and other exclusionary tools must still be justified on the grounds that they protect the public "health and welfare" and prevent the invasion of "public nuisances." But the Courts have demonstrated a willingness to go along with fiscal zoning by their acceptance of the argument that anything that lowers property values must constitute a public nuisance.[f]

The concept of cumulative districting has been replaced by the more restrictive concept of "exclusive districts." Under this system, a district can only be developed in that use for which is was zoned. Thus the concept that higher uses must be protected from nuisance-causing lower uses has

---

[e]Quoted in [1, p. 4]. The case is *Euclid* v. *Ambler*.

[f]See [16].

been replaced by a stronger concept that a "best use" (which the community can decide) exists for every piece of land. Industry therefore, has become as protected as single-family homes. Industrial zoning can be used to keep large tracts of land from being developed residentially. The next step appears to be zoning which will specify not just a functional use for each piece of land, but a specific use, i.e., a drycleaner or a research laboratory.

Thus zoning would seem to have almost fully established the power of local communities to stand at the door and rule on individual requests for admission. Lawyers appear to doubt the constitutionality of this situation, because it infringes the rights of owners, but the courts seem unconcerned. A frequent explanation for this situation holds that the courts simply dislike zoning litigation. One court, for example, made this dislike official. An Associated Press news story of December 1, 1963 went as follows, "Chief Justice John C. Bell said today the Pennsylvania Supreme Court no longer will hear zoning and other cases of little significance."[g]

Recent legal attacks on zoning have taken both direct and indirect approaches. One indirect approach has attacked the legality of local property taxes as a means of financing public education. The California Supreme Court in *Serrano* v. *Priest,* 1971, ruled that any tax that leads to higher expenditures in wealthy communities is an unconstitutional means of financing public education, since it denies the equal protection under law guaranteed by the Fourteenth Amendment. The recent busing case in Richmond constitutes another indirect attack on zoning since federal courts have threatened to bus into suburban schools exactly the central city children that suburban families wished to escape when they moved to the suburbs.[h] Such cases are indirect attacks on zoning, since if local communities lost the right to finance their own school systems and to decide who can attend, much of people's incentives to group themselves into homogeneous communities would be lost. At present, however, both the *Serrano* and the *Richmond* approaches have been rejected by the Supreme Court and legislation to the same effect appears very improbable.

The direct attack on zoning—attempts to strike down the local right to determine land-use policy—has been attempted in several court cases and in various legislative measures. A Massachusetts law passed in 1969 requires each municipality to zone at least 0.3 percent of its vacant land for low-income housing.[i] However the passage of this law has not spurred other states to follow. In New Jersey the State Supreme Court has upheld a 1971 Superior Court decision which voided a local zoning ordinance on the

[g]*The Washington Star,* December 1, 1963. Quoted in [1, p. 104]. Babcock, Chapter V, contains a review of legal views on zoning.

[h]*School Board of Richmond* v. *Board of Education of the Commonwealth of Virginia*, U.S. Supreme Court, May 21, 1973.

grounds that it failed to meet the regional housing needs of the surrounding area.[j] But the direct attack on zoning has had mixed success at best. For every case decided against exclusionary zoning, another can be cited in which large-lot zoning was upheld. For example, a recent Federal Court of Appeals decision upheld a zoning ordinance in Sanbornton, New Hampshire, that zoned all vacant land in the town for 3- or 6-acre lots. The judge was more impressed by the need to protect Sanbornton from "ugly suburban sprawl" than by the need for reasonably priced housing.[k]

Thus, for the present at least, fiscal zoning seems to be going strong. There would seem to be a sound basis in fact, therefore, for developing models of zoning that assume communities can dictate their land-use patterns.

The Tiebout and Hamilton Theories

The theory of metropolitan location choice presented by Tiebout, and its recasting by Hamilton as a theory of neutral zoning constitute a departure point for the zoning models discussed below. The Tiebout theory is discussed in the Introduction to this volume; the Hamilton extension is presented in Chapter 2 and need not be repeated here. However several properties of the neutral-zoning model should be recapitulated. Hamilton shows in particular that if enough communities exist to satisfy every consumer preference level for housing and local services, then every household can locate in a community where it consumes the same amount of housing (the minimum allowed by zoning), pays the same amount in property taxes, and consumes the same quality local services as every other household in that community. Each household in the community therefore pays the average cost (assumed equal to marginal cost) of the local public services it consumes. If enough communities exist (or can be established) to provide the necessary diversity of housing and local service options, then the budget constraint faced by households if local services are provided as a local public good will be identical to the constraint faced if they are provided as private goods. Thus the market yields a Pareto-optimum allocation of resources.

Several interesting results emerge from this allocation of households to communities. One is that in zoned communities in equilibrium, the local property tax carries no deadweight loss. The tax is a price paid for public services received by households. Another result is that no income redis-

---

[i]See [5].

[j]*New York Times,* July 15, 1973, page 57.

[k]*Zoning Digest,* Volume 24, 1972.

tribution occurs in the process whereby local communities supply local services, since all residents of a given community receive the same local services and pay the same property taxes. A tax-financed service to just one segment of the community would induce other segments to migrate to another community where such programs did not exist. Note that zoning is necessary for this result to hold. If there were no zoning, free riders could build homes worth 10 percent of the zoned level, pay one-tenth the property taxes paid by other residents, and consume the same public services. Without zoning, the poor would have an incentive constantly to follow the rich from community to community and the model would have no stable outcome. Zoning provides the means by which "fair-share" taxpayers can exclude free riders.

A third outcome of the model is a prediction that residents of the central city consume less housing, *ceteris paribus,* than residents of zoned suburbs. This results from the fact that the central city is assumed to be unzoned, whereas suburbs are zoned. Therefore the central-city property tax is not a price paid for services received, but a tax on housing which is only imperfectly related to benefits. It causes central-city residents to consume less housing with a resulting deadweight loss.

The criticism to be leveled at the Hamilton model is that it does not seem to present a realistic model of community behavior. It assumes that communities and their residents are either very altruistic or very passive—any newcomer is allowed in as long as he pays his own way and no more. Under the strict Tiebout assumption that residents can form new communities if they do not wish to locate in any existing community, it is plausible to assume that existing communities cannot exploit their new residents. Such behavior would merely induce formation of new communities. But in reality local government jurisdictional boundaries are predetermined, unlikely to change, and leave few interstices in which new communities could form, at least in metropolitan areas. Each local government has some group of existing residents, no matter how small. New residents must find their way into an existing zoned suburb or locate in the central city.

In addition, we have seen that communities have almost unlimited powers of exclusion. It is reasonable to assume that they use these powers. If a community has any monopoly power over supply of house sites, then it can collect a toll from newcomers who prefer to locate in that community. Relatively inelastic demand might exist for residences in a community with a convenient location, a status reputation, or a very good school system. But even for communities with no monopoly power, it is reasonable to assume that residents might prefer their communities' present disposition to the alternative of a larger population, higher density, and less open space. It is even more clear that without some inducement, communities would prefer to exclude businesses and factories from their borders. New firms—and perhaps new houses—lower the environmental quality of a community, and its residents demand compensation for allowing them to enter. Thus the basic tenet of neutral zoning—that communities allow new residents to enter on the same fiscal basis as existing residents—is contrary to the presumption that the residents of a community act as a group to further their self-interest.

The next section offers several alternative zoning strategies that communities might pursue if they decided to act in a more self-interested manner than is assumed under the neutral zoning theory.

Non-Neutral Zoning Strategies

The first strategy is referred to as fiscal-squeeze zoning. Communities are assumed to maximize a fiscal-squeeze transfer (*FST*) to be gained from incoming residents or firms. The transfer is equal to property taxes paid on newly developed land minus marginal public service costs,

$$FST = tQ_A(P_L + E_A) - C_AQ_A - PCT \cdot Q_A \qquad (3.1)$$

In equation (3.1), $tQ_A(P_L + E_A)$ is property taxes paid on the value of newly developed land, where t is the property tax rate, Q_A is the number of acres developed, and $(P_L + E_A)$ is the price of land per acre plus the value of improvements per acre. Costs incurred for new residents have two parts. The first is direct costs due to the provision of extra local services. The quality of local services supplied to new residents of the community is assumed to be the same as that supplied to older residents. Local public services are not pure public goods and production of an extra unit of services incurs extra costs. These are C_AQ_A, where C_A is extra service costs per acre of new development. Communities probably would not use a fiscal-squeeze zoning strategy until they were large enough to achieve a minimum efficient scale in production of local services, unless the gains from a fiscal-squeeze strategy outweigh the costs of small-scale production. However, scale is not a great constraint on community action. Often services can be bought from special-purpose agencies or nearby communities. Even assuming a community must produce its own local services, if production of education requires the largest scale of any local service, communities achieve full economies of scale at a fairly small size. Hettich [7] suggests that minimum marginal cost is achieved for elementary education when a school has 300 pupils in daily attendance. Costs are constant as enrollment increases thereafter. For a community to have one elementary school of efficient size would imply a population of 2500-3000. Provision of its own secondary school at an efficient scale requires a school of about 1,000 pupils and a population of about 10,000 to 12,000. For suburban communities in large metropolitan areas, meeting these scale requirements puts no strong constraint on the adoption of a zoning strategy.

The second cost term, $PCT \cdot Q_A$, refers to the environmental cost of new development. If new development is proposed, the community compares its environmental value to that of existing houses or of vacant land. Suppose the proposed development is new houses. If new houses would lower environmental quality, the community demands a payment, called a "pollution-compensating transfer" (PCT), to compensate it for the environmental quality loss from new construction. This payment is required to make the community indifferent on environmental grounds to the new development. In addition, the community attempts to maximize the fiscal-squeeze transfer it gets from new development.

It is reasonable to assume that the environmental effect of nonresidential buildings is always adverse, so the PCT required to make a community indifferent to a new commercial or industrial building is positive. Residential construction might have a more variable environmental effect. The community might use the value of the proposed new houses, V_N, as an index of their environmental quality, where higher value houses are assumed to be built on larger lots.[1] Houses of lower value than the community's existing houses, V_O, are assumed to be undesirable and a positive transfer is required. New houses of higher value than V_O are environmentally desirable and the required PCT level falls.

In Figure 3-1, the solid line is a possible PCT function and the broken line is a net tax revenue function excluding pollution transfers to the community. The net tax revenue function equals property tax revenues per new house minus direct local service costs incurred by the community. At all $V_N \leq V_O$, PCT is positive. At some $V_N > V_O$, PCT becomes zero (point V_C). Further to the right, environmental considerations drop out of the community's fiscal squeeze calculations since all proposed uses are environmentally desirable. PCT might even become negative in this range if the community were willing to pay to attract high-value houses.

The figure illustrates some constraints on the community's fiscal-squeeze maximization process. In particular, it is clear that the community would not permit houses of value $V_N \leq V_O$, if the marginal cost of public services is constant at $C = tV_O$. In the range $V_N \leq V_O$, property tax revenues from new houses are at most equal to the cost of providing extra local services. Therefore since the transfer required to make the community

---

[1]The community can control the lot-size-house-value relation through use of building code, setback, and square footage regulations. V_N is thus a general index of the environmental quality of new houses. However, if the community values colonial style houses and a proposed new house is modern, then a different environmental index might be necessary which would make even very expensive modern houses environmentally undesirable.

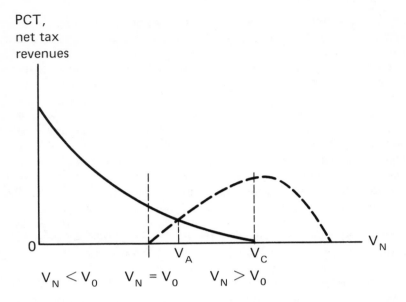

Figure 3-1. Determination of Fiscal Squeeze Transfer

environmentally indifferent to such houses is positive, the community must be made worse off if it allows these houses to be built.

The community therefore chooses a position in which it allows only new houses with value of at least V_A to be built. At V_A, net tax revenues just offset the adverse environmental impact of new development. The community is therefore indifferent to new construction. It is important to note that given the existence of environmental costs, this indifference point occurs at a value V_N greater than V_0, rather than at the point $V_N = V_0$. The community is made worse off by allowing construction of new houses of the same value as its existing houses. Such houses are excluded by zoning.

Communities that have strong monopoly power as vacant land suppliers try to set zoning regulations that admit only new construction with no adverse environmental impact, at $V_N \geq V_C$. Other communities with less monopoly power may admit new construction that does have an adverse environmental impact, but they nevertheless require that new houses have a value greater than V_0. Both types of communities exclude all new construction except that aimed at consumers who are willing to pay a premium for houses within their boundaries.

There are other reasons that communities may prefer not to admit new houses of the same value as their existing houses. Suppose there is a great deal of uncertainty concerning the future cost of maintaining the same quality local public services and that communities are risk averse. Figure

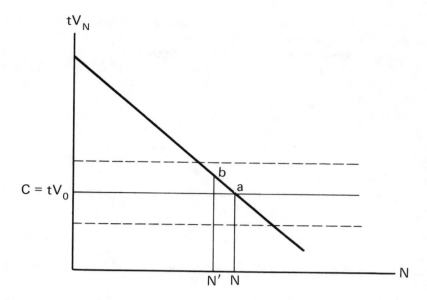

Figure 3-2. Demand for Housing Sites

3-2 shows the demand curve for housing sites in the community as a function of the zoned housing value, V_N. Given a fixed tax rate, a linear transformation of the curve makes it a function of property tax payments required on the zoned housing value, tV_N. Suppose the community provides services at a cost per house of $C = tV_0$. In the absence of uncertainty, the community would allow all houses to be built which generate tax revenues at least equal to costs, $C = tV_N$, at point a. Suppose uncertainty makes the cost of a given quality of local services fluctuate between the two dotted lines, and that the mean cost is at a. Expected surpluses on production of local services are equal to expected deficits, so in the long run the community should break even supplying local services to new houses of value $V_N = V_0$. However if the community is risk averse, it will be made worse off by taking this zero-profit bet. For the community to be equally well off allowing new houses to be built, their expected value must yield a surplus on production of local services in the long run. But for new houses to yield such a surplus they must be of higher value than V_0. Therefore the risk-averse community moves to point b which only houses of value $V_N > V_0$ are allowed and fewer are built than under certainty. In this case, bookkeeping records would show the existence of a fiscal-squeeze transfer but the community would nonetheless be just indifferent to allowing new houses or excluding them. Houses of value $V_N = V_0$ would make the community worse off and competition among communities would not induce a risk-averse community to allow them.

Finally, some communities have strong monopoly powers as suppliers of housing sites with particular characteristics. They set zoning regulations in the region $V_N \geq V_C$ of Figure 3-1 regardless of the zoning level set by nearby communities. Although there may be several hundred communities in a large metropolitan area, the lots they supply may not be good substitutes. There are several reasons for this. First, the Tiebout theory tells us that consumers seek communities whose residents have public service demands similar to their own. Therefore only communities with similar levels of public output compete with each other. Second, many consumers work in the suburbs rather than the central city. They prefer to live near their work places to save commuting costs and therefore consider locating only in communities that have the desired public output level and are near their work places. Suburban workers in addition are not indifferent among communities located in all directions from the city center. These two factors suggest that only small groups of communities compete with each other.

Third, many communities have some special attribute which may make certain consumers willing to pay a premium for admission. Certain communities may have a particularly convenient location near a major highway. Others may offer a particular mix of public services that is attractive to some consumers. Another may have a very good school system, given its tax rate, or a status reputation. If competition to cut zoning levels developed, such communities would prefer to drop out of the competition at a level where V_N is above V_C. They would then supply housing sites only to consumers with inelastic demands.

Thus competition among communities pursuing fiscal squeeze zoning strategies does not result in neutral zoning, since if competition forced zoning down to the $V_N = V_O$ level, few communities would still be willing to supply sites. Most communities would rather drop out of competition at some $V_N \geq V_O$.

An alternative non-neutral zoning strategy that communities might attempt to pursue would be to maximize the wealth of their existing residents. If most of residents' wealth is in their dwellings, this goal can be accomplished by pursuing a zoning strategy that maximizes the value of their houses. If this zoning policy also dictated that new houses generate a fiscal-squeeze transfer, then the existing houses would also increase in value due to capitalization of a tax rate drop or an increase in the quality of local services, depending on how the fiscal-squeeze transfer is used. The policy of maximizing the value of existing houses in the community is referred to as a "scarcity zoning policy." It is possible that a stable community with many owner-occupiers might favor a fiscal-squeeze zon-ing policy while a community with rapid turnover might prefer a scarcity zoning policy. Or it might want to combine elements of both policies in order to achieve some capital gain from zoning plus some flow benefits.

A third possibility is for the community to use its zoning power to maximize the value of vacant land in the community. Such a policy is in contrast to the goal of a scarcity zoning policy, which maximizes the value of nonvacant land. It also ignores the costs of new development in terms of lower environmental quality.

Assume that the residents of a community determine its zoning policy and that any major new zoning plan must be approved by vote of a majority of community residents. It is therefore unlikely that a vacant-land zoning policy would be adopted by a community, since it benefits only the owners of the community's vacant land. Such a policy is likely to be popular only if the community is populated by farmers who own its vacant land as well as its already developed housing. The farmers then might benefit more from an increase in the value of their farms than of their houses. Otherwise, a community's vacant land is likely to be owned either by outside speculators or by a few local residents. In either case, owners could influence the community zoning process only by lobbying or bribery.

It should be emphasized that all three categories come under the head-ing of fiscal zoning. Under all three zoning strategies, and under neutral zoning, the community is using its power over land use to achieve an objective other than the externalities objective of correcting inefficiencies in the free market for land. Under neutral zoning, the object is to keep out free riders who would use the community's public services without paying taxes equal to marginal cost. Zoning is used to insure that no income redistribution from existing residents to newcomers occurs within the local public sector. The other zoning policies go further than neutral zoning in pursuit of fiscal objectives. In these cases no new development is allowed unless it makes the existing residents of the community better off. Zoning insures that some income redistribution does take place through the public sector. In the case of fiscal-squeeze zoning, the redistribution is to a community's existing residents from new residents. In the scarcity zoning case, the redistribution is from buyers of new houses generally to owners of existing houses in the community.

The next several sections analyze various fiscal zoning strategies. It should be noted that the idea of a community's residents using zoning to benefit themselves at the expense of outsiders is not new. Margolis [9] pointed out the practice in 1956. The fiscal-squeeze strategy is widely employed by local officials and is well-known to land developers. The latter know the practice mostly in the context of refusals of requests for zoning variances when they wish to build high-density development projects in low-density zoned communities. However, in spite of being well-known, fiscal zoning has not been carefully analyzed.

Fiscal-Squeeze Zoning

Under the fiscal-squeeze zoning strategy, a community requires newcomers to make a transfer to its existing residents in return for the right to build a new house. The community maximizes this resource transfer over values of its zoning policy variables. These are assumed to be its required lot size and the amount of vacant land it supplies for development. Under this strategy it is assumed that the community has some monopoly power as a supplier of undeveloped land, although it competes with other communities supplying sites that are substitutable for those of the particular community. The community faces a not-perfectly-elastic demand curve for its vacant land.

The Fiscal-Squeeze Transfer Strategy

The fiscal-squeeze transfer function generally takes the form,

$$FST = t[P_L(Q_A, L) \cdot Q_A + P_H \cdot H_A(L, P_L) \cdot Q_A]$$
$$- C_A(L, W, F) \cdot Q_A - PCT \cdot Q_A \tag{3.2}$$

which says that the fiscal-squeeze transfer derived from all new residents equals the excess of property tax payments on land and housing over the cost to the community of providing extra local public services and of foregone environmental quality. The community maximizes this function over values of the lot-size requirement and over the quantity of land supplied, assumed to be its major policy variables. In contrast, under a neutral zoning policy, the community would set a lot size and quantity such that total tax payments equalled costs and the fiscal-squeeze transfer equalled zero.

In dealing with community zoning policies, several simplifications are made. The most important is that the community itself is considered the sole supplier of vacant land within its boundaries. This could be because it owns all its vacant land or because, though the land is privately owned, the community's zoning policy determines the terms on which it can be supplied. If the community sets prohibitive terms such as a fifty-acre minimum lot size, then the owners of the land will not be able to develop it themselves or to sell it for development by others.

In equation (3.2), L is the required minimum lot size on which a new unit

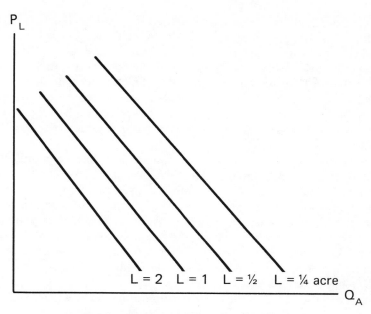

Figure 3-3. Demand for Lot Sizes

of housing can be built, expressed as a certain number of acres of land. Depending on the lot size selected by the optimizing procedure, single houses might be built (if $L = 1/2$ acre) or apartments (if $L = 1/16$ acre).

$P_L(Q_A, L)$ is the demand function for land, expressed in inverse form. The price per acre of land (P_L), depends on the number of acres of land developed (Q_A) and on the required lot size (L). $\partial P_L / \partial Q_A$ and $\partial P_L / \partial L$ are both negative; quantity demanded falls as price rises and the price of land falls as the lot size increases. In a competitive, unregulated land market the price of land per acre would be the same regardless of lot size (ignoring the price effects of distance from the central city). Here, however, we assume that the price per acre is inversely related to the required lot size, so that larger lots are sold at a lower per acre price than smaller lots. Figure 3-3 shows a family of demand functions for land of various lot sizes. As the required lot size increases, demand falls, since consumers who wish to buy small lots may prefer to buy no land at all when only large lots are offered. On the other hand, if only small lots are offered, consumers who wish to buy large lots can buy several small lots and consolidate them. (General equilibrium aspects of this price function for land are discussed on pp. 80-93.)

Communities in the following discussion are assumed to set one lot size only. That is, if the optimal residential zoning policy is determined to require one-acre lots, then the community sets one acre as the lot size requirement for all its vacant land intended for residential use.[m] Assuming that the community cannot act as a discriminating monopolist, it is optimum to set a single lot size. However, if the community could separate markets for various size lots, then it would be better off setting several lot sizes. Whether discrimination is possible depends on whether any newcomers would buy the larger lots if smaller ones were offered. Depending on their motives for entering the community, even high-income families might buy small lots if the community offered several lot sizes simultaneously.

Evidence suggests that communities are not discriminating monopolists; most set one lot size for a large fraction of their residentially zoned vacant land.[n] We can therefore assume that discrimination is not a possibility and that all of a community's vacant residential land is assigned to one lot size. In this case, newcomers to a given community are likely to be quite homogeneous. They will consume the same amount of land (L) and the same total housing value, since the latter depends on L and P_L. If housing consumption and income are closely related, then the newcomers will also have similar income levels.

P_H in equation (3.2) is the price per unit of housing, which is constant. H_A is the amount of housing built on an acre of land, which is a function of the required lot size and the price of land. $P_H H_A Q_A$ is the total value of housing built on the developed land. Assuming, initially, that the value of housing built on an acre of land—apart from the land itself—is constant, then $E_A = P_H H_A$ is constant (E_A is the value of housing per acre). This assumption is relaxed below.

No particular cost function is specified in equation (3.2) for local public services. Cost varies with the required lot size (L), the quality of local services (W), and family size (F). W and F are assumed to be invariant with respect to changes in policy variables, so they drop out of the function. W is constant because the existing residents of the community are assumed to have decided on a quality level of local services which maximizes their utility. It is assumed that they wish to retain majority control over the community in order to insure that this quality level of local services remains unchanged. Therefore they allow only a small number of newcomers to enter relative to the number of existing residents and the newcomers are unable to change W. In the long run, however, newcomers may take over majority control of the community and, if they have higher incomes than the older residents, they may raise the quality of local services.

---

[m]Presumably, it has previously made a decision concerning the allocation of its vacant land between residential and nonresidential uses. This decision is discussed below.

[n]In a sample of about 300 New Jersey communities in the New York metropolitan area, about three-quarters of the communities zoned 75 percent or more of their land for development in a single lot size. Most of the remainder divided their vacant land into regions set aside for two different, but similar lot sizes. See [17].

Some restrictions must be placed on the form of the cost function with respect to lot size. Suppose all local service costs were proportionate to lot size, so that costs per lot were $C = aL$. Then the optimum zoning strategy for a community would be to set the minimum possible lot size. Costs would approach zero, while the value of vacant land per acre would be maximized. Thus fiscal-squeeze transfers would be maximized. Since this is unrealistic, it is assumed that there are fixed costs per household in production of local services, so costs rise less than proportionately as lot size increases. Local services can be divided into two categories; these supplied to dwellings and those supplied to residents. Streets, water, sewers, and street lights are examples of the former; schools, libraries, and recreation facilities of the latter. It is assumed that services supplied to dwellings increase proportionately as lot size increases. Thus the cost function per lot is assumed to take the form $C = a + bL$, with b positive.

This cost function per lot translates into a cost function per acre, $C_A = C/L$. Thus

$$C_A = \frac{a + bL}{L} = b + \frac{a}{L} \tag{3.3}$$

Costs per acre of land fall at a diminishing rate as required lot size increases. Therefore

$$\frac{\partial C_A}{\partial L} < 0 \quad \text{and} \quad \frac{\partial^2 C_A}{\partial L^2} > 0$$

Pollution costs in equation (3.2) are $PCT \cdot Q_A$. The initial assumption here is that pollution costs equal zero, since communities have sufficient market power to exclude new development with adverse environment effects. This assumption is also relaxed below.

Finally, it is assumed that neighboring communities have predetermined zoning strategies that do not change in response to zoning changes by the particular community discussed here.

Suppose a community's fiscal-squeeze transfer function takes the form previously mentioned, except that value of buildings per acre is now constant and pollution effects are zero.

$$FST = t[E_A Q_A + P_L(Q_A, L) \cdot Q_A] - C_A(L) \cdot Q_A \tag{3.4}$$

The community maximizes the fiscal-squeeze transfer obtained from all new residents over its zoning policy instruments, Q_A and L. The first-order conditions are

$$\frac{\partial FST}{\partial L} = t Q_A \frac{\partial P_L}{\partial L} - Q_A \frac{\partial C_A}{\partial L} = 0 \quad \text{or} \quad t \frac{\partial P_L}{\partial L} = \frac{\partial C_A}{\partial L} \tag{3.5}$$

and

$$\frac{\partial FST}{\partial Q_A} = t\left(Q_A \frac{\partial P_L}{\partial Q_A} + P_L + E_A\right) - C_A = 0$$

or

$$t[P_L(1 + e_{P_L Q_A}) + E_A] = C_A \qquad (3.6)$$

Equation (3.5) says that the community's required lot size should be such that marginal property tax revenues per acre equal marginal public services costs per acre. Both $\partial P_L/\partial L$ and $\partial C_A/\partial L$ are negative. In (3.6) $e_{P_L Q_A}$ is the inverted price elasticity of demand for land. Since it is negative and C_A is positive, the optimum supply of vacant land occurs where $-1 \leq e_{P_L Q_A} \leq 0$. In this range the total value of land supplied increases as the quantity of land increases. If $e_{P_L Q_A}$ were less than minus one, the value of land would fall as more land was supplied. Fiscal-squeeze transfers would also fall, so the optimum strategy would be for communities to provide very little land. But as Q_A approaches zero, $e_{P_L Q_A}$ becomes inelastic, assuming the demand curve intersects the vertical axis. Communities are assumed to supply land in this range of inelastic demand.

Thus, as more land is supplied, property tax revenues to the community increase faster than costs, until the optimum land supply is reached. Q_A reaches its optimum at Q_A^* and the optimum lot size is L^*.

The analysis shows that communities that decide to maximize fiscal-squeeze transfers from new residents set higher required lot sizes than those in neutrally zoned communities, where lot sizes are set such that fiscal-squeeze transfers equal zero. The large lot sizes help to attract high-income newcomers who wish to buy large lots by subsidizing their land purchases. Since the price of land per acre falls as lot size increases, the subsidy increases with lot size. The subsidy is at the expense of potential small-lot consumers in the community and the region, who must pay a high land price for small lots in other communities. The large-lot community loses fiscal-squeeze revenues owing to lower land value; but if housing consumption increases with lot size, then the loss of revenue from land is made up by increased revenue from higher housing value and greater savings per acre in the incremental cost of public services.

Fiscal-Squeeze Strategies with Pollution

Until now it has been assumed that new housing built in a community has little or no adverse environmental effect. In this section, the model is generalized by assuming that communities demand pollution-compensating transfers (PCT) in return for incurring the environmental loss caused by new housing. We have suggested that PCT might vary inversely with the value of new houses built. Communities can affect the value of new houses via their control over lot sizes. Thus in the fiscal-squeeze equation, PCT might be a function of L. Further, if pollution is seen as a pure public good within the community, then every resident incurs a utility loss from pollution, regardless of the size of the community. In that case, the pollution term might be multiplied by the community's population.[o]

These considerations suggest a generalized fiscal-squeeze transfer function:

$$FST = t[P_L(Q_A, L) \cdot Q_A + E_A Q_A] - C_A(L) \cdot Q_A$$
$$- PCT(L) \cdot Q_A \left(H + \frac{Q_A}{L} \right) \tag{3.7}$$

$(H + Q_A/L)$ is the total household population of the community, where H is the number of existing households and Q_A/L is the number of new households to be admitted by the zoning policy. Maximizing (3.7) with respect to Q_A and L, we get

$$\frac{\partial FST}{\partial L} = t \frac{\partial P_L}{\partial L} - \frac{\partial C_A}{\partial L} - \frac{\partial PCT}{\partial L} \left(H + \frac{Q_A}{L} \right) + \frac{PCT \cdot Q_A}{L^2} = 0 \tag{3.8}$$

and

$$\frac{\partial FST}{\partial Q_A} = t[P_L(1 + e_{P_L, Q_A}) + E_A] - C_A - PCT \cdot H - 2PCT \left(\frac{Q_A}{L} \right)$$
$$= 0 \tag{3.9}$$

In (3.8) the two new terms on the right are both positive, since $\partial PCT/\partial L < 0$. The two terms on the left are equal to zero at $L = L^*$, so the whole expression is positive at L^*. This implies that the optimum lot size, considering environmental effects, is greater than L^*. The adverse environmental effects of new development thus imply a more restrictive zoning strategy.

Equation (3.8) can be used to investigate the effects of changes in the community's existing population on its zoning strategy. Assuming that the terms $\partial P_L/\partial L$, $\partial C_A/\partial L$, and $\partial PCT/\partial L$ are constants, (3.8) can be differentiated and solved for $\partial L/\partial H$,

$$\frac{\partial L}{\partial H} = \partial PCT/\partial L \div \left[\frac{(\partial PCT/\partial L)Q_A}{L^2} - \frac{2PCT \cdot Q_A}{L^3} \right] \tag{3.10}$$

---

[o]The community is assumed to ignore any spillover effects of pollution on neighboring communities.

$\partial L / \partial H$ is positive, implying that communities with larger populations tend to set higher required lot sizes. This suggests a testable hypothesis: that new development with adverse environmental effects tends to occur in communities with smaller existing populations, since the cost of compensating them for the loss of environmental quality is lower. Further, suppose the adverse effects of a new development are not perceived by all residents of the community, but only by its near neighbors—say those people living within a one-mile radius. Then if environmental spillovers accruing to other communities are ignored, (3.10) suggests that environmentally adverse new developments tend to be sited on the borders of the community. Its adverse effects then fall partially on people who do not need to be compensated.

Equation (3.9) also has two new pollution terms. Both are negative, so that at $Q_A = Q_A^*$, the whole expression has a negative sign. The pollution terms increase the cost of developing land but do not affect tax revenues. Therefore the community offers less vacant land for development.

Thus if a community considers the value of new houses to be an index of their environmental quality and if it controls value indirectly through L, then the effect of adding environmental considerations is to make the community's zoning strategy more restrictive. It requires larger lot sizes and offers less land for development.

Variable Housing Value

This section will consider the case in which E_A, value of housing per acre built on a community's vacant lots, is variable. $E_A = P_H H_A$, where P_H is constant; but now suppose the quantity of housing bought varies with the size of the lot: $H_A = H_A(L)$. Suppose also that $\partial H_A / \partial L > 0$. Then a community maximizing the fiscal-squeeze transfer considers the function

$$FST = t[P_L(Q_A, L) \cdot Q_A + P_H \cdot H_A(L) \cdot Q_A] - C_A(L) \cdot Q_A \quad (3.11)$$

where environmental costs are ignored. Alternatively, the value of housing might also depend on the price of land. In that case the function would be

$$FST = t[P_L(Q_A, L) \cdot Q_A + P_H \cdot H_A(P_L, L) \cdot Q_A] - C_A(L) \cdot Q_A \quad (3.12)$$

The first order conditions for (3.11) are

$$\frac{\partial FST}{\partial L} = t \frac{\partial P_L}{\partial L} - \frac{\partial C_A}{\partial L} + tP_H \left(\frac{\partial H_A}{\partial L} + \frac{\partial H_A}{\partial P_L} \frac{\partial P_L}{\partial L} \right) = 0 \quad (3.13)$$

and

$$\frac{\partial FST}{\partial Q_A} = tP_L(1 + e_{Q_A P_L}) - C_A + tP_H H_A = 0 \quad (3.14)$$

Equation (3.13) has a straightforward interpretation. We know that at $L = L^*$ the two left-hand terms are equal to zero. The last two terms in (3.13) are positive, since $\partial H_A/\partial L$ is positive by assumption, while the quantity of housing consumed is assumed to be negatively related to the price per unit of land on which the house is built. The community's optimum response is to increase its required lot size above L^*.

In (3.14) the two left-hand terms are again equal to zero at Q_A^*, and the right-hand term is positive. Therefore the whole expression is positive at Q_A^*, and the community's optimum response is to increase its supply of vacant land above Q_A^*.

These results are intuitively appealing. The community taxes both house and land value. Therefore if $P_H H_A$ is a positive function of L, the community gets a greater increase in tax revenue from a small increase in its lot size requirement than it would if $P_H H_A$ were constant. Consequently the community should increase its required lot size to a further point than L^*. Similarly, the benefit from offering a unit of land for development is increased, so the community has an incentive to increase its available land supply.

Looking now at the case in which H_A is a function of $P_L L$, the first order conditions for (3.12) are

$$\frac{\partial FST}{\partial L} = t\frac{\partial P_L}{\partial L} - \frac{\partial C_A}{\partial L} + tP_H \frac{\partial H_A}{\partial(P_L L)} P_L(1 + e_{P_L L}) = 0 \qquad (3.15)$$

and

$$\frac{\partial FST}{\partial Q_A} = tP_L(1 + e_{P_L Q_A}) - C_A + tP_H H_A = 0 \qquad (3.16)$$

The new specification of the H_A function does not affect the optimal supply of land in (3.16) if $\partial H_A/\partial L$ does not depend on Q_A. Equation (3.15) is different, however. If $\partial H/\partial(P_L L)$ is positive and $-1 < e_{P_L L} < 0$, then the last term of (3.15) is positive and the same result holds as discussed above. If the quantity of building is a function of the value of the lot, then the optimum lot size for a community maximizing its fiscal-squeeze transfer is greater than the optimum if H_A were constant.

Suppose, however, that the term $\partial H_A/\partial(P_L L)$ were negative or positive but declining (i.e., with a negative second derivative). If it were negative, then the community's optimum lot size would be lower than L^*. If H_A were a function of both L and $P_L L$ and $\partial H_A/\partial(P_L L)$ were negative, then the outcome would be indeterminate. The optimum lot size would be larger or smaller than L^* depending on whether the positive terms in equation (3.13) $tP_H [\partial H_A/\partial L + (\partial H_A/\partial P_L)(\partial P_L/\partial L)]$, or the negative terms in (3.15) $tP_H [\partial H_A/\partial(P_L L)] P_L(1 + e_{P_L L})$, were larger.

This range of possible results can be explored by deriving from utility theory a specific relationship between housing and land expenditure. Suppose consumers have Cobb-Douglas utility functions of the form

$$U = H^\alpha L^\beta X^\gamma \tag{3.16}$$

where X is demand for other goods besides housing and land. Consumers maximize utility subject to a budget constraint,

$$P_H H + P_L L + P_X X = Y$$

However because of zoning their land consumption is fixed; they can only vary consumption of H and X. The first-order conditions with respect to H and X and the budget constraint can be solved for a demand function for housing:

$$H = \frac{\alpha(Y - P_L L)}{(\alpha + \gamma)P_H} \tag{3.17}$$

The Cobb-Douglas utility function implies a demand for housing as a function of income, expenditure on land and the price of housing, which is constant. The quantity of housing demanded is a negative function of expenditure on land.

In order to substitute this demand function for housing into the fiscal-squeeze transfer expression of equation (3.12), the individual demand for housing (H) must be translated into a total demand for housing. If N is the total number of new lots in the community, then $NL = Q_A$ and $P_H H_A Q_A$ in (3.12) equals $P_H H N$. Thus the new objective function is

$$FST = t \left[P_L(Q_A, L)Q_A + \frac{\alpha Q_A}{\alpha + \gamma} \frac{Y - P_L L}{L} \right] - C_A(L) \cdot Q_A \tag{3.18}$$

The first derivatives with respect to L and Q_A are

$$\frac{\partial FST}{\partial L} = t \frac{\partial P_L}{\partial L} - \frac{\partial C_A}{\partial L} - \frac{\alpha t}{\alpha + \Gamma} \left(\frac{\partial P_L}{\partial L} + \frac{Y}{L^2} \right) = 0 \tag{3.19}$$

and

$$\frac{\partial FST}{\partial Q_A} = t P_L (1 + e_{P_L Q_A}) - C_A + \frac{\alpha t}{\alpha + \gamma} \frac{Y - P_L L}{L} = 0 \tag{3.20}$$

In (3.19) the first two terms are equal to zero at L^*, whereas the third term is indeterminate. The optimum lot size for the community can be greater than or smaller than L^*. This result derives from the fact that housing and land are substitutes for each other under the Cobb-Douglas assumption. As a result, the higher a community's land requirement, the lower the level of housing consumption chosen.

The first-order condition for Q_A, equation (3.20), is slightly different in the Cobb-Douglas case. The third term is again positive, implying an optimal supply of land greater than Q_A^*, the optimum supply of land increases when housing expenditure is variable, regardless of whether housing consumption and land consumption per household are complements or substitutes. In either case, there is greater benefit in property tax revenues to be had from supplying land, so the community should continue to supply land past its cutoff point in the constant expenditure case.

These results have interesting implications concerning the effects of zoning on the ratio of investment in buildings versus land in metropolitan areas. It has been suggested that lot-size zoning plus property-tax financing of local services leads to underinvestment in structures. Communities use lot sizes as their major zoning tool. Property owners are then free to build structures of whatever value they wish, yet they are taxed on the total value of land plus structure. They can thus gain admittance to a community by buying a lot of the required size, but generate less fiscal squeeze for the community than expected by building a low-value house.

There is obviously less scope for zoning to distort investment patterns if land and building expenditures are complements than if they are substitutes. Suppose the relation were linear, as in

$$H = b(P_L L) \tag{3.21}$$

Then the $P_H H / P_L L$ ratio is a constant and zoning at any lot size would not change the ratio of investment in buildings relative to land.

Now suppose that the relation were

$$H = a(P_L L)^b \quad (0 < b < 1) \tag{3.22}$$

This implies a declining $P_H H / P_L L$ ratio as L increases. The community then might select a zoning level which would imply a lower ratio than would prevail in the absence of zoning. However since expenditures on both land and housing rise as lot size is increased, the ratio varies less than do the two components. So the scope of possibility for distortion due to zoning is limited.

The possibilities are less limited in the substitutes case. By using the Cobb-Douglas utility function, we can establish the optimum expenditure ratio on land and capital that would prevail in the absence of zoning. We can then examine the distorting effects of zoning.

Suppose consumers maximize the Cobb-Douglas utility function (3.17) subject to a budget constraint. Assume for the moment there is no zoning. Compute the first-order conditions with respect to land and housing consumption and solve to get

$$\frac{P_H H}{P_L L} = \frac{\alpha}{\beta} \tag{3.23}$$

The optimum ratio of expenditure on housing relative to land is α/β.

Going back to the zoning model, consider the same utility function, but with a zoning constraint added. This is the condition $L \geq \bar{L}$, which says that land consumption must be at least $\bar{L}$. The new objective function is

$$Z = H^\alpha L^\beta X^\gamma - \lambda_1(P_H H + P_L L + P_X X - Y) - \lambda_2(\bar{L} - L) \quad (3.24)$$

The first-order conditions with respect to L and H are

$$\alpha H^{\alpha-1} L^\beta X^\gamma - \lambda_1 P_H = 0 \quad (3.25)$$

$$\beta H^\alpha L^{\beta-1} X^\gamma - \lambda_1 P_L + \lambda_2 = 0 \quad (3.26)$$

Solving these for the expenditure ratio, we get

$$\frac{P_H H}{P_L L} = \frac{\alpha}{\beta}\left(1 - \frac{\lambda_2}{\lambda_1 P_L}\right) \quad (3.27)$$

The ratio under zoning is equal to the unconstrained ratio multiplied by the constant expression in parentheses. $\lambda_1 P_L$ is the utility of the marginal expenditure on land, λ_2 is the utility loss at the margin owing to the zoning constraint. If the zoning constraint is not binding, then $\lambda_2 = 0$ and the expenditure ratio becomes the same as under a nonzoning regime.

If the constraint is binding, then the λ_2 term can be interpreted graphically. Figure 3-4 shows the declining marginal utility of land and the constant marginal utility of income spent on land. λ_2 is the difference between the marginal utility of income spent on land and the marginal utility of land at $\bar{L}$, denoted $U_L(\bar{L})$. In the figure this is $ac - bc$ or the distance ab.

Substituting $\lambda_2 = \lambda_1 P_L - U_L(\bar{L})$ into (3.27), we get

$$\frac{P_H H}{P_L L} = \frac{\alpha}{\beta}\left(\frac{U_L(\bar{L})}{\lambda_1 P_L}\right) \quad (3.28)$$

When the zoning constraint is binding it is clear that $U_L(\bar{L})$ must be less than $\lambda_1 P_L$; hence it must be that $U_L(\bar{L})/\lambda_1 P_L$ is less than unity. Therefore expenditure on housing relative to land under zoning is lower than it would be in the absence of zoning. Zoning does cause "underinvestment in structures."

It also follows that the ratio of physical quantities in housing relative to land, H/L, declines under zoning. Expenditure on a lot is assumed to rise or remain constant when zoning increases required lot sizes, $P_L L \leq P_L \bar{L}$. Zoning therefore has the effect of raising L and lowering P_L by the same or a smaller percentage, so that $P_L L$ rises or remains constant. In (3.28), P_H is a constant, so the ratio $H/P_L L$ declines when zoning is introduced. Therefore H must decline if $P_L L$ stays constant or must decline or rise less fast than $P_L L$ if expenditure on land rises. In any of these situations, the ratio H/L declines when zoning is introduced. It declines faster than the ratio $H/P_L L$.

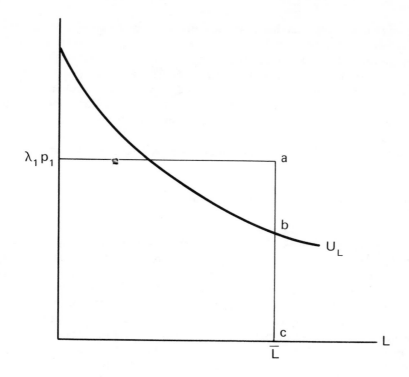

Figure 3-4. Marginal Utility of Land

Thus two results have been proved concerning the effects of zoning on investment in land and housing when consumers have Cobb-Douglas utility functions. Zoning causes a decrease in the ratio of relative expenditures on housing to land, $P_H H / P_L L$, and a decrease in the ratio of physical quantities invested, H/L. These effects are small when the lot size required by zoning is not much greater than the lot size that would prevail otherwise. The distortion increases as zoning requires larger and larger lot sizes.

Two other results can be added. From the definition of fiscal-squeeze zoning, total expenditure on land and housing under zoning ($P_H H + P_L L$) rises relative to the level that would prevail without zoning. This must be true or the tax revenues collected from new residents would be no greater than the revenues collected from previous residents of the community, who entered before zoning was enacted or when its provisions were less strict. The extra expenditure on land plus housing under zoning consists of a lower expenditure on housing and a greater expenditure on land. Under a Cobb-Douglas utility function it can be shown that the increase in land expenditure is financed by equal proportionate decreases in expenditures on housing and on other goods. The ratio of expenditures on housing relative to other goods therefore remains constant regardless of the zoning provisions adopted.

Fiscal-squeeze zoning thus has important allocation effects on investment in metropolitan areas. Under certain assumptions, it causes "underinvestment in structures" and also "underexpenditure on other goods." It transfers income from buyers of small lots to buyers of large lots and from new residents to existing residents of zoned communities. Fiscal zoning also has important effects on land value, both in individual community land markets and over the whole metropolitan area. These are examined below.

Household Location Choice under Zoning

We have analyzed the process by which communities decide to adopt a fiscal-squeeze zoning strategy. However, the process of location choice by consumers has not yet been discussed, so it is unclear whether households are willing to pay the subsidies required to enter a fiscal-squeeze community. Households might instead search for communities that do not attempt to squeeze new residents. Or they might choose to remain in the central city. The first parts of this section describe a general theory of household location choice in a fragmented metropolitan area. The last part integrates this theory with the fiscal-squeeze objective of community zoning behavior, in order to establish why some households choose fiscal-squeeze communities.

The salient fact about location choice in a large American metropolis is that households have a wide choice of places to live. Within a twenty-mile radius they generally have a choice of one or more central cities and up to several hundred suburbs.[p] Each is a separate jurisdiction. Most probably have zoning provisions that require consumption of a certain amount of housing and land as an admission requirement for newcomers. In return, each provides education and other local public services. Communities are initially assumed to follow neutral zoning strategies. The central city is an exception to this rule, however. We assume here that it provides a fixed level of public services, but has no zoning requirements.

Each suburban community sets a lot size requirement (L). The price function for land is assumed to be the same for every community, P_L is determined by distance from the central city (u). The price of housing capital (P_H) and the quantity of capital used in one house (H) are assumed to be constant.[q] Therefore when a community sets L, it determines the total

---

[p]The New York SMSA contains 438 local governments or 29,000 people per government. Data for other SMSAs are: Philadelphia, 339 or 13,000; Los Angeles, 76 or 79,000; Boston, 78 or 33,000; Chicago, 148 or 34,000.

[q]The assumption concerning H is a simplification. Alternately, a housing supply function $H(L)$

land-plus-building value of a housing unit, $P_L L + P_H H$. Newcomers to the community must buy housing of at least this value.

Communities also set a fixed quality level for local public services (E), which they provide to all residents. The average cost per household of E determines the property tax rate (t). Each household is assumed to have a preference for a certain amount of land and a certain quality of public services. Households' utility functions are defined over land, public services, housing, and a composite good (X),[r]

$$U = U(L, E, H, X) \qquad (3.29)$$

Households maximize utility subject to an income constraint,

$$Y = P_L L + t(P_L L + P_H H) + P_H H + P_X X, \qquad (3.30)$$

where public services are paid for via a property tax on land and housing. Each household determines that its utility function is maximized at some level of land and public services consumption, L^* and E^*. In the Tiebout model, consumers live on dividend earnings and do not work. Therefore they are free to locate in any suburb with L^* as its land requirement and E^* as its public services level, regardless of its location. A suburb exactly meeting these specifications always exists in the neutral-zoning model. This sorting process of households to communities therefore has the result that everyone in a given suburb owns a house of exactly the minimum zoning requirement. So all inhabitants of a community pay the same property taxes and this amount is recognized as the price of public services. Given the variety of zoning-taxing levels in many suburbs, households can buy as much land and as much public services as if their choices were unconstrainted by zoning. The resulting allocation is Pareto optimum.

The neutral-zoning case also suggests that households living in suburbs consume more housing than those in the central city. This is because in the central city, while housing choice is unconstrained by zoning, property taxes discourage housing consumption. Property taxes are not a price paid for public services, because the services received are the same regardless of the price paid. In the suburbs, however, property taxes do not discourage housing consumption, which is therefore higher.

The neutral-zoning theory of household location choice makes stringent demands on any city, even a large one, in its assumptions. Suppose some

---

could be used, which would make housing a function of required lot size. However this would complicate the exposition without materially changing the results. If the model dealt primarily with the central city, where cost and profitability factors determine the optimum capital/land ratio, then a variable housing specification would be necessary. However, the model deals primarily with suburban land use. In that context the assumption is made that whether a given house (probably owner-occupied) is placed on half an acre or two acres of land is mostly a matter of taste or of zoning.

[r]This description of consumer location choice under neutral zoning is adapted from [6].

suburbs in a metropolitan area practice fiscal-squeeze rather than neutral zoning. Then the variety of *L-E* combinations offered by suburbs is restricted, since suburbs require newcomers to consume more land than their existing residents, thus eliminating the bottom of the spectrum. In that case households might not be able to find suburbs that exactly suit their preferences. Alternately, if all suburbs practice neutral zoning but not all the desired *L-E* options are provided, then again the neutral-zoning results do not hold. Households incur a deadweight loss on land consumption even in suburbs that do not attempt to collect transfers from newcomers.

Therefore we need a more general theory of locational choice, one which dispenses with some of the more restrictive assumptions of neutral zoning. In particular, the theory must deal with the case in which the number of suburbs is less than the number of distinct housing and public service preferences. Also, it should incorporate specifically the spatial and central characteristics of the location choice problem.

The spatial aspect of consumer location choice is formulated using three special assumptions: first, that households have no preference for any particular distance from the central city, except via the effect of distance on the price of housing and the cost of commuting; second, that the marginal disutility of time spent commuting is constant, i.e., people do not dislike the second fifteen minutes spent commuting more than the first fifteen minutes, nor the third more than the second; third, that all residents of the metropolitan area work in the central city.[s]

The cost of commuting has a money and a time element. It is equal to $(wh + c)u$, where u is the distance travelled to work each way, c is the operating cost per two miles, h is the time required to travel two miles, and w is some function of the wage rate. The cost of commuting subtracts from income, so the new budget constraint is

$$Y = P_L L + t(P_L L + P_H H) + P_H H + P_X X + u(wh + c) \quad (3.31)$$

Long-run locational equilibrium requires that if all households have equal incomes, then all must derive equal utility. Households derive no satisfaction from living at any distance relative to another. If they could increase utility by living at another distance, they would move. At long-run equilibrium, therefore, a price function for land is established such that no one wishes to move.

Since the cost of commuting is linear, households that live at greater distances from the center and consume the same amount of housing must face a lower price of land. Otherwise they would achieve a lower utility level and would change locations. Therefore, when distance is added to the

---

[s]These assumptions and the spatial model described in the next few paragraphs are taken from [10].

model, both the price and the quantity of land consumed become functions of distance from the central city. As distance increases, commuting costs rise and the price of land falls. In order for households at all distances to achieve the same utility level, extra land consumption must compensate them for the higher commuting cost of locating further out.

Mills [10] shows that the assumptions just described imply a price function for land which declines slower than linearly as distance increases, as in Figure 3-5. Land consumption in the Mills model rises at an increasing rate with distance if all households have the same income, as in curve aa, Figure 3-6. Mills also shows that if there are several income classes in the city and the income elasticity of demand for land is at least unity, then higher income classes live in rings around the central city in ascending order of distance from the center. In Figure 3-6, the broken line ab shows land consumption in a multi-income city. The lowest income group lives in region I, the next higher income group in region II, and so on. Each group maximizes utility anywhere in his distance region. Land consumption increases with distance, but with discrete jumps where two income groups meet at a boundary.[t]

In order to place consumer theory in a spatial context, it is necessary to borrow assumptions amounting to a whole urban theory. However, the urban theory borrowed here is a theory of metropolitan location without zoning. For our purposes, it must be modified by adding and examining the effects of both neutral and fiscal-squeeze zoning when only a limited set of L-E options is offered by communities in the metropolitan area.

There are three separate situations in this model. One expresses the choice faced by a central-city household. Its housing choice is unconstrained, but it faces a variable property tax payment on land depending on lot value, in exchange for a fixed level of public services. This case also applies to households living under a unified metropolitan area government which provides a fixed level of public services. The second situation represents the choice of a household that considers buying a house of the minimum value required by a given suburb. The third situation applies to a household considering buying a higher-than-minimum-value house in a given suburb. This last case arises because there are fewer suburbs than there are possible choices of housing and public services levels.

Case A: The Central-City Case

When distance and a central focus are added to the central-city location problem, the household objective function becomes

---

[t]These results are derived in [10].

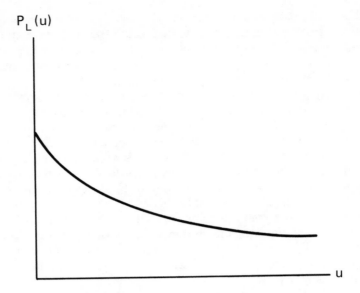

Figure 3-5. Land Price Function

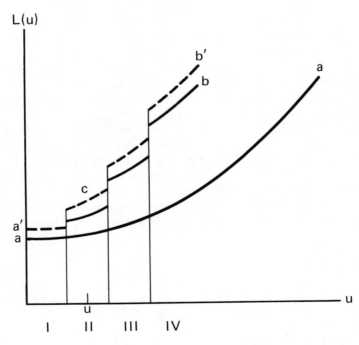

Figure 3-6. Land Consumption

$$Z = U(L, E, H, X) - \lambda\{P_L(u) \cdot L(u) + t[P_L(u)L(u) + P_HH]$$

$$+ P_HH + P_XX(u) + u(wh + c) - Y\} \qquad (3.32)$$

where $L(u)$, $P_L(u)$, and $X(u)$ are functions of distance. There is no constraint on housing consumption, but a fixed amount of public goods is provided to all residents. Payment for public goods is via a property tax levied on housing and land expenditures. No function relates the value of public services received to the price paid for them. The price of land varies over distance as shown in Figure 3-5. The individual consumer takes the land price function as given.

The household maximizes (3.32) over consumption of land, other goods and distance, but not over consumption of public services, since these are fixed in the central city, nor over housing consumption, since this is fixed all over the metropolitan area. The first order conditions, $\partial Z/\partial L$, $\partial L/\partial X$ and $\partial Z/\partial u$, are

$$\frac{\partial U}{\partial L} = \lambda[P_L(u)(1 + t)] \qquad (3.33)$$

$$\frac{\partial U}{\partial X} = \lambda P_X \qquad (3.34)$$

$$\frac{\partial U}{\partial L} \cdot \frac{\partial L}{\partial P_L} \cdot \frac{\partial P_L}{\partial u} = \lambda \left[L \frac{\partial P_L}{\partial u}(1 + t) + P_L \frac{\partial L}{\partial P_L} \frac{\partial P_L}{\partial u}(1 + t) \right.$$

$$\left. + (wh + c) + P_X \frac{\partial X}{\partial u} \right] \qquad (3.35)$$

Equation (3.33) says that the marginal utility of land is equal to the marginal utility of the combined price of land and public services, where λ is the marginal utility of income. The property tax drives a wedge into the marginal condition for land and causes central-city residents to incur a deadweight loss. This can be shown graphically. Figure 3-7 shows the declining marginal utility of land and the marginal utility of income. They intersect at a land consumption level of n, which maximizes utility. However, public services are financed by a tax on land and buildings, which lifts the price of land to $\lambda P_L(1 + t)$. Land consumption drops to m and the household loses consumer surplus equal to *defg*, composed of a deadweight loss on land consumption of *hgd* and a transfer of *efgh* via property taxes to the central city.

Equation (3.34) says that the marginal utility of other goods is equal to their price. Equation (3.35) is the distance equilibrium condition. A small increase in distance has four effects on income and consumption. On the right-hand side of the equation, the first term is the price reduction of land caused by the increase in distance; it is negative. The second term is the

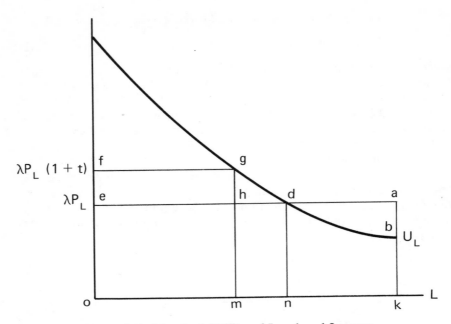

Figure 3-7. Marginal Utility of Land and Income

change in the quantity of land consumed due to its price fall; it is positive. The third term is the extra transport cost added by extra distance; it is positive. The fourth is the decreased expenditure on other goods, which offsets increased expenditure on land at greater distances. The four terms together give the net effect on utility of a change in distance from the central city. The household increases distance until the marginal utility of the extra housing and commuting and less other goods is just equal to the value of these consumption changes retained as income. Within the central city, the change in utility due to a change in distance should be equal to zero over a range of distances, since households of a given income should be on the same indifference curve at more than a single location. As households move further out, the consumer surplus from land increases, but this gain is offset by a consumper surplus loss from decreased consumption of public services and/or other goods.

Case B: The Minimum Suburb Case

This section discusses the location choice of a household considering whether to move to a particular suburb from the central city or to another suburb. The problem can be generalized to that of a household considering which of several suburbs suits its preferences best.

Suppose a particular suburb has a lot-size requirement that requires newcomers to purchase a lot of size k. Potential newcomers thus face an indivisibility. Their "marginal unit of housing consumption" is the whole value of the land plus building required by zoning. As a result, the minimum suburb case cannot be treated using Kuhn-Tucker optimization techniques.

Figure 3-7 shows the household's declining marginal utility of land curve and its constant marginal utility of income. The utility maximizing level of land consumption is at n, while the suburb's zoning requirement is k, where $k > n$. (The converse case is treated in case C). Thus the zoning requirement is a binding constraint on the household's utility maximization. The utility of buying a zoned suburban lot at a given distance from the center is the area under the curve from o to k or $\int_o^k U_L \, dL$. The utility of the income that must be spent on quantity k of housing is $\lambda P_L k$ or the rectangle $okae$. The resulting consumer surplus from suburban housing, net of deadweight loss, is $\int_o^k U_L \, dL - \lambda P_L k$. The household compares this quantity to its opportunity cost of moving. If the consumer surplus is greater, it moves. However it must also add the possible increase or decrease in consumer surplus from public services in the central city relative to the suburb. If the household decides to move, then the triangle adb represents the deadweight loss incurred due to the suburban zoning constraint.

The household deciding to remain in the central city also incurs a loss of consumer surplus from the suburban zoning constraint, because zoning prevents it from consuming a higher level of public services than is provided in the central city. This result differs from the neutral zoning case in that there is loss to the household whether it remains in the city or moves to the suburbs. This loss would not occur if all suburbs were neutrally zoned, since a suburb would exist in which the zoning constraint k equalled n.

In this discussion, the household considered one suburb at a given distance from the center. However, the effect of distance in this model means that in considering one suburb the household is implicitly considering all other suburbs in the ring around the central city occupied by its income class and perhaps suburbs in other rings. The household's equal-utility land-consumption locus over each distance in a ring is shown by Figure 3-6, curve ab, for several rings. Suppose one suburb at distance u, in ring II decided to require housing consumption at c. No households would locate in the suburb, since there is a range of land-consumption-distance combinations along ab that would place them on a higher indifference curve than u.

Thus one suburb alone cannot pursue a fiscal-squeeze zoning strategy because of the plethora of higher-utility alternatives nearby. In order for fiscally zoned suburbs to succeed in attracting migrants, there must be no better alternatives. This is shown by the dotted line $a'b'$, representing the situation in which all suburbs pursue fiscal-squeeze zoning. Each requires higher land consumption than households would freely choose at that distance. If the dotted line represents the zoning situation confronting the household, then it is forced to locate in some fiscal-squeeze suburb. Then Figure 3-7 describes its consumer surplus loss from fiscal zoning. The line $\lambda P_L(u)$ is located differently at each u, but at each distance, fiscal-squeeze zoning causes a consumer surplus loss to occur, equal to the triangle adb. This analysis assumes that the consumer derives no satisfaction from locating in a less densely populated community. If he does, then the P_L curve in Figure 3-7 shifts up somewhat as k increases. This would reduce the deadweight loss derived from zoning. However, under fiscal-squeeze zoning, only newcomers, not the older residents, consume land at k. Thus their effect on the community's overall density level is small and is ignored here.

The same analysis applies to consumer choice with respect to public goods, E, as to land. The marginal utility of an extra unit of public goods (or a higher quality of public goods) is assumed to decline with increasing quantity. Suppose E refers to public schools. The household lives in the central city, where schools of quality r are provided. In Figure 3-8 its total utility from public schools is $\int_0^r U_E \, dE$. If it pays $P_r r$ in dollars for schools ($\lambda P_r r$ in foregone utility), then it has a net consumer surplus of $abdc$ from schools. (This quantity could be negative if taxes were higher.) In a suburban location with a lower cost per unit of school quality, P_s, the household prefers quality q. For this it pays $\lambda P_s q$ and realizes consumer surplus of aef. If it moves from the central city to the suburb, its net consumer surplus gain is $aef - abdc$, shown as the shaded area on the graph.

However, quality q of schools may not exist and the household may have to choose quality s as the closest substitute. Here, marginal costs between q and s exceed marginal benefits, so the household incurs a net deadweight loss of fgh. As in the housing case, it may incur deadweight loss whether it lives in the central city or in a suburb. The consumer surplus realized on public goods in the suburb is

$$\int_0^s U_E \, dE - \lambda P_s s \qquad (3.36)$$

where marginal public goods quality past q causes a loss of consumer surplus. If the household moves to the suburb, its higher consumption of public services must be offset by decreased consumption of other goods.

It is assumed that households choose the location that maximizes their total consumer surplus from land, public services, and other goods.

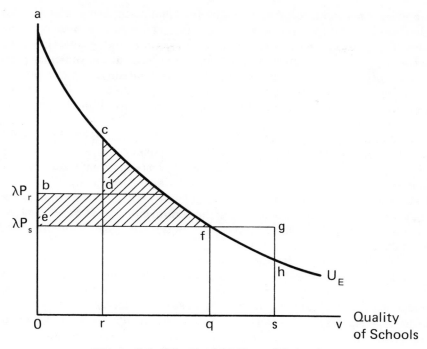

Figure 3-8. Marginal Utility of Schools

Households compare the consumer surplus to be realized in other locations to the consumer surplus realized in their present location, which would be foregone by moving. Consumer surplus in the new location is net of deadweight loss incurred from consumption of both housing and public services under constraints, if these are binding. This decision function can be represented as follows:

$$\left[\int_{o}^{k} U_L \, dL - P_L(u)k \right] - \left[\int_{o}^{n} U_L \, dL - \lambda P_L(u)n \right]$$

$$+ \left[\int_{o}^{s} U_E \, dE - \lambda P_s s \right] - \left[\int_{o}^{r} U_E \, dE - \lambda P_r r \right]$$

$$+ \left[\int_{o}^{v} U_X \, dX - \lambda P_X v \right] - \left[\int_{o}^{w} U_X \, dX - \lambda P_X w \right] \leqq 0 \qquad (3.37)$$

The first four bracket terms represent (i) consumer surplus realized from housing in a suburb, (ii) the consumer surplus opportunity cost of housing in the central city, (iii) consumer surplus realized from public services in a suburb, and (iv) the consumer surplus opportunity cost of public services in the central city. The fifth and sixth terms relate to the other goods bought with residual income. (v) is consumer surplus realized from other goods bought with income left over from land, public services, and commuting expenditures in the suburb and (vi) is the consumer surplus opportunity cost from other goods if the household stayed in the central city and had more money left over after other expenditures. The equation compares a central city and a suburb location, but two suburbs could also be compared.

In comparing a suburban with a central-city location, the household would be better off in the suburb if (3.37) is positive. The sign of (3.37) reflects partially offsetting gains and losses. Term (vi) is greater than (v), so their overall effect is negative. The terms relating to land, (i) and (ii), and to public services, (iii) and (iv), could be positive or negative. If both were negative, the household would stay in the central city. If one were negative and one positive, or both positive, the household might move or stay depending on relative magnitudes.

When the Tiebout-Hamilton assumption that a suburb exists which provides every possible L-E level is relaxed, the result that households who move to the suburbs from the central city consume more land no longer holds. We assume that the suburb which provides exactly the consumer's desired L and E levels does not exist. As a result, the household may incur a deadweight loss on land in the suburb where it chooses to locate. In particular, suppose it wishes to consume very high quality public services. The suburb providing this may have a land consumption requirement lower than or equal to the household's land consumption level in the central city. The household could buy more land than the zoning requirement, but may choose not to, since its deadweight loss from buying more land might be great. This would imply a steeply declining marginal utility of land curve. Thus, when not all land and public services combinations are available in the existing suburbs, we cannot predict whether land consumption will be greater in the central city or in the suburbs.

Case C: The Higher-than-Minimum Suburb Case

The third case is that of a household considering moving to a higher-than-minimum value house in a given suburb. If the zoning requirements of most suburbs tend to satisfy the demands of households who wish to live at that distance, then this household must have divergent tastes. It wishes to consume more land than other households with the same income, but the same quality of public services. We separate this decision into two parts: the household first chooses whether to live in a suburb with a zoned land consumption requirement of k and a tax rate of t and then chooses whether to buy more land than k and how much. The first decision is of the same form as case B. The second decision is of the same form as case A, with a constrained utility function of the form:

$$Z = U(L, E, H, X) - \lambda\{[P_L(u) \cdot L(u) + P_H H] (1 + t)$$
$$+ P_X X(u) + u(wh + c) - Y\} \tag{3.38}$$

This is the same function as in case A. Again, property tax payments cause the household to incur a deadweight loss on land if it consumes more than the suburb's zoning requirement, k. When the household buys more land than k, the extra tax it pays does not buy a larger quantity or quality of public services.

For the case C household, equation (3.37) tells it whether to move to a particular suburb. The first-order conditions, (3.34) and (3.35), tell it how much land to buy over the suburb's zoned minimum, k.

The central-city resident and the case C suburbanite have two features in common. The first is that neither incurs any loss of consumer surplus due to "excessive" land consumption. The city resident incurs no loss since central-city zoning does not restrict consumption possibilities and the suburbanite because he maximizes utility by choosing to consume more land than the zoning constraint requires. Second, both incur a loss of consumer surplus from property taxes. The central-city resident can limit this loss by moving to the suburbs if he wishes. Similarly the suburban dweller can limit his loss by moving to a suburb where the difference between his chosen level of land consumption and the zoned minimum is smallest. This difference should generally be smaller than the difference between the zoned minimum, k, at the original suburb and the zoned minimum at the next higher suburb, j. If the household wished to buy as much or more land than j, it could minimize the loss of consumer surplus by living in j rather than k.

Suppose a household chooses suburb k because it prefers the level of public services provided by this suburb. However the household wants to consume $k + \Delta$ of land, so it pays more for public services than their "price." The price of public services is tkP_L, but the household pays $t(k + \Delta)P_L$. Suppose a new suburb is formed with land requirement j, where $j > k$. If j's tax rate is also t and $k + \Delta > j$, then the household can get public services worth tjP_L by moving to suburb j, where $tjP_L > tkP_L$. It will still suffer some loss of consumer surplus in j, since j's zoning requirement is too low and its level of public services provision may be too high. Still the household incurs smaller loss in j than in k.

Some other suburb might make the household's consumer surplus loss disappear entirely. This suburb would have a zoning minimum equal to $k + \Delta$ and a tax rate s less than t, such that $tk = s(k + \Delta)$. In this suburb the household has an unconstrained housing choice and incurs no consumer surplus loss from taxes. This is because it pays the minimum amount for that level of public services which maximizes its utility. In the Tiebout-Hamilton case, enough suburbs are assumed to exist to accommodate everyone's preference without any consumer surplus loss. Here, fewer suburbs exist, so that some mixing of housing values occurs in each. But the degree of mixing is limited by the tendency of households who prefer the most expensive houses in each suburb to minimize their consumer surplus loss by moving to a suburb with a higher minimum housing value.

This three-case model of consumer location thus provides a statement of the conditions under which households move to the suburbs, as well as a new explanation as to when and why they choose to consume more housing in the suburbs than in the central city. Households compare the consumer surplus they would realize in the central city and the suburbs from both land and public services. The combined center-city consumer surplus terms are the opportunity costs. Households move if this cost-benefit calculation comes out positive, but they do not entirely avoid incurring a consumer surplus loss, even in the suburb that maximizes utility.

The model suggests that a major motive in households' moves to the suburbs is the desire to consume more public goods than are available in the central city. The household will probably pay more taxes for public services in the suburbs. But the pay-more-and-get-more combination increases utility. If tax rates are the same or lower in the suburbs, then to pay more taxes the household must consume more land. The combination either increases consumer surplus or the household stays in the central city.

Thus the motive for households to consume more housing in the suburbs than in the central city is the obligatory tying of housing and public goods consumption in the suburbs. A household that wishes to buy the higher quantity public goods of the suburbs must buy the minimum housing consumption that the suburb requires. The effect of distance in the model, however, is to give the household many choices among "tied deals." Since it can maximize utility over land consumption anywhere in a range of distances, it can avoid one suburb's tied deal by going to any other suburb in the distance range of its income class. We can therefore predict that fiscal-squeeze zoning by suburbs will only succeed if many suburbs over a whole range of distances have similar requirements.

Fiscal-Squeeze Zoning and the Consumer-Location Model

The model of household location choice developed above deals only with the choice among communities that are neutrally zoned. It remains to discuss consumer-location choice in the context of suburbs pursuing fiscal-squeeze zoning. New residents in these suburbs must pay more than the cost of services provided to them. We assume here that newcomers to fiscal-squeeze suburbs must purchase houses which conform to the suburb's current zoning requirements.

Figure 3-9 shows the declining marginal utility curve for public services. The consumer in a neutrally zoned commumunity consumes public services at q, where the marginal utility of a unit of public services equals the marginal utility of the money spent on a unit of services held as income ($U_E = \lambda P_E$). However, in a fiscal-squeeze community, only the previous residents of the community achieve this situation. The new residents must pay a fiscal-squeeze transfer. Property taxes on their higher-value houses generate more revenue than the cost of services provided. Knowing the quality of public services provided by the community (which is the same for old and new residents), the price per unit can be calculated as the total property tax payment divided by the quantity of public services provided. Suppose this calculation reveals the unit prices to be P_E and P_E' for old and new residents respectively, where $P_E' > P_E$. The property tax rate is the same for old and new residents, but new residents' houses are worth more.

Figure 3-9 shows that a household paying P_E' per unit of public services in a fiscal-squeeze community chooses to consume a lower quality of services than the same household would choose if it were not squeezed. If the household could move to a neutrally zoned community with the same housing requirement, it would demand q of public services. In a fiscal-squeeze community it demands q', where $q' < q$. It makes a resource transfer to the other residents of the community of $abcd$ and incurs a deadweight loss of cde. However, in shopping among communities, the household can minimize this transfer by looking for the community that has the highest P_E level relative to a given P_E'.

The older residents of the fiscal-squeeze community also receive public services of level q'. However they only pay the cost of these services, P_E, or less, depending on how the community uses the fiscal-squeeze transfer. If the older residents are at equilibrium at public services level q' then they must have a lower demand for public services. Their marginal utility of public services curve is the dotted line in Figure 3-9. The older residents thus have a lower demand for public services than the newer, squeezed residents.

The situation of new residents in fiscal-squeeze communities is similar to that of central-city dwellers in that both pay more in property taxes than the cost of public services received. However, the central-city dweller has the alternative of choosing to consume less housing and paying lower taxes while receiving the same services. The household in a zoned suburb cannot consume less housing in the same community. It can only move to a

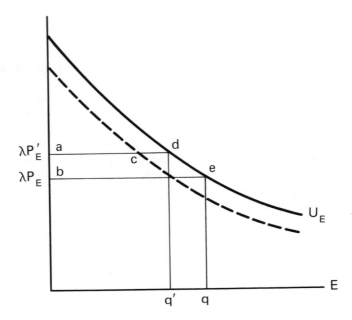

Figure 3-9. Marginal Utility of Public Services

different suburb. However, in any fiscal-squeeze community, the new resident's consumption of public services is discouraged by the community's zoning.

This conclusion concerning the allocation effect of zoning differs from those of other theories. It has been suggested that the property tax, as a non-neutral tax on housing, discourages housing consumption. The Tiebout-Hamilton theory took issue with this contention. It suggested that property taxes are considered by consumers as a price for public goods, comparable to the price they would pay for these services on a private market. Under the fiscal-squeeze assumptions, however, a different result emerges for new residents of zoned communities. Housing consumption is fixed by zoning at a relatively high level. The property tax therefore becomes a tax on public services consumption rather than on housing. Public services consumption is discouraged, since newcomers to a community must pay more than one dollar for every dollar's worth of public services received.

Thus, when a household chooses a location from among fiscal-squeeze communities, it chooses among various prices for various levels of public services provision, but all the prices are inflated relative to the cost of services received. The household therefore reduces its public services consumption and incurs a loss of consumer surplus. If it consumes the minimum zoned value of housing rather than more, it generally incurs a loss of consumer surplus on housing as well. Fiscal-squeeze zoning probably has the effect of increasing the proportion of households who incur a deadweight loss on housing, since it increases the level of zoned housing requirements generally. As a result, the number of households consuming the minimum should increase. The extra households incurring deadweight loss on housing may have the effect of causing more people to remain in the central city, relative to the number that would remain under neutral zoning. Fiscal-squeeze zoning thus bottles up more families in the central city by making the suburbs more expensive for new migrants.

The prediction of the Tiebout-Hamilton theory that suburbanites consume more housing than central-city residents is made stronger in a regime of fiscal-squeeze zoning. The higher zoning requirements mean that there are more case A and case B households in a metropolitan area, but fewer case C, who choose more housing than zoning requires. More households consume just the minimum that their community requires, thus consuming more housing in the zoned suburbs than they would in central city.

Households who consume a suburb's minimum housing requirement decide to locate in a suburb because they make a consumer surplus gain from living there relative to living in the central city or in another suburb. Their consumer surplus gain sets a theoretical maximum on the amount a zoned community can squeeze from a newcomer. The community can in theory absorb all the consumer surplus that a household gains from its move, but no more. In Figure 3-7, a household living in the central city consumes m of housing, where $U_L = \lambda P_L(1 + t)$. If the household were to move to an unzoned suburb, it would choose to consume n of housing and would make a consumer surplus gain equal to *defg*. If, however, it were forced to move to a fiscal-squeeze suburb, then the suburb could push its zoning requirement as far as some k, where $k > n$, before the household would choose to stay in the central city. At k, the suburb would have fully appropriated the consumer surplus gain the household makes in moving, since its consumer surplus gain from moving would be just equal to its deadweight loss from zoning, *dab*.

Similarly, the suburb could force the household to buy a level of public services such that its consumer surplus gain is fully offset by deadweight loss. This is the maximum that a community can squeeze from a newcomer. It is interesting to note that this theoretical amount is greater the less happy the household was with its previous situation. For example, if a household was relatively happy in the central city, then it would make only a small consumer surplus gain from moving to the suburbs and there would be less for the zoned community to squeeze. This applies in particular to low-income families who benefit from the central city's income redistribution and to those families who wish to consume little land.[u]

This theoretical maximum is likely to be constrained by more than the

[u]This suggests that fiscal-squeeze communities could profit by cooperatively increasing the information available in the consumer location area, so that each consumer could find his most preferred community, i.e., the one that can squeeze the most from him.

household's central-city alternative, since no community monopolizes the vacant land supply. In the context of the Mills model, households of a given income are indifferent among all suburbs in a particular range of distances from the central city, assuming there is no zoning. Fiscal-squeeze zoning has the effect of forcing an increase in land consumption over the level that households would choose without zoning. Thus, if one suburb in a distance range requires more land consumption than the household would otherwise choose at that distance, the household responds by choosing another suburb in the same range. Therefore if lots in various suburbs in the ring are close substitutes, all suburbs must employ fiscal-squeeze zoning if any are to employ it successfully. Furthermore, all suburbs in a distance range must choose similar fiscal-squeeze zoning requirements. Figure 3-6 shows in solid lines the land-consumption-distance function for a city in which four suburban distance rings are occupied by four income groups in ascending order. The dotted line shows a hypothetical land-distance tradeoff that would prevail if all suburbs zoned themselves fiscally to a similar degree.

These substitutions—households moving to the central city, to a closer ring, or to another suburb in the same ring—define the theoretical limits on a community's ability to pursue a fiscal-squeeze zoning strategy. In reality, the degree of substitutability among various suburbs may be much less than in this model; and thus the constraints on a suburb's freedom of action may be less severe. In particular, households may have a definite preference for one suburb over others, which would give that suburb more monopoly power.

It is interesting to note that the fiscal-squeeze zoning method of requiring households to buy large lots is a second-best method of forcing newcomers to transfer resources to the community. Suppose a community wishes to squeeze a resource transfer from each newcomer. It is constrained by law to charge the same property tax rate on new properties as old. Therefore, the only means it has of raising higher revenues from newcomers is to require them to buy more land. However, if side payments or higher tax rates on new properties than old are allowed, the community could raise the same resource transfer from newcomers more efficiently, without requiring excess housing consumption.

Suppose zoned communities allow newcomers to buy only as much land as they wish to buy. The community then assesses the value of land and computes a "pseudo-tax rate" such that tax revenues equal to cost plus a predetermined fiscal-squeeze transfer are collected on each new house. Newcomers thus incur an income loss from fiscal zoning, but zoning does not distort relative prices, nor does it force newcomers to buy too much land. The household gains because it is able to buy the amount of housing it wishes, while the community gets the same fiscal-squeeze transfer. In fact, the community should be able to exact an even greater transfer because the household's income is not reduced by the necessity of buying more land than it wants.

Thus discriminatory property tax rates or side payments could enable fiscal-squeeze communities to accomplish their objectives more efficiently. These tactics are probably used to some extent in practice by assessing newer properties at a higher percentage of market value than older properties. And they are commonly used by communities when dealing with incoming industries and firms. Firms are allowed to build the property they want, but in return they must make a contribution toward the community's new sewage system or new highway. These tactics are at least efficient, if not exactly fair.

Scarcity Zoning

A decision to exploit newcomers for the fiscal-squeeze transfers they can generate is one zoning strategy that a community might adopt. Another possibility is that communities might decide to control new development with the objective of maximizing the value of existing houses in the community. This is a more complicated strategy than maximization of fiscal-squeeze transfers, since new development affects the value of existing houses in several ways. First, the new development generates a total fiscal-squeeze transfer to the community at large. This transfer can be used by the community to lower taxes while maintaining the same level of local public services, or to raise the quality of services at the same property tax rate.[v] These fiscal benefits to the existing houses are capitalized as an increase in the value of the old houses, since the supply of old houses is constant.

A second effect is one of scarcity. Newer houses built in the community, although of higher value, are substitutable for older houses. Increased income and population in the metropolitan area cause an increase in demand for the existing houses of a given community, which causes their value to rise. However, if the supply of newer houses increases concurrently, then the scarcity premium on old houses is diminished or possibly eliminated. The supply of houses in the metropolitan area could be increased by building new houses in a particular community (community A) or in nearby communities. The effect of new construction on the scarcity value of old houses depends on the extent to which the larger, higher-value new houses in community A and in other communities are substitutes for the smaller existing houses of community A.

A third effect involves externalities. Suppose a community controlled by its older residents decided to forego new development completely in

[v]The community is assumed to balance its budget each year and to have no outstanding bonds.

order to maximize the value of its existing houses. Then an opportunity cost of the policy would be the foregone increase in value of the older houses due to the positive external effects of higher value houses locating nearby and upgrading the quality of the neighborhood.

The fiscal and scarcity effects are discussed separately below.

The Fiscal Effect

Suppose a community has two homogeneous groups of houses—old and new houses—where the total land plus building value of an old house is less than that of a new house. The value of an old house (V_o) in community A is

$$V_o = P_L L_o + E_{H,o} \tag{3.39}$$

where L_o is the fixed lot size of old houses and $E_{H,o}$ is the fixed value of the building comprising an old house. The value of an old house is related to the fiscal flows within its community in the following manner:

$$V_o = \frac{R_o}{r} - \frac{T_o}{r} + \frac{C_o}{r} \tag{3.40}$$

R_o is the rent generated by an old house, T_o is the property taxes paid on the house, C_o is the community's expenditure on local public services received by the old house, and r is the discount rate. R_o is, in effect, the rent which the property would generate in the absence of such local services as public shcools, streets, parks, sewerage, etc. An increment to the house's rent equal to $(C_o - T_o)$ is generated by the local public sector. Houses are assumed not to depreciate given a constant stream of maintenance expenditures at a predetermined level.

The taxes and expenditures received can be expressed as tax and expenditure rates on the value of the property and the expression can be aggregated over the fixed number of old houses (H_o) in the community:

$$H_o V_o = H_o \frac{R_o + c_o V_o - t V_o}{r} \tag{3.41}$$

In (3.41) the tax rate (t) is without a subscript to indicate that it must be the same on new and old houses. The expenditure rate (c_o) is the rate on old houses. Both t and c_o vary with the size and use of the fiscal-squeeze transfer generated by new development in the community.

Equation (3.41) could be used to determine the optimal zoning policy if the community wished to maximize the value of old houses in the community. In contrast, the fiscal-squeeze transfer strategy chooses a zoning policy which maximizes the excess of taxes over expenditures on new houses in the community. The equation to be maximized is

$$FST = t[P_L(Q_A, L) \cdot Q_A + P_H \cdot H_A \cdot Q_A] - C_A(L) \cdot Q_A \qquad (3.42)$$

The expression in brackets is the total value of new houses in the community. If N is the number of new houses, where $N = Q_A/L$, V_N is the value of a single new house, and C_N is the level of expenditures on a single new house, then $N \cdot (tV_N - C_N)$ is the excess of tax revenues over expenditures on all new houses. Equation (3.42) can then be rewritten as

$$FST = N(tV_N - C_N) \qquad (3.43)$$

The fiscal-squeeze transfer generated by community A's zoning policy can be used in several ways.[w] The community can lower taxes while maintaining the same level of local public services or it can raise the level of local services while keeping the same tax rate. In the latter case, the strategy could be varied by distributing the benefits differently between the old and new houses. For example, if the tax rate were held constant and expenditures increased, then the extra expenditures could be made entirely on old houses or they could be shared between old and new houses. In the latter case some of the fiscal-squeeze transfer would "leak" away to benefit the new houses. In the former, spending on new houses would be held constant and the fiscal-squeeze transfer distributed entirely to the old houses. The expenditure distribution affects the value of the old houses via the capitalization formula.

Solving (3.41) for $H_o V_o$, we have

$$H_o V_o = \frac{H_o(R_o + c_o V_o)}{r + t} \qquad (3.44)$$

The higher the value of $c_o V_o$, expenditures per old house on public services, the higher the total value of old houses in the community. It is clear that $c_o V_o$ and hence $H_o V_o$ will be at their maximum values when the entire fiscal-squeeze fund generated by newcomers is spent to provide increased benefits to the old residents. These values will be lower when the fund is split.

Suppose the community follows this strategy and assigns all the benefits from the fiscal-squeeze transfer to the old houses. (Owners of old homes must have voting control of the community for this allocation to prevail, since owners of new houses would oppose it.) In that case, the fiscal-squeeze transfer must be equal to the excess of benefits over tax payments received by the owners of old houses.

$$FST = H_o(c_o V_o - t V_o) \qquad (3.45)$$

---

[w] In the preceding sections it was assumed that expenditures on local public services per house were related to lot size, $C(L) = a + bL$, so that all old and all new houses received the same expenditure per house but new houses received more than old. The fiscal-squeeze transfer represents extra revenues for the community. We now assume that the community can choose any expenditure program for these funds, subject to the restriction that the program be approved by majority vote.

Substituting this expression into equation (3.41), we get

$$H_o V_o = \frac{H_o R_o + FST}{r} \tag{3.46}$$

where R_o, H_o and r are constants. Thus we find that if all the FST benefits are expended on old houses, a community decision to maximize fiscal-squeeze transfers is equivalent to a decision to maximize the property value of older houses in the community.

It can be shown that the result holds if the fiscal-squeeze fund is used exclusively to reduce taxes on the old houses, while benefits to both old and new houses in the community remain constant. Then maximizing fiscal-squeeze transfers is again equivalent to maximizing the total property value of old houses in the community. It might be noted that either of these two extreme allocations of benefits and taxes would be unconstitutional and therefore difficult to achieve. In practice, however, communities can lower tax rates differentially on old and new properties by assessing old properties at a lower fraction of market value than new properties. Benefits spending can also be allocated mainly to old residents by choosing particular projects that benefit them. For example, if most of the school-age children live in the newer houses of the community, then the fiscal-squeeze transfer fund could be used for such projects as street repaving in the older areas of the community or for centers for senior citizens. But if part of the total fiscal-squeeze fund is spent on benefits for both groups or on a tax reduction, then that part of the fund will be capitalized as an increase in the property value of the new houses. Its potential effect on the value of the old house is then foregone.

The Scarcity Effect

The scarcity effect on the value of old houses works in the opposite direction from the fiscal effect. Under the fiscal effect, the more new houses that exist in a community, the higher the property value of the old houses, as long as the new houses are of higher value than the old. Under the scarcity effect, the more new houses that are built, regardless of their value, the lower the value of the old houses. Old houses are most valuable when no new houses exist. If new houses are built, their effect on the old depends on their value. The greater the value of new houses, the less substitutable they are for old houses. Finally, the effect on the value of old houses depends in which community the new houses are built. If they are built in community A, then their degree of substitutability with community A's old houses is greatest. If they are built in other communities, then their substitutability with community A's older houses is less.

The scarcity effect on value of older properties in community A, therefore, depends not only on the actions of community A itself in allowing new houses to be built, but also on the actions of nearby competitor communities. In addition, the scarcity value of old buildings in community A depends on the general rate of growth of demand for housing in the metropolitan area market.

Assume temporarily that community A can determine any zoning requirements without causing nearby communities to change their zoning policies. Then the scarcity and fiscal effects on the value of old houses in community A can be shown graphically in Figure 3-10. The top portion of the diagram shows the fiscal effect of new construction on the value of old houses $(H_o V_o)$. The horizontal axis shows values of L, the zoned lot size for new houses in community A. When community A determines a value of L and Q_A, it determines the value of $P_L \cdot Q_A$, the total land value of new housing. This in turn determines the effect of the zoning strategy on the value of old houses via the fiscal mechanism (assuming a fixed division of the FST fund among old and new properties). The lot size of the older houses in the community, L_o, is the minimum lot size considered by the community.

The graph shows that the fiscal effect on $H_o V_o$ is positive and rises initially as L rises. It reaches a maximum at L^* and then declines. The decline is caused by the smaller demand for new houses in community A as its required lot size increases.

The scarcity effect on $H_o V_o$ is shown by the solid line in the lower half of Figure 3-10. The scarcity effect on the value of old houses is always negative, although it becomes less negative as the community's required lot size increases. When $L = L_o$, the number of new houses built in the community is at its maximum and the scarcity effect on $H_o V_o$ is most negative. At the other extreme, at some $L = L_{max}$, community A's lot-size requirement is so large that no new houses are built. At this point, the fiscal-squeeze transfer is zero. Also at this point the scarcity effect is at its maximum, which is zero. When no new houses are built, existing houses are most scarce.

Figure 3-10 is drawn such that the maximum point of the scarcity effect and the minimum point of the fiscal effect coincide at L_{max}. These points coincide only if (i) new houses in other communities are not substitutes for new houses in community A *or* (ii) if all nearby competitors to community A face the same demand curves by prospective residents and follow the same zoning strategy. If the latter condition holds, then when community A sets L_{max} as its lot size, all competitor communities also set L_{max}. Then no new houses are built in the region and the scaricity value of old houses in all communities is at a maximum.

If neither of these two special conditions hold, then the fiscal and

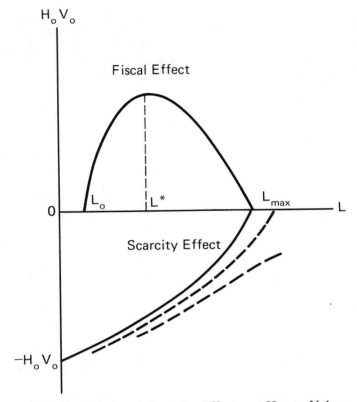

Figure 3-10. Fiscal and Scarcity Effects on House Values

scarcity effects on old houses in A are not both equal to zero at the same point. Suppose community A sets a lot-size requirement of L_{max}, to insure that no new houses are built. The fiscal effect is then equal to zero. The scarcity effect of community A's zoning policy is also dependent on the reactions of other communities whose lots are substitutes for those in A. If nearby communities set lot sizes that allow new construction, then this lessens the scarcity value of old houses in A. The scarcity curve of Figure 3-10 then moves to the right (shown as the dotted lines). In that case it might reach zero at some lot size greater than L_{max} or might never reach zero. A scarcity curve that never reaches zero implies that competitor communities to A allow new construction to take place regardless of what zoning policy is followed by community A. This implies a strong degree of independent action by competitive communities.

Alternately, suppose community A decreased its zoning requirement to L^* in order to maximize its fiscal-squeeze transfer. Suppose this induced community B also to lower its zoning requirement to meet A's competitive threat. In this case, less construction would occur in A than would be the case if B did not react. A would realize a lower fiscal-squeeze transfer, so the fiscal effect on the value of A's old houses would be lower than is shown in Figure 3-10. On the other hand, the old houses in A would be more scarce and therefore more valuable. So the scarcity effect would be greater than is shown in the figure. The scarcity line would shift upward.

Scarcity effects on communities are thus more difficult to treat than fiscal effects, since they involve to a greater degree the problems of interdependence among competing communities. Communities wishing to pursue a strategy that maximizes the value of their existing old houses must also balance conflicting fiscal and scarcity effects. Ignoring again the problems of community interdependence, we can explore the characteristics of a value-maximizing zoning policy. Substituting (3.42) into (3.46), we get

$$H_o V_o = \frac{1}{r} \{H_o R_1 + t[P_L(Q_A, L) \cdot Q_A + P_H H_A Q_A]$$

$$- C_A(L) \cdot Q_A\} \tag{3.47}$$

The terms H_o and r are constants. The entire fiscal-squeeze fund is assumed to be spent to increase the level of local service expenditures on the community's old houses. The community's zoning instruments are the required lot size for new houses and the quantity of vacant land supplied for new house construction.

Taking partial derivatives of $H_o V_o$ with respect to L and Q_A, we get

$$\frac{\partial H_o V_o}{\partial L} = \frac{1}{r} \left(H_o \frac{\partial R_o}{\partial L} + t \frac{\partial P_L}{\partial L} Q_A + t P_H Q_A \frac{\partial H_A}{\partial L} - \frac{\partial C_A}{\partial L} \cdot Q_A \right)$$

$$= 0 \tag{3.48}$$

and

$$\frac{\partial H_o V_o}{\partial Q_A} = \frac{1}{r} \left[H_o \frac{\partial R_o}{\partial Q_A} + t(P_L(1 + e_{P_L Q_A}) + P_H H_A) - C_A \right]$$

$$= 0 \tag{3.49}$$

Both equations consist of fiscal-squeeze terms plus one term relating to the scarcity effect on the value of old houses. We know from the "Fiscal-Squeeze Zoning" section that considering the fiscal effect alone, $H_o V_o$ is maximized at a lot size of L^* and a land supply of Q_A^*. This is so since we have shown above that maximizing FST and maximizing $H_o V_o$ are the same when only fiscal effects are considered and the entire fiscal-squeeze transfer fund is expended to benefit the old houses.

Therefore the last terms in (3.48) and (3.49) equal zero at L^* and Q_A^*. The scarcity term in (3.48) is positive since $\partial R_o/\partial L > 0$. Hence (3.48) equals zero at some lot size greater than L^*. The scarcity term in (3.49) is negative since $\partial R_o/\partial Q_A < 0$. Thus (3.49) equals zero at some land supply smaller than Q_A^*.

We see, therefore, that the scarcity effect on the value of a community's stock of old houses works in the opposite direction from the fiscal effect. While the fiscal effect encourages new development (as long as the new houses are of greater value than the old), the scarcity effect countervails this and encourages the community to adopt a more restrictive policy toward new development. Adding the scarcity effect to the community's equation pushes it even further in the exclusionary zoning direction, with an even larger required lot size for new houses and fewer new houses built.

The Value of Land under Zoning

This section deals with two hitherto neglected questions. First, the effect of fiscal zoning on land value in a community and in a metropolitan area is examined. Second, the results of this examination are used to explore the third zoning strategy posed as a possible model of community behavior. This strategy assumes that the community uses its control over land use to maximize the value of its vacant land. Since the ownership of vacant land is generally concentrated in a few hands, the benefits from such a strategy are equally concentrated. It is therefore not likely to be popular except in farming communities or communities in which land speculators hold an extraordinary amount of power.

Fiscal Zoning and Land Value

Suppose there are several groups of land users in a particular market whose demand curves are unrelated. One group demands land as an input in the production of single-family houses, another group demands land as an input in the production of factories which produce manufactured goods. The relevant land market is an entire urban area.[x]

Figure 3-11 shows the demand curves for land for houses and factories, as well as the aggregate demand curve for both sectors. The total supply of land in the market is S. In an unzoned competitive market, the equilibrium price of land is P_1, determined by the intersection of the supply curve and the aggregate demand curve, $S = D_1 + D_2$. Single-family houses consume

---

[x]Parts of the following discussion are taken from [12].

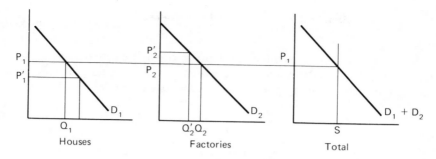

Figure 3-11. Demand Curves for Land

Q_1 units of land and factories consume Q_2 of land, where at equilibrium $S = Q_1 + Q_2$ and $P_1 = P_2$. The total value of land in the market is

$$V = P_1Q_1 + P_2Q_2 = P_1(Q_1 + Q_2) \qquad (3.50)$$

Suppose zoning is introduced into the land market. Assume for the moment that zoning has the effect of setting aside a certain area that can be used only for houses. If this area is smaller than the competitive allocation to housing, Q_1, and if cumulative districting is used,[y] then zoning has no effect on land use since land allocated to factories is used for houses. If the area set aside for houses is greater than Q_1, then zoning has the effect of reducing the land available for factories from Q_2 to Q_2'. In Figure 3-11, Q_2' is less than Q_2 and a segmented market for land is created. The price of land used for factories rises to P_2' and the quantity falls to Q_2'. The amount $Q_2 - Q_2'$ of land is shifted to the housing submarket where it has the effect of driving down the price of land used for housing to P_1'. Zoning effectively taxes the use of land for factories by $P_2 - P_2'$ and reduces the price of land for houses by $P_1 - P_1'$. After zoning, the aggregate value of land is $P_1'Q_1' + P_2'Q_2'$. It is not clear a priori whether zoning increases or decreases aggregate land value.

The effect of fiscal zoning on land value in the general case can be shown algebraically. The value of land before zoning is given by (3.50). The change in value after zoning is calculated by totally differentiating (3.50) and substituting $dQ_1 = dQ_2$.

$$dV = \left[P_1 + Q_1\left(\frac{dP_1}{dQ_1}\right) \right] dQ_1 - \left[P_2 + Q_2\left(\frac{dP_2}{dQ_2}\right) \right] dQ_1 \qquad (3.51)$$

The prezoning price of land is the same for either use, so $P_1 = P_2$, or, substituting,

---

[y] Under this system, land allocated to a "lower use," factories, can be developed for a "higher use," housing, as its owner wishes, but not vice versa.

$$dV = P\,dQ_1\left(\frac{1}{e_{Q_1P_1}} - \frac{1}{e_{Q_2P_2}}\right) \tag{3.52}$$

where $e_{Q_1P_1}$ and $e_{Q_2P_2}$ are standard price elasticities of demand. In the example, Q_2 is land for factories, which has decreased. Therefore the condition for the zoning policy to increase aggregate value ($dV > 0$) is

$$\frac{1}{e_{Q_1P_1}} > \frac{1}{e_{Q_2P_2}} \tag{3.53}$$

The zoning policy raises land value in a market if demand for land for the restricted use, factories, is more inelastic (or less negative since both are negative) than demand for land for the encouraged use, houses. If the converse holds then zoning lowers aggregate land value.[z]

Suppose now that the two groups of demanders for land are developers of houses and of apartments. In this case their demand curves for land are interrelated, since apartments and houses are substitutable. If zoning forces up the price of land for apartments, part of the apartment demand shifts to houses. The two demand curves are represented in inverse form as

$$P_1 = P_1(Q_1, Q_2) \quad \text{and} \quad P_2(Q_1, Q_2) \tag{3.54}$$

As above, we wish to derive the conditions under which a zoning policy that shifts land from one submarket to another increases aggregate land value. The prezoning land value is

$$V = P_1(Q_1, Q_2) \cdot Q_1 + P_2(Q_1, Q_2) \cdot Q_2 \tag{3.55}$$

To calculate the postzoning land value, we take a total differential of (3.55) and substitute $dQ_1 = -dQ_2$ and $P_1 = P_2$. Collecting terms, the result is:

$$dV = P\,dQ_1\left(\frac{1}{e_{Q_1P_1}} + \frac{Q_2}{Q_1} \cdot \frac{1}{e_{Q_1P_2}}\right)$$
$$- \left(\frac{1}{e_{Q_2P_2}} + \frac{Q_1}{Q_2} \cdot \frac{1}{e_{Q_2P_1}}\right) \tag{3.56}$$

Once again the change in aggregate value is ambiguous; it depends on the relative elasticities and cross-elasticities of demand in the two submarkets. The condition for aggregate land value to increase when zoning is instituted is

---

[z]This formulation can be extended using the same procedure to a more than two-sector land market. In that case, land taken from one sector by zoning is distributed among the others such that

$$dQ_1 = - \sum_{i=2}^{n} dQ_i$$

for n sectors.

$$\frac{1}{e_{Q_1 P_1}} + \frac{Q_2}{Q_1} \cdot \frac{1}{e_{Q_1 P_2}} > \frac{1}{e_{Q_2 P_2}} + \frac{Q_1}{Q_2} \cdot \frac{1}{e_{Q_2 P_1}} \qquad (3.57)$$

The condition depends on the elasticities and cross-elasticities of demand weighted by the initial relative land allocation. Note that if the cross-elasticities are equal to zero, (3.57) is identical to (3.53).

These results are counterintuitive in that a competitive, unregulated land market might be expected to maximize land values. Rather it is possible for fiscal zoning, which has the effect of creating separate submarkets for land, to increase aggregate land value. Zoning enables suppliers of land to act as discriminating monopolists. They charge a high price in that submarket where demand is inelastic by using zoning to restrict supply. The left-over supply is channeled into the market with elastic demand. In general, aggregate land value can be increased even when the two submarkets are interrelated if demand for the restricted used (in this case apartments) is sufficiently inelastic.

Land Value in a Metropolitan Market

Having failed to establish a theoretical prediction as to the effect of fiscal zoning on land value, it is necessary to turn to arguments of a lower level of generality in order to say anything about the actual effect. The analysis in the previous section suggests that the key parameters in determining what effect zoning has on land value are the elasticities and cross-elasticities of demand for land. This section offers some theoretical speculations concerning the empirical effects of zoning on land value in a metropolitan market, assuming that the overall effect of fiscal zoning by many independent communities is to restrict the availability of land for apartments and small dwellings and to increase the supply of land zoned for large-lot houses.

Since land is an input in the production of housing services, the theory of derived demand is relevant in considering the magnitudes of the elasticities. The theory suggests that demand for land is more inelastic (i) the less there are good substitutes for land in the production of housing, (ii) the smaller is the ratio of the cost of land to the total cost of housing, (iii) the more inelastic is demand for housing, and (iv) the more inelastic is the supply of other factors used in the production of housing.[aa]

In examining condition (i), we need to ask whether there are better substitutes for land in production of apartments or large houses. The obvious substitute for land is capital. It is likely that land is more substitutable for capital in production of apartments than houses. This is because a

---

[aa]See Rees [14, pp. 70-73].

single-family house must be surrounded by at least a certain amount of land, while the capital-to-land ratio in apartment construction can be varied widely. An acre of apartment land can be developed as 16 garden apartments or as several hundred high-rise units. Condition (i) thus suggests that demand for land for houses is more inelastic than demand for land for apartments.

Condition (ii) says that demand for land is more inelastic the smaller the share of land in the total cost of housing. Data from the Kaiser Committee [13] puts the share of land in total cost at 13 percent for elevator apartments and 25 percent for single-family homes. This condition, therefore, points in the opposite direction as the previous one: it suggests that demand for land for apartments is more inelastic.

Condition (iii) suggests that demand for land is more inelastic the more inelastic is the demand for the final product. Research on price elasticities of demand for housing has not settled the question whether demand for houses is more or less elastic than demand for apartments. DeLeeuw's survey [4], for example, gives data on the price elasticity of demand for apartments. His elasticity figure for apartments is a range from -0.7 to -1.4. The major studies of the price elasticity of demand for housing also fit within this range, so that no clear differential can be established.[bb]

Condition (iv) says that demand for land is more inelastic the more inelastic is the supply of other factors used in production of housing. Since the other factors used—lumber, labor, glass, etc.—are mostly the same in production of both apartments and houses, this condition is also ambiguous. It is possible that apartment construction uses relatively more processed inputs such as prefabricated concrete walls or elevator units than does house construction, which may use more unprocessed inputs such as lumber. If unprocessed inputs were more inelastically supplied, then condition (iv) would suggest that demand for land for houses should be more inelastic.

Marshall never gave a formula that tells how to add up the score on his four derived demand conditions. Two of the conditions suggest that demand for land for houses should be more inelastic, one suggests the opposite and is based only on conjecture. Condition (iii), which concerns the elasticities of demand for apartments versus houses, is silent. Finally, we have even less feel for the magnitudes of the cross-elasticities of demand for land for apartments and houses. Thus the theory of derived demand yields at best a weak presumption that zoning may decrease aggregate land value. A decrease in land value becomes more likely under fiscal zoning as demand for land for the restricted use is less inelastic and smaller in absolute value relative to demand for land for the encouraged use.

[bb]Muth [11, p. 72] and Reid [15, p. 27] find the price elasticity of demand for housing to be about -1.0; however, their studies combine demand for houses and apartments.

Vacant-Land Zoning Strategies in an Individual Community

The analysis of zoning and land value in a metropolitan area market, though indeterminate, suggests that the effect of zoning on an individual community's value can be predicted with greater confidence. We assume that fiscal-squeeze zoning by many communities in the area has the effect of restricting the amount of land available in small parcels for apartment construction and of creating separate submarkets for large and small lots. Further, the price of land per acre for small lots is higher than the price for large lots and higher than the no-zoning (or neutral-zoning) equilibrium price of land.

It is clear that demand for land in a single community for either large or small lots must be much more elastic than is demand for land in the metropolitan areas as a whole. Land zoned for large houses in one community is highly substitutable for land zoned for the same use in other communities. Similarly, though land zoned for small lots is generally in short supply, builders of apartments or small houses can easily substitute land in one community for land in another. If land for either use in one community were priced significantly higher than the price prevailing in the metropolitan area generally, large numbers of demanders would shift their demands to other communities.

These assumptions of substitutability are consistent with a land market in which the demand curve for land in an individual community is either perfectly elastic or just elastic. The former says that each community is sufficiently small and all communities are sufficiently alike that changes in zoning by one community do not significantly affect land prices in the urban market. The latter says that not all communities in the metropolitan area supply land in competition with each other. Communities compete mostly in small groups and some communities may have unique features that enable them to maintain a slightly higher price for their land and still sell some lots. The effect of zoning on land value and the optimum zoning strategy for vacant-land owners is considered below for both these situations. Zoning under flat demand curves is discussed first and under sloped demand curves second. It should be noted that the conclusions concerning aggregate land value in a community or a metropolitan area are unchanged by fiscal-squeeze transfers which cause capitalization effects to occur. The transfers cause expenditures on local services to be greater than taxes paid on older houses and taxes to be greater than expenditures for the newer houses. Both effects should be capitalized, thus raising the value of old houses and reducing that of new houses. But since the new total fiscal-squeeze transfer paid by new houses must be equal to the total transfer received by the old, then the positive and negative capitalization effects must cancel out for the community as a whole and for the metropolitan area.

Land-Value Zoning under Perfectly Elastic Demand for Land

The collective zoning decisions of communities essentially create distinct submarkets for land zoned for different uses and for residential land zoned for different lot sizes. Through its zoning, an individual community chooses the market in which it makes its vacant land available. It was demonstrated above that the price of land per acre is generally higher in apartment or small-lot use than in large-lot use. Therefore, a community clearly maximizes its land value by making all its land available for apartments. However, the discussions of fiscal-squeeze and scarcity zoning suggest that the residents of a community may find their own interests best served by zoning that permits only large-lot development. A community that zones all its land for large lots clearly has a lower land value than a community zoned for apartments. Thus fiscal-squeeze zoning in general is inconsistent with maximization of land values. The effect of a community's decision to restrict or ban high-density uses is to decrease the value of its land.

The interests of vacant-land owners thus are clearly sacrificed to further the interests of existing residents when a community adopts a fiscal-squeeze zoning policy. They are even worse off under a scarcity-zoning policy where a very large lot size is chosen in order to discourage new construction from occurring at all. Suppose vacant-land owners somehow take control of a community and attempt to formulate a zoning policy that maximizes the value of vacant land. First, they must obviously prevent the community from adopting fiscal-squeeze or scarcity zoning. Either no zoning or zoning for high-density uses should be sought. A second consideration is less controllable by vacant land owners; the extent to which they profit from their own community's policy depends on the value of land per acre in the restricted use. This value is higher as less land is offered for the restricted use, or as more communities in the region adopt fiscal-squeeze zoning and require all their land to be developed as large-lot houses. If, however, all other communities decide against fiscal-squeeze zoning, then a unified metropolitan market for land in all uses develops and an intermediate price per acre must emerge. This price is above the price of large lots but below the price of small lots under zoning. If other communities adopt fiscal-squeeze or scarcity zoning, then a single unzoned community is better off since it monopolizes the supply of land for high-density uses.

A community controlled by its vacant-land owners and attempting to maximize the value of its land should adopt a no-zoning policy. But the gain to be made from this policy depends directly on the number of other communities that adopt fiscal-squeeze or scarcity zoning policies. The occasional community controlled by its vacant-land owners provides an enclave for land uses generally seen as undesirable. The enclave community has very high land value per acre. But since high-density uses may yield negative fiscal-squeeze transfers, the older residents of the enclave may be made worse off.

Land-Value Zoning under Sloped Demand for Land

We need to examine the case in which communities' demand curves for land are not perfectly horizontal and individual communities have at least some degree of monopoly power. This is not an implausible case since in reality effective substitutability of land in different communities may be confined to overlapping groups of nearby communities. The Tiebout model, for example, tells us that a given household prefers to locate in a community whose existing inhabitants have income levels and public service demands similar to its own household. The Mills model goes further and suggests that, in the absence of zoning, households of different income levels tend to locate in rings around the center city, with the highest-income families in the most distant ring. In addition, if some employment is located in the suburbs, then the household of a worker holding a suburban job is not indifferent among suburbs located in various directions from the center of the city. Rather the household would prefer land in a community on the portion of the relevant ring that is nearest its employment location.

Given these limitations on substitutability, an individual community's lots are probably only competitive with the lots of a few nearby communities with similar income levels. Figure 3-12 shows how a metropolitan area might be divided into groups of competing communities. The division into rings separates income classes. The division by radiating spokes indicates that for suburban workers, direction from the center is important. These spokes might be located differently for households with different suburban work places. The ring pattern in Figure 3-12 is produced by urban models that require all workers to work in the center city. In order for a ring-spoke pattern to prevail, *most* jobs must be in the center, so that center-city commuting determines the prevalent land-price-distance function. If most jobs were in the suburbs, then there might be subsidiary land price peaks in the suburbs and different income level consumers might locate at the same distance from the center. Also, due to the influence of zoning, new residents of a given income level locate at different distances from existing residents of a community with the same income level. Under

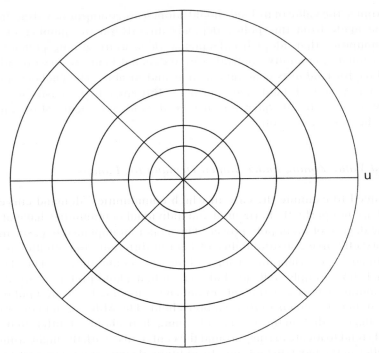

Figure 3-12. Metropolitan Community Structure

these circumstances, demand for land is not perfectly elastic since many demanders can only choose among a few communities in the metropolitan area.

Suppose once again that there are segmented submarkets for land zoned large lot residential and zoned for apartments. As communities shift from no zoning or neutral zoning to fiscal-squeeze zoning, the value of large lots falls and of land zoned for apartments rises. A community still minimizes its land value by making all its land available for the encouraged use—low-density housing. The larger the required lot size, the lower the land value in the community. But depending on the form of the demand function for land, the community may be able to maximize its land value by selling some land for apartments but maintaining the value of apartment land by restricting its availability and selling some land for single-family houses. The alternative policy of making all land available for apartments might drive down the value of apartment land, if demand curves are not perfectly elastic.

Suppose demand curves for a community's land are linear. In that case, as more land is transferred from apartments (A) to single-family (SF) houses, the elasticities of demand for each use shift. Suppose the elasticities were originally $e_A = -1.22$ and $e_{SF} = -0.85$. Then as more land is shifted to apartment use, e_A becomes more inelastic and e_{SF} more elastic. Overall land value rises with the shift as long as e_A is more elastic than e_{SF}. Past that point, further shifts of land to apartment use lower overall land value in the community. In contrast, if demand for land is log-linear, and if e_A is more elastic than e_{SF}, the value-maximizing strategy for the community is to make all its vacant land available for apartments. In general the best strategy depends on the form of the demand curves for each land use. In addition, the maximum value of land in any community also depends on the zoning strategies of nearby communities whose land is substitutable for that of the community in question. In general a single community's maximum land value level is determined by the degree to which it has a monopoly on the supply of land for the restricted use.

Spot Zoning and Land Value within a Community

This section considers whether and when a developed community in an urban area changes the zoning on a specific parcel of land.[cc] The parcel is assumed to be located in a community already zoned to preserve its present density level. The owner of a specific parcel of land asks for a zoning variance. It is assumed that the variance must be approved through a majority voting procedure.

In terms of a static urban model, it does not matter whether the parcel of land is presently vacant or is developed differently from the way the owner now wants to use it. In a static model, as some change in parameter values shifts the model each period, all land can be redeveloped costlessly. In that case there is no reason for vacant land ever to exist within the metropolitan area. Although the fact that the area is zoned may create exceptional factors which would make it profitable to leave a parcel vacant temporarily. The owner might feel, for example, that the parcel is more likely to be granted a variance if it is presently vacant than if it is developed as a conforming use. Suppose the parcel is in Community C, which is developed as single-family houses, all of which are of the same value. The owner of the parcel wishes to develop it for some higher-density use, such as apartments or stores. It has been pointed out by many writers that in a zone devoted to a single land use, it may be profitable to develop some nonconforming use even though adverse external effects cause a capital loss to neighboring parcels. Suppose the owner of the parcel is prepared to compensate nearby owners for their losses. This takes externalities considerations out of the picture and concentrates attention on the fiscal effects of the zoning change.

It is easy to see why the interest of the community and that of the parcel

---

[cc]Parts of this section are discussed in [12].

owner may conflict. Suppose the owner wishes to maximize his capital gain from the development or

$$\Delta(P_L L) = L \cdot \Delta P_L \tag{3.58}$$

He considers all possible uses for the parcel and perhaps chooses a high-rise apartment as the best use. The community, on the other hand, wishes to maximize the fiscal-squeeze transfer from the parcel to the community at large or

$$\Delta V = t \Delta(P_L L + P_H H) - \Delta C = t(L \Delta P_L + P_H \Delta H) - \Delta C \tag{3.59}$$

The community's objective function is different from the owner's. It taxes both land and building, so it is concerned about how much capital is invested in the land in its new use. (The owner, on the contrary, ascribes all the increase in value of the parcel to the land, while the return on capital is constant.) The community is also concerned about the extra public service costs, ΔC, generated by the new development.

Suppose the rezoning proposal is put to a vote in the community. We wish to establish the conditions under which a majority of residents vote for the proposal. Suppose residents' voting behavior is determined by the net effect of the zoning variance on their fiscal positions: they vote yes if they benefit from the change and no if they are hurt. If there is no net effect then they are indifferent and the proposal then has a 50 percent chance of approval. Vote counting is easy in this community, since in the absence of externalities all residents are affected alike by every variance.

Variances affect residences fiscally via the capitalization formula, since the supply of housing in community C is completely inelastic.

$$V_i = \frac{R_i}{r} - \frac{T_i}{r} + \frac{C_i}{r} = \frac{R_i}{r} - \frac{t V_i}{r} + \frac{c V_i}{r} = \frac{R_i}{r + t - c} \tag{3.60}$$

These formulas were discussed under "Scarcity Zoning." As shown here, the value of a house is related to its rent (R_i), the property taxes it pays (T_i), and the services it receives from the community (C_i). In a neutrally zoned community with no nonconforming uses and all houses of equal value, expenditures equal taxes, so the two terms, t and c—tax and expenditure rates—drop out.

If the zoning variance has no effect on the fiscal position of other residents, then this condition remains true. The value of residents' houses is unchanged by the zoning variance, which indicates that benefits and costs to households remain unchanged. For this to hold, the variance must cause the rezoned parcel to rise in value just enough to generate extra taxes equal to the extra public service costs created by the use change. From (3.60) this implies that

$$\Delta C = t(L \Delta P_L + P_H \Delta H) = t \Delta V \qquad (3.61)$$

On either side of this indifference point, the extra costs generated by the zoning variance are greater than or less than the extra revenues generated by the parcel's increased value. If costs are greater than revenues, the community incurs a deficit in supplying the redeveloped parcel with services. It must meet this deficit by increasing the tax rate (t) or reducing the expenditure rate (c). Either of these changes are capitalized as a decrease in the value of residents' houses. If this occurred, the residents of the community would vote against the zoning variance. They must absorb the cost of the variance since the parcel does not pay its own way in terms of local services. Yet they do not share in the capital gain generated by the variance, which goes entirely to the owner of the parcel. Their rational course of action is therefore to vote against the rezoning proposal.

Conversely, if the extra costs generated by the zoning variance are less than the extra tax revenue, then the rezoned parcel subsidizes the community as a whole. The net revenues generated can be used to lower the tax rate on residents' houses or to raise the quality level of local services. In this case residents benefit from the rezoning proposal and they vote for it.

A proposed zoning variance for a single parcel of land can, therefore, fall into one of three categories: it can benefit the residents of the community; it can effect them adversely; or it can have no effect on them. These categories can be expressed as conditions on the parcel of land. If the parcel has no net effect on the residents, then it must generate revenues equal to the costs or

$$\Delta C = t \Delta V$$

If the parcel was previously developed as a conforming use (a single-family house), then we also know that $C = tV$ for the parcel. Dividing these two equations we get:

$$\Delta C/C < \Delta V/V \qquad (3.62)$$

The condition for residents to be indifferent to or favorable to the rezoning of a parcel of land is that the percent increase in the parcel's value must be at least as great as the percent increase in costs after rezoning. This, however, holds only if the parcel was previously a conforming use. If it previously was a net drain or a net surplus to the community, then the rezoning condition would be less strict or stricter respectively.

With these assumptions about the voting behavior of residents on zoning variance proposals, several results can be derived about the effect of zoning on land value. We have already shown that zoning an entire community must decrease its overall land value relative to the no-zoning alternative, if land markets function efficiently and no externalities are present. Concerning spot zoning two further results can be shown. One is that the community never adopts, by voting, a zoning proposal that decreases its overall land value. The second is that the converse of this statement is not true: communities sometimes reject zoning variance proposals that would increase their overall land value.

However it is possible that certain rezoning proposals which would not pass when applied to one parcel would pass if applied to all or most parcels in the community. Suppose the residents realized that all or most of them could redevelop their land for a capital gain of $2000 per parcel if rezoning were applied generally. In this case, the proposal might pass even if each redeveloped parcel caused a fiscal drain from the community. Then each owner's benefit from a capital gain would outweigh his share of the capitalized fiscal drain. Those that could redevelop their parcels at a net profit would vote for the proposal. If they were in a majority, the rezoning would be adopted.

This argument is basically the one made in the previous section, that zoning is irrational from a landlord's point of view because it depresses land values. In a perfect-land-market context it is difficult to see why zoning would be adopted. However, an already zoned community is unlikely to give up its zoning because of an argument such as this one. Contrary to an urban spatial model's prediction, all land at a given distance from the center is not normally expected to make the same capital gain from redevelopment at a higher density at a given time. It is more likely that a few parcels, such as those on major streets, could benefit greatly from redevelopment, while other parcels in residential areas would make a loss. In this case the main-street owners are likely to ask for spot rezoning because they would lose on a vote for a general rezoning. The bulk of property owners then judge the proposals on the basis of the rezoned parcel's net surplus or deficit position on local services.

We have thus established that spot rezoning proposals, if adopted by rational voters in a zoned community, must increase the overall community's land value, that is, assuming that externalities have no effect on the process, since adverse effects are compensated by the owners of the rezoned parcel. Voters act according to the effect of fiscal zoning on their individual interests. It is worth noting, however, that this is not the usual decision-making apparatus used for rezoning proposals. To start with, zoning variances are usually granted by a zoning board, not by majority vote of the residents. Second, nearby owners affected by externalities are not usually compensated for their windfall losses. Therefore more of the "voting" at zoning board meetings may be influenced by nearby owners affected by externalities than by disinterested owners acting on fiscal considerations. Third, a decision by a zoning board not too unusually dominated by realtors and developers is hardly representative of the voting outcome that would prevail if all owners had a voice in board decisions.

Finally, even if all owners did participate, it might not be reasonable to expect them to predict which rezoning proposals would generate a surplus and which a loss.

Zoning and Property Taxes in a Spatial Model

Most theoretical urban models have no local public sector. To investigate the effects of adding a public sector to an urban model, the assumption is made that local services are provided by a center city and by a large set of independent local communities located at various distances from the center. Schools are assumed to be the only locally provided public good and they are financed by a local property tax. Constant costs prevail in the educational production function. Suppose all households have the same number of children attending school. Suppose temporarily that they also have the same income and demand the same quality education. Then there is constant expenditure per student on education at all distances from the central city.

Neutral zoning in this situation must raise equal revenue per household. If each household demands S dollars of spending per student-year and pays S dollars in property taxes, then taxes are recognized as a price paid for schools, just as though education were bought on the private market. The outcome is therefore efficient and the local government sector has no distorting effects on resource allocation.

This situation requires a tax rate that varies with distance. Households in the Mills model [10] for example, trade off higher housing consumption against higher commuting costs at greater distances. Since housing consumption rises with distance but revenue per household to be raised by the community is constant, the tax rate must fall with distance. This tax rate can be derived for the Mills model. In the model, land consumption per household, $L(u)/N(u)$, rises at an increasing rate with distance. The price of land per acre, $P_L(u)$, declines faster than linearly. The product of these two quantities is a linear expression in u:

$$\frac{L(u)P_L(u)}{N(u)} = \frac{k^{-1}}{r} \ [\bar{R}^B + Bkc(\bar{u} - u)] \tag{3.63}$$

where k and B are constants, and $B = \alpha(1 + \Theta_2)$ where α is the share of land in housing and Θ_2 is the price elasticity of demand for housing; r is the interest rate on capital; $\bar{R}$ is rent on land at the edge of the city; $\bar{u}$ is the distance to the edge of the city; and c is the cost of commuting two miles. The first derivative of the expression with respect to u is positive when B is a negative number, which occurs when housing demand is price elastic—a condition that also holds under fiscal-squeeze zoning. (This derives from the fact that $e_{P_L,L}$ must be between -1 and 0 in order for fiscal-squeeze zoning to be successful. Mills' notation has been changed slightly.)

Equation (3.63) says that expenditure on land rises linearly with distance. In the Mills model, capital and land take constant shares of a household's total housing expenditure. Therefore if communities must raise constant revenues per household for education (S) by taxing housing expenditure, they should set tax rates equal to

$$t(u) = \frac{S}{\dfrac{k^{-1}}{ra}\ [\overline{R}^B + Bkc(\overline{u} - u)]} \tag{3.64}$$

In (3.64) the denominator is housing expenditure, capital plus land, owned by a household at any distance, where the share of expenditure going to land is α. S is a constant while housing expenditure increases with distance. Therefore the efficient tax rate in communities that span a range of distances is not constant. To maintain their Tiebout efficiency properties in a spatial model, communities must levy a tax rate that falls with distance at a declining rate. At each u, taxes equal the cost of education for all households (S), so no net capitalization effects occur. This result has rather perplexing implications for public policy, however, since it implies that communities should not treat their households equally.

Equation (3.64) can be easily extended to the Mills model with several income classes. Figure 3-13a shows the land consumption per household curve for a city with three income groups. Group I is the poorest, group III the richest. The L function rises at an increasing rate and makes discrete jumps at the income group boundaries. Expenditure on land per household, shown in 3-13b, rises linearly with jumps at the boundaries. School expenditures, also shown in 3-13b, are constant within each income group, but increase with income, producing jumps at the boundaries.

The tax rate necessary to raise the desired level of school expenditure declines with greater distance from the center within each income ring. Across rings, the tax rate rises or falls with greater income depending on whether the income elasticity of demand for education is greater than or less than the income elasticity of demand for housing. Figure 3-13c shows a declining tax rate across several income classes, where demand for housing is assumed to be more income elastic.

If communities raise the specified amount of revenue per household at each distance for schools and if households at each income level benefit equally from schools, then the operation of the local public sector does not introduce any distortions into the urban land market. Communities in this situation can be of any size; but each community must be fully contained within one income ring. Since each community provides only one level of school spending, it cannot satisfy the demands of more than one income class.

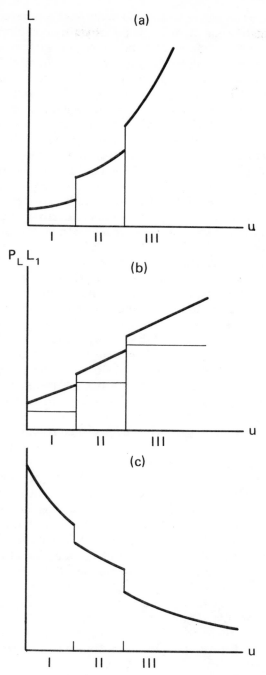

Figure 3-13. Land Consumption per Household

Thus a local government sector and neutral zoning have been incorporated into a spatial urban model. It is possible for communities to exist in this model and to provide local public services without disrupting the efficient allocations of resources in the urban land market. But a practical difficulty is introduced: variable housing consumption by households of the same income at different distances necessitates a nonconstant property tax rate within communities. In the noncentrally defined model of neutral zoning presented by Hamilton [6], a community could levy the same property tax rate on all of the equal-value houses within its boundaries. In the centrally defined model discussed here, a community must attempt to raise equal revenues per household from a nonequal property base. Since property tax rates cannot legally vary within a community, this suggests that communities in the model might have to be crescent shaped—they would extend around the center but cover only a narrow range of distances. Or a community might vary its assessment ratios by distance.

The optimum tax-rate-distance relation becomes problematic when communities pursue fiscal-squeeze zoning strategies. The spending of already realized fiscal-squeeze transfers may affect communities' tax rates differently at different distances. Since, as discussed earlier, communities may spend fiscal-squeeze transfers either on higher quality local services or on a lower tax rate at the same benefit level, all transfers could be used to lower tax rates. Then the shape of the tax-rate-distance relationship would be altered depending on which communities collect the highest fiscal-squeeze transfers per household. If wealthy communities collected the highest transfers, then tax rates would decline faster between income classes (or rise less quickly) under fiscal-squeeze zoning than under neutral zoning.

The variable tax rate result that emerges when zoning is considered in a spatial model provides another qualification to a Tiebout-type model considered as a description of the real world. But this objection is probably more important in theory than in practice. The steeper portion of a metropolitan area's rent-distance function is within the central city, which does not tax households according to the cost of providing their services in any case. In the suburbs, variation in housing consumption within a community due to mixing of income levels may be larger than variation due to changes in the price of land. If the flat portion of the function is divided among several income classes and several communities, then a flat tax rate in each community should introduce only a small distortion. In addition, the more high-income classes the metropolitan area has, the larger its land area and the flatter its price of land function at the fringes. Thus the more separate, small communities there are in a metropolitan area and the flatter the P_L function, the less distortion is introduced by constant property tax rates within communities. It is interesting to note that while recent court decisions have emphasized the equity violation inherent in variable property tax rates among communities, equity (and efficiency) calls for a variable rather than a constant tax rate within communities.

Conclusion

The preceding sections have attempted to show that independent suburban communities that are relatively homogeneous in terms of housing consumption levels have no incentive to remain so. Rather they take advantage of the Tiebout "voting" mechanism to attract newcomers and firms who can be forced to pay more than their share of the costs of local public services. Newcomers who wish to enter a suburban community can be forced to pay subsidies to the community as long as many of the competing communities in the area pursue the same zoning objective. Competition among communities to attract new residents and firms does not bid the subsidies down to zero, since communities would prefer that their land remain vacant over having it developed at a zero net transfer.

Suppose a group of communities in a metropolitan area sucessfully pursues fiscal-zoning strategies. They acquire housing of several value levels and perhaps a concentration of commercial or industrial firms. What are some of the long-term consequences of fiscal-squeeze zoning for the communities and for the metropolitan area as a whole?

First, the model offered here suggests that subsidies paid by owners of the new houses to owners of the old are capitalized as increases in value of old houses. They also may affect the value of the new houses. These capitalization effects tend to wipe out the fiscal-squeeze transfers as the houses are sold and their property tax liabilities change. If housing value (V) is

$$V = \frac{R}{r} + \frac{(C - T)}{r} \tag{3.65}$$

then the existence of net fiscal-squeeze transfers paid to old houses causes local expenditures to be greater than the tax bill for the old houses or $C > T$. At constant rent and interest rates, value rises sufficiently to wipe out the subsidy. This occurs because as the house increases in value, it pays higher property taxes $(T = tV)$, but the expenditures on local services it receives from the community (C) stay constant. Thus the owner's flow benefit $(C - T)$ is partly converted to a capital gain. When the house is sold, the new owner should pay a price such that his higher property taxes plus the yearly cost of the house's capital gain $(r \Delta V)$ wipe out his subsidy on local services. In a perfect housing market, close to full capitalization of fiscal-squeeze transfers should be observable in the value of older houses. But it is in fully developed communities that the capitalization effects should be most pronounced. For, in these communities, no new houses are built which could serve as substitutes for the older houses from the viewpoint of demanders. Also, underassessment of older houses in many communities may hide unrealized capitalization effects.

Similarly, capitalization of the net fiscal subsidies paid by new houses should eventually occur. In that case, a loss of value of new houses reduces property values to the point that the subsidy flow from new to old houses is wiped out. It is unclear when these capitalization effects might be perceived, since by definition the supply of new houses is not constant. It is possible that the developer of new houses might realize some of the capital loss when the new houses are sold. Alternately, the capitalization effects might not be perceived until the area is fully developed.

If the subsidies paid by new houses to old are wiped out by capitalization effects, does fiscal-squeeze zoning have any permanent effects? The capitalization effects themselves are the key to this question. They cause the value of the land developed as lower-value old houses to rise and the land developed as higher-value new houses to fall. The normal market response to this situation in the absence of zoning would be to increase the supply of lower-value houses sufficiently to lower their land value to the equilibrium land price under no zoning. Higher-value houses would not increase in supply since their value is depressed.

This market response is prevented by zoning. Assuming that the community's fiscal zoning regulations are still in effect, only high-value houses can be built. Under zoning, therefore, a shortage of lower-value housing persists, while high-value housing is oversupplied on artificially low-value land.

Fiscal zoning, then, causes the market to undersupply low-value housing. The situation has effects on the entire metropolitan area. We have discussed the effect of this situation on the location choice of potential new house buyers. Under fiscal zoning, they can choose from only a narrow range of housing qualities and they lose consumer surplus on housing or local public services or both. If they move from the center city to a fiscally zoned suburb, they make a smaller utility gain than they would if the suburb were neutrally zoned. Under fiscal zoning, more households remain in the center city, causing center city households generally to be housed at higher densities, with less space per household and higher land rents. Owners of central-city land make a capital gain on their land holdings, but most central-city households and firms may be renters.[dd]

Ironically, "the plight of the center city" may be worse under neutral zoning by suburbs than under fiscal-squeeze zoning. In the neutral zoning

---

[dd]This is a price intermediate between the value of land devoted to high-value and low-value housing under zoning.

model, a household can find a suburb that requires its desired level of housing consumption and provides just its desired quality of local services. Thus all center city households with higher than the minimum income have an incentive to desert the center city, which then becomes a homogeneous "suburb" of the very poor. In contrast, under fiscal-squeeze zoning the transfer (and deadweight loss) that a new household must incur to gain admission to a suburb may be as high as the subsidy (and deadweight loss) it must pay via property taxes to the central-city poor. Fewer households therefore choose the suburbs and the center city under fiscal-squeeze zoning should remain a more heterogeneous, viable entity. Similarly, the center city should retain more firms under suburban fiscal-squeeze zoning.[ee] In the discussion of suburban exploitation of central cities, it is the suburbs "bottling up" the poor in central cities that is always emphasized. But the discussion suggests that suburban large-lot zoning may also "bottle up" a profitable industrial tax base and many nonpoor families in the central city as well.[ff]

Fiscal-squeeze zoning as a system has far-reaching and perhaps long-lasting effects on resource allocation in metropolitan areas. This study has attempted to pinpoint a few of them.

References

[1] Babcock, Richard, *The Zoning Game* (Madison: University of Wisconsin Press, 1966).

[2] Bassett, Edward, *Zoning* (New York: Russell Sage Foundation, 1936).

[3] Coase, R. H., "The Problem of Social Cost," *Journal of Law and Economics* 3 (October 1960): 1-44.

[4] DeLeeuw, Frank, "The Demand for Housing: A Review of Cross-Section Evidence," *Review of Economics and Statistics* 53 (February 1971): 1-10.

[5] Davidoff, Linda, Paul Davidoff, and Neil Gold, "The Suburbs Have to Open Their Gates," *New York Times Magazine,* December 7, 1971.

[6] Hamilton, Bruce, "Property Taxes and the Tiebout Hypothesis: Some Empirical Evidence," Chapter 2 this volume.

[7] Hettich, Walter, "Equalization Grants, Minimum Standards, and Unit Cost Differences in Education," *Yale Economic Essays* 8 (Fall 1968): 5-55.

[ee]See [19] for a two-sector general equilibrium model of zoned suburbs and unzoned central city in which the effects of zoning on metropolitan area size and total land value are explored.

[ff]See [20] for a model of firm location under zoning.

[8] Makielski, S. J., *The Politics of Zoning* (New York: Columbia University Press, 1966).

[9] Margolis, Julius, "On Municipal Land Policy for Fiscal Gains," *National Tax Journal* 9 (September 1956): 247-257.

[10] Mills, Edwin, *Urban Economics* (Glenview: Scott, Foresman, 1972).

[11] Muth, Richard, *Cities and Housing* (Chicago: University of Chicago Press, 1969).

[12] Ohls, James C., Richard Weisberg, and Michelle J. White, "The Effect of Zoning on Land Value," *Journal of Urban Economics* 1 (October 1974): 428-444.

[13] President's Committee on Urban Housing (Kaiser Committee), *Report: A Decent Home,* 1968.

[14] Rees, Albert, *The Economics of Trade Unions* (Chicago: University of Chicago Press, 1963).

[15] Reid, Margaret, *Housing and Income* (Chicago: University of Chicago Press, 1962).

[16] Sager, Lawrence, "Tight Little Islands, Exclusionary Zoning, Equal Protection and the Indigent," *Stanford Law Review,* 21 (April 1969): 767-800.

[17] State of New Jersey, Department of Community Affairs, unpublished land use survey, 1971.

[18] Tiebout, Charles, "A Pure Theory of Local Public Expenditure," *Journal of Political Economy* 64 (October 1956): 416-424.

[19] White, Michelle J., "The Effect of Zoning on the Size of Metropolitan Areas," forthcoming.

[20] White, Michelle J., "Firm Location in a Zoned Metropolitan Area," Chapter 6 of this volume.

4 The Tiebout Hypothesis and Residential Income Segregation

Bruce Hamilton,
Edwin Mills, and
David Puryear

There is a growing concensus among economists, the courts, and the public that local public services, most notably primary and secondary education, are distributed largely according to ability to pay. In the language of economists, the local public economy resembles a market. Whether this system is praised or condemned depends on the goals one has in mind. Economists are fond of pointing to the efficiency attributes of a market or market analogue. Civil liberties lawyers, on the other hand, have argued that provision of education by ability to pay violates the Equal Protection Clause of the fourteenth Amendment to the Constitution. Similar arguments in the past have struck down the poll tax and have guaranteed legal counsel to defendants in criminal cases.[a]

Our main purpose here is to present empirical evidence on whether such a quasi market exists. By way of introduction, we outline the theoretical arguments and include a brief discussion of some possible reasons for relying on such a system.

The Tiebout Mechanism

Economists' treatment of the local public economy as a market is based upon a classic article by Tiebout [9].[b] The following sketch is based upon Tiebout's original article, but also contains more recent elaboration on the theory.

Consider an urban area in which there are many municipalities, each of which provides its residents with a local public service. The level of provision varies among communities but not within a community. Each community charges a user fee, or head tax, just sufficient to finance the public service. Communities are identical in all ways relevant to household location except in their public service provision. A household selects its community of residence on the basis of its public service demand, and the demand is efficiently restrained by the user fee. Such a system of local governments is transformed into a market for local public services. The

---

[a]Legal Services, an attempt to guarantee the same services for plaintiffs, has met with serious opposition.

[b]The same model is presented in Chapter 2 of this volume.

efficiency of the system is clearly contingent upon consumers facing a marginal cost price for the local public service.

In a recent paper [5] and in Chapter 2 of this volume, Hamilton has shown that proper use of minimum house-value zoning and property taxation will, in a perfectly divisible and flexible world, generate a set of implicit prices which accurately reflect the average cost of production.[c] If a community establishes a minimum-house-value zoning ordinance, a floor is placed under housing consumption, and hence under the property tax liability. Anybody whose housing consumption is above this floor subsidizes the remainder of the community through the local tax system, and the subsidy can be avoided by moving to a more restrictively zoned community. So everybody whose housing consumption is above the statutory floor has an incentive to migrate out of the particular community (or, to put the matter somewhat differently, such a household would have had an incentive not to locate in the community in the first place.) If this sorting-out process goes on in all communities, the urban area will be characterized by a set of communities within each of which house values are uniform.

This being the case, all households in a given community pay the same amount in property taxes, from which it follows that every household pays the average cost of the public services it consumes. If the appropriate mix of zoning constraints and offerings of public service is available, any combination of housing and local public service can be purchased at prices consistent with production cost. The system of local governments is a perfect market for local public services, and the institutions of this market, namely zoning and property taxation, do not distort the market for housing. Within this framework, there are two motivations for households to segregate themselves by jurisdiction; first, they segregate themselves by demand for the local public service; and second, they segregate themselves in their efforts to avoid paying more than the average cost of the local public services they consume.

Realism of the Tiebout Model

Although it is theoretically possible for a system of local governments in a metropolitan area to provide a perfect market for local public services, many observers doubt that they will do so in practice.

First, the market-clearing device in the Tiebout model is extremely cumbersome. The Tiebout model requires that families make interjurisdictional moves of their residences as their tastes, income, and positions in the life-cycle change. Such moves are far from costless so that the presumption

[c]Of course, we must assume that the average cost curve is flat or U-shaped in the relevant range in order to claim efficiency for average cost pricing.

of equilibirum in the market for local public services is less strong than in most markets.

Second, there is a question of numbers of jurisdictions. Local governments provide a vector of public services, each of which can be provided in several qualities and quantities. Thus, many local governments may be needed in a metropolitan area to satisfy all demands for public services. Furthermore, residents are by no means indifferent among alternative residential locations in a metropolitan area. Locations of workplaces and other trip destinations, as well as the trade-off between commuting costs and housing costs, drastically limit the number of residential locations among which citizens are indifferent. Thus, there must be not only many jurisdictions in the metropolitan area, but also many jurisdictions in the parts of the metropolitan area among which the resident is indifferent, if Tiebout considerations are to dominate residential location decisions. Clearly, scale economies in public service production limit the number of separate jurisdictions there can be in a metropolitan area.

The foregoing considerations raise doubts whether local public service demands dominate residential locational choice in a metropolitan area. It is also possible to doubt whether such a system would be efficient if it did exist. The Tiebout model is one in which local public services are priced at average production cost. That can be efficient only if marginal cost equals average cost. But among the reasons that services are produced publicly rather than privately is that marginal cost is less than average cost. That happens if scale economies are such that the production of the service is a classical natural monopoly or if the service is a pure or public good.[d] These situations might indicate the desirability of large local government jurisdictions or of a method of financing local government other than average cost pricing.

Finally, there is a peculiarly American institutional arrangement that indicates that average cost pricing of local public service may be inefficient. Local taxes are deductible from the federal personal income tax, whereas expenditures on private goods and services are not. Thus, average production costs of local services are perceived by local residents to be less than their true opportunity cost, thereby inducing residents to vote for excessively large and high quality supplies of these services.

Thus, there are reasons to doubt both the predominance and the efficiency of a Tiebout-like organization of local government. However, the most casual observation of the postwar process of metropolitan suburbanization suggests that it has been in part a search for particular mixes of local public services. In this situation, only the facts can tell us how important

[d]Contrary to some views, congestion costs with impure public goods does *not* serve to offset any scale economies that may exist. Congestion is a special case of the law of diminishing returns (capacity held constant), and diminishing returns to one input are perfectly consistent with increasing returns to scale.

the Tiebout model is. The purpose of the next section is to seek some facts bearing on this question.

Evidence

Our major purpose here is not to present an analysis of the wisdom of providing some kinds of services through a local public sector which approximates a market. The answer to this question depends on the complicated questions of equity and efficiency relating to merit goods, interjurisdictional spillovers, distortive influences of various kinds of tax and zoning schemes, and scale economies. We are concerned with the more modest and logically prior question of whether the local public economy approximates a market. The merits of distributing some services by a Tiebout-type market analogue need not be debated if such a market analogue is found not to exist in the local public economy.

The major previous attempt to test the Tiebout hypothesis is a study of the determinants of residential property values by Oates [6]. Using the fact that property value equals price times quantity, Oates attempts to explain statistically the variation in median house value among a sample of communities in northeastern New Jersey. His explanatory variables can be broken down into two groups: those that are proxies for the price of housing, and those that are proxies for the quantity consumed. Having corrected for the quantity of housing purchased and for other determinants of price (such as distance from New York City) Oates poses the following question: Do local tax rates and level of expenditure on local public service influence the price of housing? The predictions are that the price of housing is negatively correlated with tax rates and positively correlated with local public expenditure levels. These predictions were verified in the regression, leading Oates to the conclusion that people do indeed respond to the forces suggested by Tiebout. Although there are some difficulties with the procedure (see [4] and [7]), there is no ready alternative explanation for these results. His work appears to lend strong support to the Tiebout hypothesis.

The most direct implication of the Tiebout model is that households will segregate themselves among communities by their demands for public services. In the specific formulation of the model discussed above, households are also segregated by housing demand as a result of zoning. We will argue below that some metropolitan areas in the United States have fiscal environments that are more conducive to the functioning of a Tiebout system than do other metropolitan areas. Through the use of standard regression analysis, we will attempt to determine whether the degree of segregation is a function of the local fiscal environment.[e]

We have not tried to estimate demand equations for public services. Instead, we have chosen family income as a crucial determinant of demand for public services,[f] and education as our crucial public service. Undoubtedly, education is the public service most likely to fit the Tiebout hypothesis. It accounts for more than half of local government expenditures and its income elasticity of demand is substantially greater than zero.[g] Thus, our basic hypothesis is that there should be relatively little variability of income within suburban school districts to which the Tiebout model is applicable.

We have computed Gini coefficients of family income as a measure of income inequality.[h] Ideally, Gini coefficients should be computed for school districts, but these data are not available.[i] Instead, we have computed Gini coefficients for census tracts. Census tracts are small relative to the average school district and therefore we assume that each tract is within a single school district. (Our observations include no tracts that are "split," that is, tracts that extend into more than one jurisdiction.)

There are many reasons for expecting homogenity within census tracts, whether the Tiebout model is empirically valid or not. In particular, census tracts are to some extent defined by homogeneous neighborhoods. Each of our regressions contains several explanatory variables which are of no interest for testing the Tiebout hypothesis, but which are included in an effort to allow for other effects on income segregation. These variables are not derived from a rigorous theory of residential location patterns. We simply include all variables for which we could gather data and which we thought might influence census-tract Gini coefficients. This is an unfortunate way to do statistical work, but in the absence of a well-developed

[e]For another study with basically the same motivations, see [3].

[f]Other considerations may of course be important. For example, it is reasonable to believe that a major purpose of retirement communities is to capture an important advantage of a Tiebout-world, to avoid paying taxes to educate other people's children. Retired people are ideally placed to achieve their purpose because their residential locations are not constrained by their places of work. But this is too narrow a test of the Tiebout model for our purposes.

[g]Recent estimates of the income elasticity of demand for education include those of Barlow [1], Bradford and Oates [2], and Peterson [8]. These estimates range from 0.4 to 0.7.

[h]This is calculated from Census data in the following way: The Census gives the number of households within each of a number of income classes (mutually exclusive and jointly exhaustive), with the top interval of course being open. We assume that the income distribution is flat within each interval, enabling us to treat the midpoint of the interval as the mean. For each interval we calculate the percent of households in the census tract, and the percent of aggregate income, from which we construct a Lorenz curve and a Gini coefficient. For the open-ended interval, we assume a simple triangular income distribution.

[i]It should be pointed out that school districts are not in general coterminous with the zoning authorities who largely determine the degree to which a community is homogeneous.

theory of patterns of income segregation there seems little alternative. A listing of these nuisance variables, along with explanations for inclusion and predicted coefficients, appears in Appendix 4A.

Our data are from the 19 SMSAs which satisfy the following criteria:[j] (i) a single school district serves all or most of the central city (at least 3/4 of the central city residents); (ii) there are 25 or fewer suburban school districts; (iii) the entire SMSA is within a single state; (iv) state aid to education data are published in the 1967 Census of Governments; (v) the SMSA has a single central city; and (vi) the SMSA has at least 5 suburban census tracts with 300 or more families and tract population densities of at least 100 per square mile.

Within each of the 19 SMSAs we selected a random sample of 5 suburban census tracts which met our nonrural criteria and 5 central-city census tracts. We regressed the suburban census tract Gini coefficients on a large set of variables including three that represent the Tiebout hypothesis and a number of control variables. For comparison, we regressed the central-city census tract Gini coefficients on the same set of variables. Our predictions and results for the central-city regressions are discussed below.

For purposes of testing the Tiebout hypothesis, we are particularly concerned with the effect upon income segregation of the following variables:

Range of Public Service Offerings Available

The local public economy can hardly be said to approximate a market if there is not a substantial range of consumption bundles available. Segregation of households by public service demand is futile if the supply is not responsive. We predict, therefore, that the greater the range of choice within an SMSA, the greater will be the income segregation of our sample census tract. We have selected the number of noncentral-city school districts within the SMSA as our index of the range available. It might be argued that the appropriate measure is not the number of school districts but rather the number of school districts per capita. But since SMSA population is included as one of our explanatory variables, the regression equation is free to take account of this influence (although in a particular functional form). A more appropriate measure of the range of choice available would explicitly account for the *types*, not just the number, of

_____

[j]The 19 SMSAs are: Ann Arbor, Atlanta, Binghamton, Denver, Kalamazoo, Little Rock, Macon, Mansfield, Monroe, New Orleans, Ogden, Orlando, Reading, San Antonio, Shreveport, South Bend, Springfield (Illinois), Terre Haute, and Waco. That part of an SMSA outside the central city is defined as suburban.

school districts. We assume that the number of school districts is a reasonable proxy.

Intergovernmental Aid to Education

To the extent that intergovernmental aid breaks the link between tax liability and public service consumption, the rationing-through-price aspect of the market is destroyed. Households with low demand for public service do not avoid residence in high public service communities that are not also characterized by high tax burdens. Similarly, communities will be less vigilant in their exclusionary behavior, since the funds for public service provision come not from local coffers but from the state. Therefore, we predict that our sample census tracts will be more income-integrated, the higher the reliance on intergovernmental aid. Our representation of reliance on intergovernmental aid goes through several incarnations, which are reported chronologically below.

Our first measure of intergovernmental aid was simply the fraction of expenditures on education financed by intergovernmental grants.[k] The results of this regression were not encouraging. Our first regression contained as explanatory variables all those listed in Appendix 4A, plus the number of school districts in the SMSA and the fraction of school budgets (in the state) financed by intergovernmental aid. The school districts coefficient was negative, as predicted, with a t statistic of 1.60. The aid coefficient, contrary to prediction, was negative and insignificant. We recognized at this point that the single variable we had included was too crude. Intergovernmental aid had been included on the assumption that increased aid would weaken the link between tax burden and public service provision, a link that is necessary for the working of the market-type mechanism. But the degree to which intergovernmental aid weakens this link depends upon the manner in which the aid is distributed. There are three different types of aid formulae, each of which has a different effect on the relationship between taxes and expenditure.

Compensatory Aid. Dollar for dollar, compensatory aid goes furthest in breaking the tax-burden-expenditure link. The price of admitting poor people (people who pay little in local taxes) is reduced for the community if state aid compensates local governments for their poor residents, or if it is distributed in inverse relation to the tax base. So a dollar of compensatory aid should lead to more income integration than other kinds of aid.

---

[k]These data are available only by state, so the explanatory variable is the ratio of total intergovernmental aid granted in the state to total public education expenditure in the state. Throughout this chapter our aid variables will be state aggregates of averages, rather than census tract or school-district-specific observations.

Flat Aid. If aid is granted on a flat per-pupil basis, an extra dollar of local taxation still brings forth an extra dollar of expenditure, and the presence of a low-income household, with its low tax liability, requires an extra tax effort on the part of the high-income members of the community in order to maintain public service levels. Of course, if the flat grant is large enough relative to total expenditure, then the local effort becomes a trivial consideration. Our prediction, then, is that flat grants, unless they become very large, will have only a minor impact on segregation patterns.

Matching Aids. A formula which matches (according to some ratio) local revenue effort serves to magnify the differences between the contribution to the local fisc of the rich and the poor. This is simply because, when two unequal tax burdens are matched by intergovernmental aid, the absolute difference increases. In simple algebra, $T_1(1 + m) - T_2(1 + m) > T_1 - T_2$, where T_1 is the tax burden of a wealthy person, T_2 is the burden of a poor person, and m is the fraction of local taxes which are matched by the grant. Since matching grants increase the cost of admitting poor people to the community, we predict that an increase in the amount of matching aid will increase the segregation of our census tracts.

In our first attempt to account for differences in aid formulae, we separate intergovernmental aid into two categories: matching and all other.[1] The vast majority of the matching formula money appears under state foundation programs. These programs match local revenue effort up to some cutoff point, after which local effort is not matched. The purpose of the program is to establish a floor, or foundation, under per-pupil expenditures in the state.

Results

For each specification reported below, we ran two separate regressions; one over all our central-city observations, and another over the suburban observations. The suburban regressions are our best test of the Tiebout mechanism and its responsiveness to local fiscal structure. The central-city regressions were run to determine the effect of the workings of the suburban public economy on the structure of the central city. It seems reasonable to expect that our "Tiebout variables," would affect central-city coefficients in the same direction as suburban Ginis. Efficient working of the Tiebout mechanism is likely to attract high-income residents to those areas where they are most able to exclude the poor, namely the suburban fringes.

---

[1]The Census does report gross rent by rent class, so we could have converted these figures to present value by a gross rent multiplier. But we felt that the distortions inherent in such an approach were greater than those caused by omitting rental property.

On the other hand, a well-functioning Tiebout mechanism will leave the poor facing restrictive zoning in the suburbs and confined to the central-city. If the suburbs are highly segregated for public economy reasons, the central city is likely to be homogeneous because a large share of the rich have been attracted to the suburbs and a large share of the poor find themselves restricted to the central city.

We report the central regression results for all specifications, but will discuss the findings only for the final regression runs.

The results of these regressions are reported in Table 4-1, columns 1 and 2 for the suburban and central-city equations respectively. As can be seen, the matching aid coefficient is positive but not significant ($t = 1.01$). The other aid variable is also positive as predicted, and just significant at the 0.95 confidence level ($t = 1.69$, degrees of freedom = 74). The number of school districts is significant at the 0.99 confidence level and negative, as predicted. We discovered after running these regressions that our break-down of total intergovernmental aid was inappropriate. It was pointed out to us that almost invariably the statutory ceilings on the foundation pro-grams are binding, which means that at the margin the grants are not matching. Under the provisions of the law, an increase in the number of pupils gives rise to a flat increase in state aid, and is independent, over the relevant range, of local effort. So the aid we had included under the matching heading should be treated as flat-grant aid.[m]

In an attempt to correct this error, we divided the aid variable into two new categories: compensatory, and all other. As indicated above, the "all other" category is almost exclusively flat-grant aid. Our two new explana-tory variables, then are compensatory aid and all other aid, both as frac-tions of total school expenditure. We predict a positive coefficient for the compensatory aid variable and an insignificant coefficient for the other aid variable. The results for suburban census tracts are reported in column 3 of the table. The compensatory aid coefficient is positive as predicted, but significant only at the 0.88 confidence level. The other aid coefficient is negative and insignificant. And the number of school districts coefficient is negative as predicted, but less significant than in the previous equation (0.93 confidence level).

The final change in our regression equations involves an interaction between the number of school districts and intergovernmental aid vari-ables. If as hypothesized, and as our regression results indicate fairly weakly, segregation is advantageous only in the presence of a large number of alternatives to choose from, the amount and type of aid should influence segregation patterns only if there is a reasonably large number of school districts to choose among. To test this hypothesis, we generate a dummy variable equal to zero if the SMSA has three or less suburban school

---

[m]This was pointed out to us by Harvey Galper.

Table 4-1
Regression Results

Variable	Suburb (1)	City (2)	Suburb (3)	City (4)	Suburb (5)	City (6)
(1) Constant Term	−146.9	−199.4	−847.10	−2114.53	−1154.67	−1760.31
(2) State Aid on Matching Basis as a Fraction of School District Revenue in the State	308.3 (1.01)	−55.8 (0.17)	⋯	⋯	⋯	⋯
(3) Other State Aid as a Fraction of School District Revenue in the State	46.40 (1.69)	47.00 (1.66)	⋯	⋯	⋯	⋯
(4) Flat-grant aid as a Fraction of School District Revenue in the State	⋯	⋯	−3.55 (0.57)	5.11 (0.75)	⋯	⋯
(5) Compensatory Aid as a Fraction of School District Revenue in the State	⋯	⋯	3.40 (1.12)	6.06 (1.92)	⋯	⋯
(6) Variable (4) times Dummy[1]	⋯	⋯	⋯	⋯	−3.57 (0.89)	−2.42 (0.51)
(7) Variable (5) times Dummy	⋯	⋯	⋯	⋯	4.51 (1.98)	2.49 (0.96)
(8) Number of Suburban School Districts in the SMSA	−1.70 (2.82)	−0.80 (1.25)	−12.40 (1.54)	−10.17 (1.16)	⋯	⋯
(9) Variable (8) times Dummy	⋯	⋯	⋯	⋯	16.38 (1.92)	−10.77 (1.15)
(10) SMSA Population (in 100,000's)	−25.90 (2.54)	15.04 (1.29)	−18.48 (1.54)	−13.43 (0.97)	−27.32 (1.94)	−16.91 (1.02)

(11) % SMSA Population Growth, 1950-1970	9.80 (0.95)	-8.21 (0.82)	-0.02 (0.01)	-0.97 (0.78)	0.13 (0.10)	-1.21 (0.88)
(12) SMSA Fraction Black	-91.37 (0.97)	-129.0 (1.29)	-15.33 (1.70)	-14.69 (1.50)	-14.24 (1.62)	-12.83 (1.29)
(13) SMSA Gini Coefficient of Family Size	1160.9 (2.92)	1125.0 (2.70)	1012.1 (2.51)	1171.3 (2.57)	1174.2 (2.77)	1175.1 (2.38)
(14) Number of Families in Tract (1,000's)	-2.01 (0.30)	9.42 (1.26)	5.50 (0.08)	99.94 (1.20)	2.75 (0.04)	105.79 (1.24)
(15) Mean Family Income in Tract ($1,000's)	5.63 (1.40)	19.9 (6.97)	71.52 (1.62)	199.08 (6.63)	58.50 (1.36)	192.50 (6.35)
(16) Fraction of Families in Tract with Income of $15,000 or More	38.8 (0.55)	-200.0 (3.45)	-8.44 (1.14)	-21.92 (3.42)	-7.28 (1.03)	-20.81 (3.22)
(17) Fraction Black in Tract	15.50 (0.49)	14.48 (0.91)	3.72 (1.14)	1.27 (0.77)	3.46 (1.08)	1.03 (0.60)
(18) Distance from Tract to Central Business District of SMSA	0.91 (1.30)	4.09 (1.09)	9.91 (1.55)	37.53 (0.92)	9.75 (1.55)	39.25 (0.95)
(19) Fraction of Homes in Tract Built before 1950	44.22 (3.15)	43.10 (2.91)	4.69 (3.07)	3.55 (2.12)	3.90 (2.44)	3.34 (1.96)
(20) Fraction of Homes in Tract Occupied by Owner	47.41 (2.33)	-123.8 (5.66)	-2.49 (1.15)	-12.42 (5.21)	-2.73 (1.29)	-12.42 (5.10)
(21) Dummy Variable = 0 if SMSA in South	13.50 (0.60)	-10.61 (0.45)	-194.72 (1.11)	-58.65 (0.31)	-159.70 (0.196)	-134.00 (0.70)
R^2	.387	.565	.4129	.5691	.4268	.5564

Dependent variable: (Gini coefficient of income) $\times\ 10^3$.

districts, and equal to unity if it has more than three. This dummy is multiplied by both of the aid variables which appear in regressions 3 and 4 (columns 3 and 4), and also by the school districts variable. The results for the suburban equation appear in column 5. This has the effect of assigning both aid variables a value of zero if there are three or less school districts. If as we hypothesize, the level of aid has no influence on segregation if there are three or less school districts, this change in specification should have the effect of increasing the magnitude and the significance of the aid coefficients. In order to remain consistent in our theory, we also multiply the number of suburban school districts by the dummy. The reason for multiplying the aid variables by the dummy is that such a small number of choices makes the Tiebout mechanism unworkable. Then it is also appropriate to assign a value of zero to the school districts variable in this range. As can be seen, all three coefficients (two aid variables and the number of school districts) became larger numerically and more significant as a result of multiplication by the dummy. The flat-aid coefficient changed only trivially, and is still insignificant statistically. This is consistent with the hypothesis that flat aid never makes much difference, but the other two coefficients increased by roughly 25 percent and the t statistics both showed substantial increases, both now being near 2.0. Both coefficients are significant at the 0.95 confidence level.

Our results correspond fairly well with a priori predictions. Flat-grant aid to school districts had an insignificant effect upon residential income segregation in the suburbs. Compensatory aid reduces income segregation significantly if we consider only those SMSAs with more than three suburban school districts. Inclusion of SMSAs with three or less districts greatly reduces both the significance and the magnitude of this effect. This is consistent with the notion that the level of compensatory aid should not influence income segregation when the paucity of school districts prevents the Tiebout mechanism from working anyway. The number of school districts also significantly influences the degree of suburban income segregation, and again both the significance and magnitude of the correlation increase if we consider only those SMSAs with more than three school districts.

Central-City Regression

For the final set of regressions, all the central-city "Tiebout" coefficients are smaller in magnitude and significance than their suburban counterparts. Compensatory aid and number of school districts are significant only at about the 0.85 confidence level. But, all have the same sign. This provides some fairly weak evidence that the Tiebout variables influence central-city income segregation in the same direction as suburban segregation. It seems likely that this is brought about by the fact that, the more attractive the suburban alternatives relative to the central city, the more homogeneous (low income) will be the remaining central-city population. But much more sophisticated analysis would be necessary to have confidence in such a hypothesis. We emphasize that the central-city findings presented here are highly tentative and are intended to be no more than suggestive.

Segregation by House Value

It will be recalled that, in the version of the Tiebout model outlined above, households are segregated both by demand for public service and by house value. The latter form of segregation, enforced by zoning, ensures that all households pay the same amount for the public services they consume. To test this hypothesis, we regressed the Gini coefficient of house value on the same explanatory variables that appear in regressions 5 and 6. In the suburban regression, both aid variables were negative and moderately significant, indicating that an increase in intergovernmental aid increases house-value segregation. The school districts coefficient is positive and significant. The signs of all three Tiebout variables are contrary to prediction.

These findings are contrary to the Tiebout hypothesis and to our findings on income segregation. The striking divergence of these results from those on income segregation is particularly surprising, given that the sample is the same in both regressions, and given the high correlation between income and house value. One would have thought that, even in the absence of a theoretical prediction about house-value segregation per se, the substitution of one dependent variable for the other (which is presumably highly correlated with the first) would change the regression results very little.

The only explanation that occurs to us is this: Within each census tract, the family-income Gini coefficient is constructed over all families in the tract, whereas the house-value Gini excludes rental property. Although we are at a loss to explain why, it would appear that homeowners are a biased sample of households, and that the bias is a function of our Tiebout variables.

We feel that the regression in which the income Gini is the dependent variable are the more reliable, for two reasons. First, as has been pointed out, the income Gini is constructed from information on all households in the census tract, whereas the house-value Gini is derived from a subset of households. The size (and, it would appear, the composition) of this subset varies according to the census tract. Second, the income Gini regressions test a far more general form of the Tiebout hypothesis than do the house-value regressions. If the local public economy resembles a market, people *must* be segregated by demand for public service. But house-value segregation is predicted only in the special Hamilton formulation of the Tiebout hypothesis presented in section 2 of this paper. It is not difficult to imagine a Tiebout-type world in which such segregation is not necessary.[n]

Conclusions

The results, we believe, provide some support for the hypothesis that the degree to which households segregate themselves by demand for public service depends upon the degree to which the local public service delivery system resembles a market. We have found that, on the whole, both the range of choice available and the degree to which there is an effective pricing system are crucial aspects of this market analogue.

References

[1] Barlow, Robin, "Efficiency Aspects of Local School Finance," *Journal of Political Economy* 78 (September/October 1970): 1023-1040.

[2] Bradford, D. F., and W. E. Oates, "Suburban Exploitation of Central Cities and Governmental Structure," in H. Hachman and G. Peterson, eds., *Redistribution Through Public Choice* (New York: Columbia University Press, 1974), pp. 43-90.

[3] Branfman, Eric J., Benjamin I. Cohen, and David M. Trubek, "Measuring the Invisible Wall: Land Use Controls and the Residential Patterns of the Poor," *The Yale Law Journal* 82:483 (1973): 483-507.

[4] Hamilton, B. W., "The Effects of Property Taxes and Local Public Spending on Property Values: A Theoretical Comment," *Journal of Political Economy* (forthcoming).

[5] Hamilton, B. W., "Zoning and Property Taxation in a System of Local Governments," *Urban Studies,* (forthcoming).

[6] Oates, W. E., "The Effects of Property Taxes and Local Public Spending on Property Values: An Empirical Study of Tax Capitalization and the Tiebout Hypothesis," *Journal of Political Economy* 77 (November/December 1969): 959-970.

---

[n]Assume, for example, that every community has a property tax, but that assessment practices are carried on in such a manner that all households in a community pay the same amount in taxes regardless of housing consumption. Here fiscal zoning is superfluous, since tax liability is unrelated to house-value. And the tax is obviously a head tax, with all the attendant efficiency properties.

[7] Peterson, George E., "The Demand for Education," Urban Institute Working Paper, 1973.

[8] Peterson, George E., "The Use of Capitalization Effects to 'Test' the Tiebout Hypothesis," *Journal of Political Economy* (forthcoming).

[9] Tiebout, Charles, "A Pure Theory of Local Public Expenditure," *Journal of Political Economy* 64 (October 1956): 416-424.

Appendix 4A

Metropolitan Population. Formation of homogeneous neighborhoods of a reasonable size is obviously facilitated by a large population, whether the demand for segregation arises from fiscal or other considerations. It is particularly important to include this variable to ensure that the school districts variable is not simply picking up the effect of population. The coefficient has the predicted sign and is quite significant in the suburbs.

Percent Population Growth, 1950-1970. A rapidly growing SMSA presumably has a relatively new housing stock. A new housing stock should be more in line with current demand patterns for housing and segregation (whatever these patterns may be). The estimated coefficient is not significant.

Percent Black in SMSA. For obvious reasons the black population in an SMSA is likely to influence the geographic distribution of people, but the sign of this coefficient was not predicted. Segregation by race is to a large extent segregation by income. But if racial animosity is extreme, avoidance of blacks may be the overriding location consideration of whites, causing them to ignore at least partially the fiscal benefits of income segregation. Our estimated coefficient indicates that an increase in the fraction of the SMSA population that is black does intensify income segregation, with a confidence level of about 0.9.

SMSA Gini Coefficient of Family Income. The predicted effect of the SMSA Gini on census tract Ginis is obvious. Interestingly, a given rise in the SMSA Gini is associated with an even greater rise in census tract Ginis. Heterogeneous SMSAs give rise to heterogeneous neighborhoods with a vengeance.

Number of Families in the Tract. We expect tracts with larger populations to be more heterogeneous than tracts with small populations. But the estimated coefficient is never very significant.

Family Income. This variable is included for two reasons. First it is possible that high-income communities have more access to exclusionary mechanisms, and are therefore more homogeneous. Second, a variable which is constrained to be non-negative, such as income, is likely to have a larger Gini coefficient the higher the mean, because a high mean implies more room between zero (the lower limit of the distribution) and the mean. Since the coefficient of this variable is positive, the latter effect seems to dominate.

Percent of Families in Tract with Income of $15,000 or More. This variable is included as a second attempt to capture the greater incentive of high- than low-income communities to exclude. The predicted sign of the variable is negative.

Percent Black in Census Tract. There is widespread evidence that many housing options are closed to blacks on the basis of race. This may reduce the ability of blacks to segregate themselves by income, implying a positive coefficient for this variable. The estimate is positive but not very significant in both city and suburban regressions.

Distance from the CBD. Census tracts tend to get larger with distance from the CBD. This variable was included partly as a proxy for geographic size. To the extent that segregation is brought about by demand for segregation per se, a large census tract (reduced physical proximity to neighbors) should tend to reduce segregation. Thus the positive coefficient observed in both city and suburb was predicted.

Fraction of Homes Build before 1950. The age of the housing stock in a census tract is likely to be a direct determinant of the distribution of house values since not all housing units deteriorate at the same rate. It is to be expected that old neighborhoods are more heterogeneous than new ones. This appears to be the case, with the estimate being positive and significant.

Fraction of Homes Owner-Occupied. The percent of houses owner-occupied is highly correlated (positively) with the intensity of income segregation.

South Dummy. It is frequently claimed that housing patterns are different in the South than elsewhere. State governments are heavily involved in educational finance in the South. Also, there are in general few suburban school districts in the southern SMSAs. To ensure that our aid and school district variables are not simply picking up regional differences, this variable is included. It is insignificant in regression 5.

5

Fiscal and Environmental Considerations in the Location of Firms in Suburban Communities

William A. Fischel

This chapter is an extension of the Tiebout model to include nonresidential land use. The term nonresidential land use refers here only to taxable commercial or industrial activities for which location decisions are determined by profit considerations. The Tiebout model and the variations on it do not deal specifically with firms, but they do not exclude them either. This is an understandable oversight, as the areas which seem most amenable to the workings of the model are the fragmented suburbs which surround many U.S. metropolitan areas, particularly those outside the South [39].Location theories usually predict or assume that suburbs are ordinarily used for residential housing, and indeed, suburban tax bases are largely residential. In the highly developed suburban communities of northeastern New Jersey used in the empirical work here, less than 20 percent of the tax base consists of commercial or industrial property.

However, several trends have made the existence of firms in suburbs a matter of greater importance than current averages would indicate: (i) The proportion of metropolitan (SMSA) employment which is outside central cities has been increasing. (ii) Concern about the neighborhood effects of firms, as well as of other land uses, has grown. (iii) Firms have frequently been regarded as a source of tax revenues. In a period when the expenditures of local governments have risen more rapidly than average incomes, this serves to focus on their potential to help residents pay their tax bills.

Another current issue that has emphasized the financial role of nonresidential property is the legal question of differences in the distribution of local services among communities. The possibility of communities seeking fiscal gains from businesses was apparently an important consideration in the U.S. Supreme Court's 1973 decision to uphold the constitutionality of local financing of public schools. In his opinion for the majority, Mr. Justice Powell wrote:

Changes in the level of taxable wealth within any district may result from any number of events, some of which local residents can and do influence. For instance, commercial and industrial enterprises may be encouraged to locate within a district by various actions—public and private. [35, p. 4423]

On the other hand, Mr. Justice Marshall, in his dissent, said that the amount of taxable property within a district "is a factor over which local voters can exercise no control." [34, p. 4446] The controversy is not without policy

119

significance even though the court upheld local financing. It was emphasized by the court that any state could choose to substitute state-wide school financing for any localized system. Although we are not directly concerned here with the school financing issue, it is hoped that the approach to the location of commercial and industrial enterprises will lend a useful perspective to this problem.

Basic Hypotheses

The theory will be formally presented later in the chapter, but the basic ideas and their rationale may be outlined here. The political structure of many metropolitan areas in the U.S. is characterized by a large number of residential suburbs surrounding a central city. Most states vest local municipalities with various means of control over land use. This control will be referred to here as zoning, though zoning is only one of several means of land-use control.[a] Zoning gives communities some control not only over the construction of new residential housing, but also over the number and types of firms that may enter.

Although most suburban communities are initially largely residential, a change in the urban rent-offer curves may make many of them attractive locations for firms. Firms are widely regarded as contributing more to the local treasury than they subtract from it, at least in terms of direct municipal costs. In consequence, a common desire of many suburban governments is to attract certain types of firms to the municipality or to the school district "to help pay the taxes." Whether firms *do* create net fiscal benefits of some sort is by no means resolved. This question is dealt with later.

Suppose for now that firms are beneficial to the community in the sense that residents *could* have more of the public services they desire, even accounting for firms' consumption of services, with no reduction in private goods. In a Tiebout world of many similar communities, such a condition would be short-lived. If the firms are footloose, in an analogy to perfectly mobile residents, and if communities act as proprietary agents, there would be gains to be had by communities with firms. They could "underbid" other communities by charging lower taxes or providing more local services of interest to particular firms. Either action would cut down on the fiscal benefit until, in analogy to economic profits under perfect competition, it approached zero. Zero fiscal benefits from firms are, however, contrary to many residents' belief and to the empirical findings of this and some other studies.

[a]Among the other means of land use control are master plans, building codes, sanitation requirements, "environmental impact" studies, land coverage ratios, and off-street parking requirements. Along with these normal "police powers" of local government are the more recent de facto controls such as refusal to expand essential services such as sewage disposal and water mains.

An explanation of positive fiscal benefits is that firms may not be very mobile, so that some communities could gain fiscal benefits from some firms before they move.[b] While plausible, this hypothesis is short-run. Firms have been moving to suburbs for many years, so that windfall fiscal benefits should constitute only a small part of the explanation. There is also evidence that communities respond to threats by firms to relocate in other municipalities [23], an observation that not only confirms the possibility of mobility, but also suggests that firms do make residents better off in some way.

An explanation consistent with the Tiebout hypothesis is that the fiscal benefits created by firms represent the minimum compensation demanded by residents for living with the undesirable neighborhood effects many firms generate. Tax payments by firms may be viewed as side payments to gain entrance to the community. The paradigm of this model is the zoning board hearing at which the firm requests a variance to put up a facility in a largely residential community. Households near the property where the firm wishes to locate may offer objections that the residential character of the neighborhood will be compromised by the firm. The firm's advocates, on the other hand, point out that the property tax revenues that the firm will generate are enough to educate several children a year in the local school system or provide tax relief for the town of so many dollars. One cannot predict how any given hearing will be resolved, or even that issues will be that clear. However, a trade-off between fiscal benefits and adverse neighborhood effects can be assumed to exist in the minds of the zoning authorities who make decisions concerning the location of firms in the community.

The Nature of Neighborhood Effects of Firms

It is assumed throughout this chapter that all firms create some neighborhood effects, or externalities, which at least a few residents find objectionable and none find desirable. This does not preclude firms from being desirable for other reasons. Aside from fiscal benefits, residents may want some firms in order to decrease shopping or commuting distance or to serve as a barrier against even less desirable land uses. Other things being equal, though, residents would prefer not to have firms in their neighborhoods.

There may be many reasons for not wanting firms. There may be air or water pollution; some activities may produce excessive noise; certain buildings may appear unsightly; some industries, such as gas storage or electricity generation, may be regarded as dangerous because of fires or explosions. Traffic congestion with its accompanying noise, smell, and

[b]A recent study [36] suggests, however, that the turnover of manufacturing establishments may be almost as rapid as that of households.

hazards is a frequent objection. Furthermore, some firms may not even generate revenues to pay for the direct public services they use.[c]

The above factors are obvious physical externalities which may disturb residents. However, firms can internalize or mitigate many of these problems. More important than any of the physical externalities may be the class of people attracted by the firm, either as employees or as consumers. This is difficult to establish, but some casual evidence is available [1, p. 57], [12, p. 21]. Even if residents are not concerned about the daytime presence of outside workers or shoppers, they may feel that the presence of large employers may create pressures for lower-income housing within the community. Perfect zoning control by each community would enable present residents to screen out "undesirable" residents, but the realities of the law and the ambitions of real estate developers make such control a matter of degree.

Nonfiscal Considerations

It has been assumed that the only reason residents might grant permission for firms to locate in their community is fiscal gain. Residents in effect sell part of their environment in return for lower tax shares for local public services. But there are other reasons for communities to permit firms to enter. The community may desire to reduce local unemployment, it may wish to shorten the journey to work for its residents, or it may want to reduce the cost of shopping trips by allowing retail stores to locate there. For suburban communities, it is argued presently that only the last motive is likely to be strong, and none is as likely as the desire for fiscal gains.

Treatment of local unemployment problems by trying to attract industry assumes that some labor is less mobile than some capital.[d] This is most likely in areas where labor mobility means a permanent change of residence rather than a change in commuting patterns. Such areas are likely to be entire metropolitan areas or relatively isolated rural center of employment, such as mining towns or farming communities.

Because a suburb is only a small part of the metropolitan labor market, many jobs created within it would be filled by people who live outside the community. A suburb that attracted firms would create a desirable spillover for other communities. Public goods theory suggests that activities

---

[c]Each of these considerations has been mentioned in newspaper articles on zoning and suburban firms. Any reader can confirm this list and expand it indefinitely by perusal of any suburban newspaper for a few months.

[d]For a theoretical treatment, see [34]. Their analysis of industrial location policies to reduce unemployment has several parallels to the theory presented here.

which have positive externalities will be underproduced. There are costs to inducing firms to locate in a particular community. A community that could not reap all the benefits of its inducements would be unlikely to offer them. Only larger governments, such as counties or states, would be able to internalize most of the benefits of such activities.[e]

Residents of suburbs, while often homogeneous with respect to income, are usually heterogeneous with respect to specific occupations. Few suburbs have a substantial number of residents who could be employed by a single firm or group of firms which might locate in the community. Even if it were decided to try to attract industry to a specific community to alleviate local unemployment, it is unlikely that specific firms could be found to satisfy the job preferences of more than a small percentage of the workers in that suburb.[f] For the same reason, suburbs are less likely to desire industry in order to reduce commuting costs. Many workers might be willing to accept the neighborhood effects of their particular place of employment if it reduced commuting costs, but it is unlikely that they would do so for other workers in their community.

Firms might choose to locate in suburbs to have greater access to labor markets. However, metropolitan suburbs usually include many municipalities. In weighing the community costs and benefits of permitting a firm to enter, the fiscal and externalities considerations are more likely to dominate employment and commuting considerations.

The previous argument may not hold for retail firms that provide goods or services primarily to local residents. Although residents of a particular suburb may be diverse in their job categories, they are likely to have similar demands for many goods. Thus food stores, drug stores, banks, and gas stations would find more advocates at zoning board hearings than other land uses, as they reduce nearly every resident's shopping costs. However, it is likely that such stores do not constitute a large proportion of all commercial property. There are substantial economies of scale in retailing and in other services which often require a market area larger than any one suburban community. Shopping centers are one example. Because many nonresidents patronize such facilities, a large proportion of their business is also for export from the community. In any case, environmental considerations are still present. Communities prefer tasteful, well-planned shopping centers to neon-lighted strips; and they may be willing to forgo the convenience of nearby stores for preservation of residential amenities.

[e]The attempts are aimed at structural unemployment. Local governments cannot deal with deficiencies of macro-economic policies [31, ch. 1].

[f]It must be noted that the people in residence *before* the firm moves in make the decisions. After the firm locates in a community, there would be a tendency for employees of the firm to buy housing in that community, so that the proportion of residents employed by the firm would naturally go up.

Fiscal Considerations by Firms in Their Location Decisions

Several economists have dealt with the effect of fiscal variables on the firm's choice of location; very few claim to have detected a systematic effect of either tax rates or local expenditures on locations decisions by firms [14,28]. Although no comprehensive review of this literature is offered here, an obvious criticism of such studies is that the fiscal criteria are often incomplete. Firms are interested not only in the taxes they pay but also in the expenditure pattern of the local government. A high-tax rate community may be attractive to a firm because it offers services that are of interest to it. A careful fiscal study involves calculating the effective tax price of public services in which firms are interested. If a firm received extra services it valued equally with its extra tax payments, the effective price would be unity; if it received services it valued only half as much as its tax payments, the effective price would be two, and so forth. The community with the lowest effective tax price (not necessarily unity) would be the most advantageous to firms.

Calculations such as these are possible but difficult because they involve assigning local services to either firms or residents. Unfortunately, the present hypothesis further complicates the theoretical issue because of zoning restrictions regarding neighborhood effects. A community which has the most favorable tax price of public services for a particular industry may not get any firms. Zoning restrictions may exclude firms altogether, or they may require them to alter their production processes so that location elsewhere is more profitable.

In the model that follows, it is assumed that all firms are indifferent to all public services. This is to focus on the externalities-fiscal-benefit relationship. The assumption is not true, but the importance of local school expenditures in suburbs may justify its use for the time being. In addition, the relationship enables us to view communities as rational suppliers of commercial and industrial sites. It is hoped that this will be a contribution to the literature on fiscal influences on business location, which has largely focused on the demand for sites by firms. A theory of the interaction of firms, environment, and municipal services is presented later.

Introduction to the Model

The basic premise here is that the fiscal benefits firms confer on suburban communities represent compensation for the undesirable neighborhood effects of firms. If this premise is valid, then one of the frequently alleged inefficiencies of the market system is substantially modified. The inefficiency causes undesirable neighborhood effects for which no compensation is made. Firms cause pollution or congestion in the process of producing goods for the market, the argument goes, but no market exists to compensate those who suffer from the local external effects. In the following model, it is shown how such a "pollution market" might exist in the form of fiscal benefits to residents.

Our intentions in this chapter parallel those of Tiebout, who sought to show how a system of local governments could overcome the problems of allocating public goods described by Samuelson and others [38, p. 416]. We wish to show how local government can overcome the classic externalities problem. Just as Tiebout claimed that his model applied only under certain conditions and for certain types of goods, so the efficiency conditions of this model are derived from restrictive assumptions. Although evidence supporting some of the necessary conditions and implications for this theory is presented on pages 149-163, it must continue to be regarded as a tentative hypothesis.

Assumptions of the Model

The setting for the model is the atomistic suburban government structure of many communities surrounding a central city. These suburbs are initially entirely residential, and residents of a particular community are homogeneous in their demand for housing and local public services. This homogeneity is enforced by zoning requirements that effectively require new residents to construct or purchase houses of value such that the property tax paid will at least cover the marginal (= average) cost of the municipal services they may demand. This process has been described in detail by Hamilton in [17] and in Chapter 2 of this volume.

Local government activity in this model is directed toward production of only two goods—public schooling, denoted by S, and "environmental quality," denoted by E. Government of a community thus consists of a school board and a zoning board.

The utility function of the ith resident of any community is given by $U_i = f(X_i, H_i, S_i, E_i)$ in which H represents housing and X represents all other goods. School boards are required to supply equal amounts of schooling to each household, so that $S_i = S_j$ for any two households i and j in a community. Total schooling demanded is NS_i, where N is community population (of households). In order to prevent free riders, the zoning board requires that all residents live in housing of some minimum value such that tax shares are equal. Thus $H_i = H_j$ in a given community, and the total stock of housing is NH_i. At a given real tax rate, t, $tH_i = tH_j$ and $tNH_i = NS_i$ in any community. Other goods, X, are independent of location. In particular, the services and transfers of nonlocal government received by any household do not vary by community of residence.

Environmental quality, E, is defined as the absence of neighborhood effects from firms. Such effects may result from concomitant side effects from firms rather than from the firms themselves. However, it is assumed that the only way such effects may be controlled is to exclude the firms that might wish to locate in the community. The "best" level of E is E_r, in which the community is entirely residential.

The method of exclusion is zoning. Zoning is assumed to be entirely local and absolute in its power over changes in land use designations. Zoning boards reflect the unaminous will of the residents of the community. A unanimity requirement is not necessary for the analysis, but it seems more realistic than majority rule, and it makes explicit the relationship between individual preference and community decisions.[g] Several writers have been impressed by how frequently a small group of suburban residents can cause the location plans of even innocuous firms to be blocked or substantially modified [1,37].

All firms have identical production functions and identical neighborhood effects. The price of land is the same in every community (one may assume equal distance from some desirable central location), and capital and labor are also equally available in every community. Firms thus have the same optimum mix of inputs in every location. Their neighborhood effects are uniform, and these externalities accumulate linearly: two firms have twice the impact on local E as one.

The externalities of all firms are uniformly distributed over every household in the community. Environment is a pure public good, so that $E_i = E_j = E$ for any residents i and j within a given community. In addition, it is necessary to assume that there are no intercommunity spillovers. If there were, the level of E in one community would be affected by that in any other community. These two extreme assumptions will be reexamined later.

The subscript notation could become cumbersome in later sections, so it will be dropped at this point. The terms X, H, S, and E refer to individual households, subject to the conditions of additivity or equality set forth in the previous paragraphs of this section.

In each community there is an equal amount of vacant land on which firms can locate. The vacant land is entirely owned by persons not living in the community, so that residents of the community have no proprietary interest in its value except as it relates to their utility. Firms are also aliens to the community. They are owned by outsiders, no residents are employed by them, and all production is for export from the community. Firms are also indifferent to each of the arguments of residents' utility functions in their choice of location.

---

[g]A "median voter" analysis of majority decision making for local public services is examined in [3].

The foregoing discussion of firms, environment, and zoning implies some simple functional relationships which are given here to emphasize the basic relationships among these variables and to use in later sections. $E = E(F)$, where E is environmental quality and F is the number of firms in the community. $\partial E / \partial F$ is a negative constant: the more firms, the less environment is available. This is also written as an inverse function, $F = F(E)$, meaning the number of firms permitted in a community is a function of the demand for environment. This demand is discussed in the next section.

These relationships may also be expressed in terms of community decisions about vacant land. If Z denotes the amount of land community residents may keep vacant in order to maintain a high quality E, or which they may allow firms to use in return for some compensation, then $E = E(Z)$, where $\partial E / \partial Z$ is a positive constant. This illustrates the direct relationship between land and firms: there is no substitution of capital for land observed. This is not because the production functions do not allow for it, but because no community can force a competitive firm to operate at other than its optimum mix of inputs. If the community did this, the firm would choose another community or go out of business.

Direct Payments and the Price of Environment

Given the situation outlined above, no firm will be permitted to locate in any suburb unless it offers some compensation to the residents. The compensation is required because firms reduce residents' consumption of E. Let us propose, contrary to most institutions, that compensation is made by means of direct cash payments to the zoning board, which is required to divide the total equally among residents. The firm pays *no* property taxes or other charges. This system will be referred to as the DPS, the direct payment system of compensation. Because neighborhood effects accrue equally to every resident and because unanimity is required for zoning variances, the direct payment by each firm must at least compensate each resident for his loss of E caused by the firm.

The direct payment will not exceed the minimum amount, however, because of competition among communities. If there are many communities with identical plots of vacant land, then firms will "shop around" among communities in an attempt to reduce the compensation they must pay. Barring a monopoly agreement among communities, the process will push the direct payments toward the minimum acceptable to residents.[h]

hWhite, in Chapters 3 and 6, analyzes the strategies communities may adopt if they do have some monopoly power. Everything in this presentation proceeds from the assumption of perfect competition among communities.

It is now possible to define the price of environment. In this situation, P_e is the direct payment a resident forgoes by commanding the zoning board to exclude a firm that wants to enter the community. In short, it is the opportunity cost of zoning decisions. It is this opportunity cost which operates the "pollution market" referred to when we introduced the model above. This price corresponds to a good with no precise units. It is only assumed that each firm causes some reduction in availability of environment to each resident in the same way that every other firm does and that the effects are directly proportional to the number of firms.

The problem for each resident is to maximize $U = U(X, H, S, E)$ subject to the income constraint

$$Y = P_x X + P_h H + P_s S + P_e F(E)$$

in which $F(E)$ is the number of firms permitted in the community. The functional notation, $F(E)$, indicates that firms reduce the availability of E to residents in the manner described in the previous section.

One may object that P_s is actually a tax rate on housing, but in the model used here, Hamilton has shown that the property tax combined with zoning causes schools to be allocated as if they were available on the private market. The solution to the consumer's problem regarding choice of environment is the usual one of equating the rate of commodity substitution of E for a given good to their price ratios.

The term $P_e F(E)$ represents the income from an asset, environment, which is owned in partnership by the community. (The analogy to a partnership is appropriate because of the unanimity required to reach any decision.) Ordinarily, one would not observe a cash flow of the entire rental value of the asset. Although some E may be exchanged for direct payments from firms, one would expect that communities that are largely residential would hold much of their environment in reserve for their own use. That residents might decide not to sell any of it, however, does not reduce its positive opportunity cost.

The definition of P_e for a community is the payment forgone by the resident who demands the most E, since the zoning board only grants variances on the unanimous consent of existing residents. The total compensation paid by all firms in a given community is $N P_e F(E)$, where N is the number of residents. Firms must deal with the zoning boards, not individual residents, and the zoning board is required to allocate compensation equally among residents.

Residents who demand less E than do their neighbors have incentives to move. (If zoning boards operate by majority vote, then those who do not demand the same E as the median voter move.) This adds another dimension to community choice. Instead of matching only housing and schooling demand as Hamilton suggests, potential residents must match housing, schooling, and environment. This would greatly add to the required number of communities if there were little correlation between demand for housing and demand for environment.

In the following sections, it is assumed that individual utility functions and budget constraints are identical with community preferences and budget constraints. The preceding paragraph suggests that residents of a given community will tend to be homogeneous in their demand for housing, schooling, and environment. Even if households are identical, however, there are problems of aggregation, one of which is discussed in the section on community sizes below. For now, the reader may wish to think of single-household communities.

It may be noted that under the restrictive and unrealistic assumptions of the DPS, the problem of external effects of firms is solved in a Pareto efficient way. Firms must pay residents exactly the value the latter put on their environment. Zoning insures that firms do not pay too little, and intercommunity competition insures that residents of any community are not paid too much. Payments go only to those affected by the externalities, so the least-cost input combinations of firms and the choice of goods by residents are not affected. Thus the DPS serves as an efficiency benchmark for the following sections, in which some measure of reality is introduced.

The Property Tax System

Direct payments by firms to residents or to any subset of them are illegal in most of the United States. Bribes to local officials for zoning variances are not unknown and are sometimes notorious, but this work is confined to approved behavior.[i] The principal method which remains as legal compensation is the local property tax. Firms are able to generate local tax revenues in excess of the value of local government expenditures they receive, the difference being known, among other things, as the "fiscal dividend." Such a residual may be used to lower taxes or increase local government expenditures. In this way, the fiscal dividend is analogous to the aforementioned system of direct payments.

The analogy of the fiscal dividend method of compensation to direct payments is not formally correct, but if certain qualifications are added, the systems give the same results. The modifications and new assumptions of the following paragraph will give a compensation system named the "property tax system," or PTS.

Recall that firms in this model can receive no local services; local government consists only of a school board and a zoning board. There are

---

[i] Many of the hypotheses in the next three sections were developed simultaneously by White [40], and this author benefited from conversations we had on the topic.

three new assumptions: (i) Local governments are required to use all property taxes for schools. (ii) Property taxes, the sole source of local revenues, are assessed at a fixed ratio to the market value of all real property. Residential housing and the structures of firms are treated equally by the tax assessor. Although the ratio of assessed value to market value cannot vary by class of property within a community, it can vary among communities. (iii) Tax rates must be the same for all classes of property within a community.

Such a system causes the tax base of residents, who are the sole decision makers regarding school expenditures, to be increased in those communities with firms. The result is for the "tax price of public schools," that price perceived by decision makers, to be reduced. For example, if industrial property in a community equals total residential property under the conditions of the model, then the tax price of schools is exactly half what it was when the community was entirely residential. If this situation persists, that is, if there is no adjustment in realty consumed by households or used by firms, then residents' decisions about schools will be based on a perceived price which is lower than the marginal cost of the real resources to society at large.

The framework above places the fiscal dividend in an analytically useful perspective. It indicates that the decision to lower taxes or increase school expenditures as a result of the presence of firms can be analyzed in terms analogous to income and substitution effects. In Figure 5-1, the horizontal axis measures schooling, S, and the vertical axis measures Q, a composite of X and H.[j] Environment is represented in a third dimension, not drawn in Figure 5-1.

In initial residential equilibrium, established before any firm demanded any suburban location, residents of the community are presumed to choose point A on budget line Q_1S_1 of Figure 5-1. The composite good Q is relevant rather than H because migration and zoning force public school expenditures to be market choices, regardless of the residential tax base. Now suppose that firms are permitted to move into the community so that half of real property is represented by industry. This results in a new budget line, Q_1S_2, with a slope one half that of Q_1S_1. Communities could, if they wished, choose point B, keeping school expenditures the same and taking a reduction in taxes, which is the same as an increase in Q. This is analogous to the income effect of a lower price in any market.[k] If the community chose point

[j]We can add X and H in this way only if it is assumed that demand for housing is unaffected by any community decisions about environmental quality. This is discussed in the following section.

[k]The analogy to price theory is not exact, however, since something is being exchanged for the lower price line, namely environment.

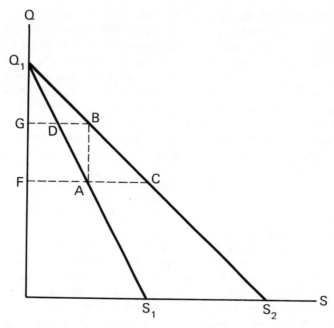

Figure 5-1. Effect of Firms on Community Budget Constraint

C, keeping *Q* the same but consuming more *S*, it is analogous to a substitution effect. Presumably, though not necessarily, communities would choose some point on the new budget line between points *B* and *C*, evincing some income and some substitution effects.

This formulation puts the notion of a fiscal dividend in a different perspective. No fixed cash payment is extracted from firms, as in the DPS, because the amount firms pay depends on residents' choices about schools. At *B* in Figure 5-1, firms pay *DB*, while at *C* they pay *AC*. Firms pay the same proportion of all taxes in both cases ($AC/FC = DB/GB$), because assessments are applied equally to all property, but their payments depend on how much residents are willing to pay. This implies that fiscal benefits cannot be measured in terms of what firms actually pay in taxes; benefits must be measured with reference to the consumers surplus gained by the firms' lowering the effective tax price of local public services consumed by residents.

The compensation mechanism of the PTS is necessarily less efficient than that of the DPS because the effective tax price of schools is less than marginal cost, so that too much will be consumed relative to income. This may seem a peculiar result for any characterization of the local property tax system, but easy to see if one considers that payment in the DPS is equivalent to a general block grant to the community while in the PTS it is like a specific matching grant. An additional difficulty of the PTS is that the extra schooling demanded by residents might exceed the amount firms would be willing to pay. Firms do not care what use is made of their payments, so they will offer the same amount in the PTS as in the DPS. The exogenously determined (by intercommunity competition) maximum payment in school taxes in the PTS cannot exceed the maximum direct cash payments in the DPS. This causes line Q_1S_2 to be discontinuous in the lower right of Figure 5-1, at a point that would be chosen by the community at that tax price.

A clear advantage of the DPS is that it not only does not cause distortion of choices among goods, but that it also enables residents to exploit the entire value of their asset, E, regardless of their preferences for schools. As an example, consider a community with no children. No firm can compensate residents by lowering the effective tax price of schools, as residents demand none. Residents might accept some firms, however, if they could get some direct payments. Both firms and residents are worse off under the PTS inasmuch as firms are denied access to some locations because they have no legal means of compensating residents for their external effects.

On the other hand, communities which demand more schooling might find that they cannot attract any firms because the school tax rate would extract too large a payment. Under the DPS, such communities could attract as many firms as their demand for E allowed and use the cash payments toward schooling or other goods as they saw fit.

Figure 5-2 illustrates the aforementioned difficulties. It shows the cross-section of a budget surface for some level of E not shown. The line Q_1S_1 is the budget line when there are no firms, $E = E_r$, and it is the same for the PTS and the DPS. When some E is sacrificed by letting in firms, however, the budget lines no longer coincide. With the addition of firms, the budget line under the DPS shifts out parallel to Q_1S_1, representing, for some reduced level of E designated E_2, the line Q_2S_2'. Under the PTS, the budget line at E_2 is Q_1S_2. The slope of line Q_1S_2 is smaller than line Q_2S_2' because the community cannot convert firms' tax payments into any good other than S. Line Q_1S_2 is discontinuous for the segment LS_2 because firms will not be willing to pay more than segment S_1S_2', the maximum they will part with in the DPS. Thus the *only* point at which the DPS and the PTS give the same choices to residents is at point L. Point L cannot be varied by communities because all firms are exactly the same: each firm maps into the same unique level of taxable property as any other. It would be the luckiest of coincidences that a community would choose L under the DPS. If it did, there would be no welfare loss due to the PTS.

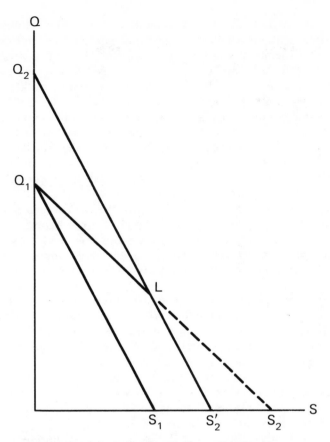

Figure 5-2. Community Budget Constraints

Modifications of the Property Tax System[1]

However more efficient the DPS may be relative to the PTS, the property tax system is the primary mechanism of compensation by firms to community residents in the United States. The inefficiencies of the PTS are the result of some restrictive assumptions, which may not be valid. The PTS can be equivalent to the DPS through five modifications of the basic PTS assumptions. Although each modification is considered independently, together they may account for many of the variations in municipal budgets and land use patterns among suburban communities.

---

[1]The next four sections involve none of the empirical hypotheses tested in this chapter. The reader more interested in the empirical work may go directly to the section on Variations on the Price of Environment.

The first modification is to assume that any number of goods may be included in local government budgets, not just schools. In this situation, residents tax themselves and the firms to the maximum that firms will allow without moving away, and the revenues are used to purchase goods which residents would otherwise have bought on the private market. This could explain why many apparently "private" goods provided by local government in some communities are left to be paid by individual households in other communities. A logical extreme of this practice would be to assess property taxes on firms and households so as to collect the largest sum and then redistribute the revenue as cash payments to each household. The limit to such a practice is only that taxes must not exceed the payment which would cause firms to migrate.

In terms of Figure 5-2, this practice involves selecting a desired E, and then levying taxes to achieve point L. If point L is not an optimum bundle of Q and S, the community simply transfers goods from the Q axis to the S axis until the optimum is reached. (For high tax rate communities, it might require transferring goods from the S axis to the Q axis so as not to drive off firms.)

The previous modification is limited in practice by law, custom, and the difficulties involved in coming to agreement on the scope of local expenditures. Municipalities in the United States are creatures of the states, and the larger bodies tend to restrict the scope of activity of the smaller.[m] Even if the range of local activities were not limited, it is much less plausible that residents could be brought together on the basis of their demand for, say, garbage collection than their demand for schools.[n] The latter is a substantial and critical expenditure for many families, while the former occupies a relatively small proportion of a household's budget.

A second modification of the PTS relaxes the requirement that assessments bear the same relationship to market value for every class of property. If each community were permitted to assess each firm at any value it chose or, equivalently, establish a higher or lower tax rate for firms than for residents, then firms could pay their compensation to residents in school taxes without residents also paying higher taxes. In this situation, the maximum payment by firms could be obtained simply by assessing firms at a value such that their tax payments yield the same amount as they would pay in cash in the DPS.

If firms' school tax payments do not exceed the school payments residents would have made had they simply been given direct cash payments, then no distortion is present. Residents' decisions are made by

[m]Buchanan [7] has suggested some strategies that central-city municipalities might adopt to extract the largest payments from potential emigrants, which include firms.

[n]Even if it were, it greatly increases the number of communities necessary to achieve an optimum distribution of public services.

assuming they are T_f richer, where T_f is the maximum tax payment from firms, and then getting firms to pay T_f for one particular good which they have chosen. The only inefficiency is caused if residents would not demand T_f worth of schools in the DPS. In this case, firms are assessed at 100 percent and residents at 0 percent, but tax revenues still exceed the amount of school expenditures residents want. In such a situation, which is not implausible, the effective tax price of schools is once again below the marginal cost of the real resources involved.

In terms of Figure 5-2, this modification allows the community to shift line Q_1S_2 for any given level of E, so that point L coincides with the point that would have been chosen on line Q_2S_2', the budget line for the DPS. The restriction is that no budget line can have a positive slope, so that if very low levels of S were chosen in the DPS, the PTS budget line could not possibly intersect it.

The foregoing modification is not equivalent to a constitutional or legislative act which requires that *all* communities assess commercial or industrial property a certain percent above or below residential property. Such a system still requires residents to tax themselves more to get higher payments from firms. It is necessary to allow *individual* communities to raise or lower assessments according to the size of the direct payment they wish to extract.

There is some evidence that firms are not treated the same as residents in every community, even in areas where the law requires such equal treatment [30]. That such disparities persist despite the law may be taken as *prima facie* evidence that some firms may feel it is desirable to pay a large proportion of local taxes to forestall local action against their neighborhood effects. However, there is no evidence that such motivations are in fact responsible for the disparities.

A third modification of the PTS assumes that housing consumption is not fixed at the level chosen prior to any demand by firms for suburban locations. Recall that housing and schools are chosen simultaneously in this model. After firms demand locations, all residents are faced with higher budget surfaces in the DPS. This may cause them to demand more housing, more schooling, and/or more of other goods. The only incentive to change communities, however, is differences in demand for E, because residents are already homogeneous in their demand for housing and schooling.

The basic PTS, however, imposes the requirement that compensation be made through lowering the effective tax price of schools. It was shown that differential assessments could resolve this restriction in most cases, but this is usually illegal. A possible response to this restriction is for the housing market to vary so that the proper differential market values would be produced. For example, if firms occupy 50 percent of the taxable property of the community for a given level of E, but equivalence to the DPS demands that they be 70 percent, then a market adjustment would occur such that housing values would shrink to 30 percent of the taxable realty of the community.

The difficulty with such an adjustment, should it take place, is that now housing consumption is distorted. That is, residents in the PTS are consuming less (or perhaps more) housing than they were in the DPS just so they can achieve the same level of E and S in both systems. Efficiency implies that residents can have exactly the same set of goods X, S, H, E in both the DPS and the PTS.

A fourth modification of the PTS assumes that firms may vary their productive inputs so as to use more or less taxable property at a given site. This enables an individual community to achieve the same result as differential assessments. All it needs to do is command the firms that wish to locate in the community to purchase more or less taxable property, until the firms occupy such a proportion of the tax base as makes the firms' property tax payment equal to what would have been demanded in the DPS. Thus, a firm whose property tax payment does not quite yield the amount it would pay in the DPS would be required to purchase more taxable property, which would add to taxes but not subtract from residents' consumption of E. A maximum land coverage ratio could be used to achieve this condition. In terms of Figure 5-2, this is again the same as causing adjustments in the slope of line Q_1S_2 so that point L coincides with the efficient point on line Q_2S_2, the DPS budget line.

The variation in taxable property requirements is efficient for residents, providing that residents' demand for schooling is at least as great as the maximum firms are willing to pay. Such a system is not efficient from the firms' point of view, however. In very low tax rate communities, they would be forced to use much more taxable property than in high tax rate communities in order to equalize their direct payments to residents in each community. (We still assume that external effects are the same for all firms so side payments per firm must be equal in all communities.) In this case, most firms will be forced to use other than their optimum mix of inputs because community zoning boards demand that their tax base be larger or smaller than in the DPS.

Variation in the External Effects of Firms

A final variation provides the necessary conditions for making the PTS equivalent to the DPS for both residents and firms without recourse to the four previous modifications. Assume that firms differ in their external effects at their least-cost combination of inputs in any given location. That is, some firms may be associated with more noxious external effects under a given set of circumstances than other firms. Also assume that there is a continuous range of such firms, from the very obnoxious to the virtually park-like. (Subsequent discussion will refer only to "noxious" and "pleasant" firms, but there can be any number of categories.) Furthermore, it must be assumed that there are enough of each type of firm for the variations in demand for E of each community. For convenience we continue to assume that each firm adds the same value to taxable property, but this is not crucial to the argument.

In a direct payment system of compensation, there is no longer a uniform payment associated with each firm. Firms are charged according to their effect on the environment of the community, so that the "noxious" firms pay larger amounts than the "pleasant" firms for the zoning board's permission to locate in the community.

Consider two communities in the DPS which have exactly the same demand for housing and environment, differing only in their demand for schooling. In the DPS, both communities have houses of the same value, both get direct payments from firms of exactly the same amount. The only difference is that one community, call it A, demands more schooling than the other, B. If we suddenly switch to the rigid PTS in which all firms are the same, it is likely that both A and B are made worse off. If by chance one were left at the optimum point L in Figure 5-2, the other community could not possibly achieve an optimum, since it demands the same E but a different level of S.

With the present modification of the PTS, the aforementioned communities can achieve the same bundle of goods as they had in the DPS. Community A, with the higher tax rate, simply gets a few noxious firms, whereas community B, with the lower tax rate, gets many of the pleasant firms. Since the effect of firms is cumulative, many pleasant firms have the same environmental impact as a few noxious ones, so E is the same. Community A gets the same total in tax payments because it taxes the few noxious firms at a higher rate. The noxious firms each pay more because otherwise they are unwelcome anywhere. The pleasant firms are attracted to B because it has a lower tax rate, so that the payment per firm is lower than in A.

The mechanics of the calculation by each community are as follows:[o] Solve the following two equations for t and V_f. Then select the most pleasant category of firms which are just willing to pay that tax rate and allow them to enter until the necessary value of V_f has been achieved. The equations are:

---

[o]Each of the following terms is for a single "decisive" resident. This avoids, but does not solve, the problems of determining a community welfare function and budget constraint.

$$t(V_h + V_f) = P_sS \qquad (5.1)$$

and

$$tV_f = P_eF(E_i) \qquad (5.2)$$

In these equations, t is the school tax rate; V_h is taxable value of housing; V_f is taxable value of firms; P_sS is expenditure on schools in the DPS; and $P_eF(E_i)$ is total direct payments from firms in the DPS, E_i being the level of environment chosen in the DPS.

The first equation states that school expenditures in the modified PTS must be the same as in the DPS. The second states that the total tax payments of the firms in the PTS must equal their payments in the DPS.[p] Because there is a continuous range of external effects associated with firms and a perfectly elastic supply of every class of firms, the community should have no problem finding a class of firms which satisfies these two equations.

There is also an implied constraint that the environment associated with the necessary V_f in the PTS equals E_i, the environment chosen by the community in the DPS. The community does not have to worry about this, however, because, under the assumptions stated, the firms associated with E_i will be the most pleasant (least noxious) of those willing to pay t. This must be because the payment differentials which prevailed among classes of firms in the DPS must also prevail in the PTS.

A numerical example may clear up some issues. Assume there are two communities, A and B, which, in the DPS demand identical housing and identical environment. Houses are valued at \$30,000 and the payoff from firms is \$50 per household for the privilege of location. This payoff may be from a few noxious firms or several pleasant ones or some mixture of categories. The difference is that school expenditures per household in A are \$1000 per year and in B only \$600 per year. The local tax rate on housing in the DPS (firms are not taxed in the DPS) is

A : $t = \$1,000/\$30,000 = 0.033$

B : $t = \$600/\$30,000 = 0.02$

The issue is as follows: Is it possible in the PTS for residents to obtain exactly the same set of goods (H, S, X, E) as in the DPS without differential assessment, local government budget changes, capitalization of housing, or forcing firms to produce using other than their optimal (DPS) mix of inputs? The answer involves solving (5.1) and (5.2) for each community. Community A must find a tax rate and value of firms such that

---

[p]Actually, community decisions are based on "greater than or equal to" considerations in both (5.1) and (5.2). We assume that competition among communities works the same in the PTS as it did in the DPS, eliminating any excess fiscal benefits.

$$t(V_f + 30{,}000) = 1000 \quad \text{and} \quad tV_f = 50$$

Community B must find a tax rate and value of firms such that

$$t(V_f + 30{,}000) = 600 \quad \text{and} \quad tV_f = 50$$

The numerical solution for A is $t = 0.03166$ (down from 0.0333) and $V_f = \$1579$. For B the solution is $t = 0.01833$ (down from 0.02) and $V_f = \$2727$. These tax rates and values of firms yield exactly the same set of values for goods S and E as were obtained in the DPS without any reduction in H or X or change in the input mix of firms.

Community A, with \$1578.95 worth of firms, can get the same environment as community B has with \$2727.28 worth of firms, even though each firm has the same taxable property, because community B has many pleasant firms, while community A has a few noxious firms. Environmental effects are cumulative, so that the sum of many pleasant firms is the same as the sum of a few noxious firms. Both communities get the same total tax payment from their firms because their tax rates are different: Community A charges a higher rate to firms (and residents) to get more schooling. The individual firms in community A must tolerate the higher tax rate because their external effects are more moxious, so they are unwelcome anywhere if they do not pay more than the pleasant firms. Note the implication of this theory. It is high tax rates which cause noxious firms to locate in a community, because it is only in high tax rate communities that they can offer enough compensation. The typical reaction to the observation that noxious firms are associated with high tax rates is that noxious firms cause those high tax rates.

If either community lowers taxes still further, as might be supposed, it will not be getting as much S as it demanded in the DPS, even while getting more disposable income. It would be inconsistent to choose a different bundle of goods in two systems in which the possible combination of goods is the same (that is, the budget hyperplanes are identical). This is the whole point of equivalence between the DPS and this modification of the PTS.

An interesting result of this analysis is that communities with more valuable homes get more of the pleasant firms than an otherwise similar community with less valuable residences. This is because communities with large residential tax bases will have a lower school tax rate than another community with the same demand for S. If both communities want the same E (and thus the same total payment from firms), the wealthier community must get many pleasant firms and the other community must get fewer, more noxious firms. This is not to say, however, that wealthy communities will always get the pleasant firms, or any firms, for that matter. This actually depends on the relative income elasticities of demand for housing, schooling, and environment.

It may be argued that distortions are present in the PTS because firms have incentives to reduce their external effects so as to get into a lower tax rate community, but they had exactly the same choice in the DPS. In both the DPS and the modified PTS, the question of whether a firm should internalize its external effects is a matter of determining which course of action causes the least reduction in profits.

The previous example demonstrates how the modified PTS may be equivalent to the DPS in any situation, so that there is no distortion caused by the "matching grant" nature of the compensation by firms. This is qualified by the requirement that school expenditures in the DPS are at least as great as the total direct payments from firms.

It may be suspected that a fixed supply of a given type of firm would cause them all to locate in the same community, if it had enough vacant land. This will probably not happen because environmental effects are cumulative, even for the most pleasant firms, so that eventually the rate of commodity substitution of environment to other goods will equal their price ratios.[q] If the supply of firms is very small relative to a community's tolerance for their neighborhood effects, however, the lowest tax rate community will get all of the most pleasant firms.

It is not clear that every firm which found a place in some community in the DPS will also find a place in the modified PTS. That depends on the distribution of tax rates. To guarantee that all communities would be satisfied in their demand for E, we had to assume a perfectly elastic supply of every category of firm.[r] In order to guarantee that every firm can be satisfied in its demand for location, we must assume a sufficient supply of communities with tax rates that allow the firms to compensate the residents properly. In general, the larger the variety of communities, the more likely each firm will be satisfied; and the larger the variety of firms, the more likely each community will be satisfied. Metropolitan areas with many communities should thus have a larger variety and number of firms than areas of similar size with only a few communities.

The land use pattern of the PTS differs significantly from those of the DPS in that PTS causes communities to be homogeneous with respect to type of firm. Although this may not affect each firm's production function, it might reduce total output because of lost agglomeration economies.[s] In the DPS, the unsightly factory may be permitted to locate in the same

---

[q]An excellent example of the diminishing marginal rate of substitution between fiscal benefits and environment is Greenwich, Connecticut. With plenty of "vacant land," this town has begun to deny variances even to the most attractive and lucrative firms. The situation is ably described in [2].

[r]We could also assume that the activities of each firm are divisible among any number of communities with no loss in production.

[s]Economies of agglomeration are advantages that accrue to one firm as a result of its physical proximity to many other firms. For a discussion, see [27, pp. 16-17].

community as the bank; the factory needs only to pay a higher direct payment. In the modified PTS, the factory cannot locate in the same community as the bank unless differential assessment is allowed or the factory alters its input mix to use excessive taxable property or emit less noxious external effects.

Different Community Sizes

An important difficulty in the model stems from the assumption that E is a pure public good. Aside from logical difficulties (how does E stop at boundaries?), this causes communities with smaller populations to have an inherent advantage over more populous communities. Consider two communities, A and B, each with households having identical demands for E. Community A has but one household and community B has one hundred households. A given firm must compensate community B one hundred times as much as community A. This is because every household is affected identically by the externalities of the firm, and thus will demand the same compensation as every other household. Firms will prefer the smaller communities in this model because they wish to minimize their side payments.[t]

The result in the DPS is that smaller communities can get larger direct payments for the same sacrifice of environment. In the PTS, this means that small communities with a demand for relatively large amounts of schooling can still get the more pleasant firms, since they can demand less tax revenue per firm to compensate the residents.

It is apparent, then, that all communities must be of equal population if either the DPS or the PTS are to operate efficiently under the stated assumptions of the model. If populations are not equal, then households in different communities will get different compensation for the same sacrifice in E.

If a small population is of such advantage to a community, there are surely incentives to keep its population from growing. Fiscal advantages are not the only consideration for a community, but many proposals to restrict population growth in individual communities have local financial advantages in mind [18]. Communities do grow, nevertheless, and even with the permission of zoning boards. We submit that this growth occurs when the proprietary interests of the community are still represented by local owners of property who would stand to gain either by selling land to new residents or by providing services for them. This interest is eventually

---

[t]If one proposes that E affects only immediate neighborhoods rather than whole communities, then community distribution of housing is more important than total population. Such distribution may be correlated with some measure of residential density, but this is not always the case. If it is, one can think of B as the dense community, A the sparse one.

reversed, once enough new residents arrive to tip the political balance of the zoning board toward the objective of maximizing residents' utility rather than maximizing the value of land.[u] This is, not to suggest, of course, that the proprietary interests of zoning boards will tip toward a restrictive attitude at the same population for every community; but it does offer some explanation for the tendency of more developed residential communities to restrict their population growth.

The difficulty of unequal populations is compounded by a more realistic situation which arises when residents and firms arrive at different times: first some residents, then some firms, followed by more residents, and so forth. Consider an entirely residential community which requires that new houses at least equal the value of each existing house, just enough to pay for the (constant) marginal cost of schools of the new household. Now sometime before all designated housing lots are sold, some of the vacant land in the community is sold to some firms. The environmental trade is such that a large part of the tax base is now nonresidential. At this point, the community has incentives to raise the minimum housing requirements much above the average of existing houses. This is because new residents will "dilute the tax base," lowering the tax payment of the firm per household since there are more people to be compensated. The firms cannot be asked to contribute more to the tax base because they could choose to go elsewhere. The answer is to ask new residents to bring their own additional tax base by requiring them to consume more housing. When firms enter *before* a community achieves residential equilibrium, then, the efficiency conditions for residential mobility are violated.

The reason for this is as follows. The good E is a pure public good, but compensation for E is not. New residents consume the same E as old, but they are asked to contribute more to the tax base than older residents. This is an objection that Buchanan and Goetz [8] had to the Tiebout model, one which Hamilton evaded by making local government services essentially "private" goods with public-sharing arrangements [17]. In reintroducing a pure public good to the analysis, we meet a serious efficiency limitation of the Tiebout system. This can be evaded only by supposing that all residents are placed first and then all firms.

There are some current examples of the difficulty caused by firms arriving before all residents. The Township of Mahwah, New Jersey, has about 35 percent of its taxes paid by commercial and industrial uses, primarily an automobile assembly plant. With an area of 25 square miles and a population of 10,539 (1970) it is hard to think of it as being over-

---

[u]This theory may explain an apparent political paradox: Conservative residents in rural areas oppose zoning because it lowers their land values; conservative residents in urban areas favor it (locally) because they have no interest in vacant land and wish to maximize utility, not profit. Babcock [1] points out the paradox.

crowded. Yet it has two-acre minimum lot size zoning, requiring housing of value considerably greater than the average of the existing housing stock.

Unequal Distribution of Neighborhood Effects

A more realistic alternative to equal populations is to drop the assumption that E is a pure public good within a given community. In this case, both the DPS and the PTS are inefficient, inasmuch as they require that every resident be compensated for external effects when in fact only a few residents actually suffer from them. This will force firms to pay more than their marginal social cost, because they must not only compensate immediate neighbors but also everyone else in the community.

Because of this increased cost to firms, communities will get lower fiscal benefits and better environment than they would under a different compensation scheme (to be described) and firms will find fewer locations available to them in suburban communities. Those firms that do locate there in the PTS are likely to have to alter their inputs to emit fewer external effects and/or purchase more land than otherwise. The communities with the greatest advantage would be not only those with smaller populations but also those with large amounts of vacant land which is far away from the residential areas.

Several writers have proposed systems which could force firms to compensate residents only in their immediate neighborhood [1, 11, 37]. The amount and the distribution of the compensation would be determined by some empirical estimation of the noxiousness and extent of the neighborhood effects. If such a system is indeed technically and politically feasible, it is superior to the property tax system of compensation.

Evidence from a study in Pittsburgh [9] suggests that physical externalities do not affect residents outside of their immediate neighborhood. However, we submit that a suburban community's environment can be thought of as a pure public good in an important sense. Just the knowledge that there are no undesirable firms admitted to the community may be something for which a resident is willing to pay, even if none of the firms' externalities affects him. It is necessary to suspend economic rationality to explain this behavior. When a household purchases a home in a suburb, it is typically the largest single expenditure that household will make, and usually the owner's largest asset once some equity is acquired. Inasmuch as most other households in the same community face the same circumstances, there is an implied compact that no group in the community shall threaten the value of residential property of any other group. If this implied compact were broken by the zoning board's permitting firms to enter so as to cause capital losses by some residents in order to reduce tax shares of others, it is conceivable that other residents would feel sufficiently insecure of their own property values that they would force the board to rescind the action. While no evidence for this hypothesis is offered, there seems no better way to account for a near unanimity rule in a system where most other decisions are made by a simple majority.

Variations in the Price of Environment

The assumption of an infinitely elastic supply of firms is abandoned in this section. It is replaced with an assumption that is only slightly less restrictive but enables the price of environment to vary within the metropolitan area. The discussion will be in terms of the DPS rather than the PTS, but it is valid for the latter as well.

Suppose that there are many firms that wish to locate in the suburbs of a metropolitan area. Instead of being indifferent among suburban locations, however, the firms prefer communities which are close to the central city. This preference causes firms to offer large direct payments to these communities. If demand for E does not vary among communities, direct payments from firms will be larger in communities closer to the central city, but they will not vary among communities that are equidistant from the central city. Once variations in demand for E are introduced, however, the direct payments per firm could vary among communities the same distance from the central city because some communities may value E more than others and hence be more restrictive in allowing firms to enter.

Having established that the potential direct payments vary according to distance from the central city, it is apparent that the price of environment varies in the same way, since P_e was defined as the payment forgone by excluding a firm. A community is only one mile from the central city and which decides to remain purely residential forgoes more payments from firms than a community twenty miles from the central city which chooses to do the same thing.

An interesting implication of this result is that it buttresses a theorem regarding location of residents by income class in a metropolitan area. The argument is that wealthier people will, under certain plausible assumptions about the income elasticity of demand for housing and transportation cost, tend to locate further from the CBD than poor people [27, pp. 85-88]. They locate there to take advantage of the lower price of land. For analogous reasons one can also argue that they locate there because of the lower price of environment.[v]

---

[v]It may be that firms will also find that the environment in the further suburbs is cheaper to purchase. These suburbs are not as populous or at least not as densely populated, so there are less people to compensate. This suggests that noxious firms may also move to the suburbs to take advantage of the cheaper E. It is known that manufacturing employment is more

Municipal Services and Environment

A community that is located near the central city and desires good environmental quality is in a quandary: It can have a given E only at a relatively large loss of direct payments from firms. This is because it has been assumed that the only input to E is exclusion of firms (see page 000). A community can do nothing to mitigate the effects of the firms on residents, nor is there anything that a household can do to improve its personal environment. In this city-planner's nightmare, there is only one way to produce environmental quality, and that is to exclude firms from any vacant land in the municipality. If Z denotes the amount of the community's vacant land withheld by zoning, a production function for environmental quality can be written $E = F(Z)$, as already noted. In other words, E is a function of a community's decisions about vacant land.

The assumption that E can be produced only by exclusion of firms is now relaxed. In addition to zoning, a vector of services designated M, a mnemonic for municipal services, is defined. The particular activities these services entail are diverse, but their object is to control the external effects associated with the activities of firms in a community. Examples of such activities would be extra police services to control traffic, fire protection, sewage treatment, health inspection, and garbage disposal. Although only public schools have been considered, in reality each of these activities is one which a purely residential community might provide. Thus only the increments in public services due to firms are actually of interest. It is assumed, however, that none of the activities which M entails enter directly into residents' utility functions except through their effects on E.[w]

Suppose that the unit costs of municipal services do not vary within the metropolitan area and that provision of each service is subject to uniformly increasing costs for every community. Thus one community has no advantage over another in production of E, abstracting presently from any location considerations.

The production of E by a given community may now be described by the general function $E = E(Z, M)$ in which Z, as before, represents vacant land and M is a vector of municipal services. The addition of M as an input to production of E changes the decision process for the community. Instead of just choosing the number and type of firms it will allow to use its vacant land (i.e., zoning), it must now choose among a least-cost combination of inputs Z and M. This process can be analyzed in terms of optimizing behavior

---

decentralized than commercial employment, and this is consistent with the present hypothesis.

[w]A useful discussion of how municipal services enter into residents' utility functions appears in [5]. An important difference from the present discussion is that they consider E to be exogenous to community decisions.

derived from the theory of the firm. The firm in this case is the government of the community, acting on behalf of the residents.

The price of the input zoning, P_z, is defined as the side payment forgone by excluding a firm. This opportunity cost of zoning is exactly what P_e was defined as previously. The terms P_e and P_z are not the same any longer, however, because E is produced not just by Z, but also by M, so that P_e is derived from the unit costs of these two imputs and the technical combination by which they produce E.

The community's optimum procedure is to minimize fixed total expenditure,

$$C_i = (P_e E_i) = P_m M + P_z Z$$

subject to the constraint $E(M, Z) = E_i$, where E_i is any level of E. The Lagrangian of this expression is

$$L = P_m M + P_z Z + \lambda[E_i - E(M, Z)]$$

and the first-order conditions for a minimum result in the equations

$$\frac{P_m}{\partial E / \partial M} = \frac{P_z}{\partial E / \partial Z} = \lambda$$

As the first two terms are the ratios of input prices to marginal products, they represent the marginal cost of producing E at the least-cost combination of inputs, assuming that second-order conditions are met. Thus the Lagrangian multiplier, λ, can be interpreted as the price of E faced by the community at the level E_i.

The price of E at E_i may be interpreted as P_e at *all* levels of E, not just E_i, if the production function, $E = E(M, Z)$, is homogeneous. This is shown as follows. Using the total expenditure relation, $P_e E = P_z Z + P_m M$, substitute from the cost-minimizing conditions

$$P_m = \lambda \frac{\partial E}{\partial M} \quad \text{and} \quad P_z = \lambda \frac{\partial E}{\partial Z}$$

Thus

$$P_e E = \lambda \left(\frac{\partial E}{\partial Z} \cdot Z + \frac{\partial E}{\partial M} \cdot M \right)$$

If the function is homogeneous of degree one, the term in parentheses equals E by Euler's theorem, so that $P_e = \lambda$. If the production function is homogeneous of degree r, Euler's theorem still holds, but $P_e + r\lambda$. Thus for any homogeneous production function, P_e is a constant for each level of E chosen.

There is no assurance that the production function is in fact homogeneous. If it is not, then communities will face different prices for E at different levels of E. Such a situation would make intercommunity comparisons of demand for environment very difficult, even without locational considerations.

So far it has been assumed that all communities face the same input prices for production of E. However, a slightly more realistic variation was introduced in the previous section. It was assumed that the opportunity cost of excluding a firm depended on proximity to a central city because firms might be willing to make a larger side payment to communities located nearer the CBD. Thus the price of zoning can be defined as $P_z = P_z(u)$, with $\partial P_z / \partial u < 0$, u being the community's distance from the CBD.

u is exogenous to a given community, but varies from one community to another. (The fact that it also varies within a community will be ignored.) Thus P_z is lower the farther from the central city the community is. This causes the optimal combination of M and Z to shift as u increases.

Figure 5-3 illustrates the effect of differences in u for two communities. Isocost line Z_2M_2 represents the input costs for Community #2, say two miles from the CBD. Point B is its optimal input combination for producing E_i. (E_i is not necessarily chosen.) Isocost line Z_1M_1 represents the higher relative costs of input Z to Community #1; say one mile from the CBD. In order to produce E_i, Community #1 will rely less on zoning restrictions and more on municipal services. Excluding firms is more costly in Community #1 because it forgoes larger direct payments per firm.

Note that the farther on the Z axis the more exclusive is the zoning; more land is preserved from use by firms. Close to the origin there are very few zoning restrictions, and almost every firm that wants to locate there is permitted, generating very poor E unless a very high level of municipal services is maintained.

If the production function for E for all communities were specified, it would be possible to estimate how the optimal input ratio (Z/M) would change for a given change in u. This is done by determining the effect of change in u on P_z and then determining the elasticity of substitution for the specified production function. For example, if the elasticity were unity, as in a Cobb-Douglas function, then a 10 percent increase in P_z (in response to some change in u, P_m constant) would indicate a 10 percent increase in the ratio of municipal services to zoning restrictions in order to maintain the same E.

There are two additional points. First, because P_m is constant, any function with diminishing returns causes E to become less expensive as u increases, so that one would not expect the level of E chosen to be the same from one distance to another. This restates a previous result, but it implies that even with municipal services, it is efficient for some communities to choose less E than others.

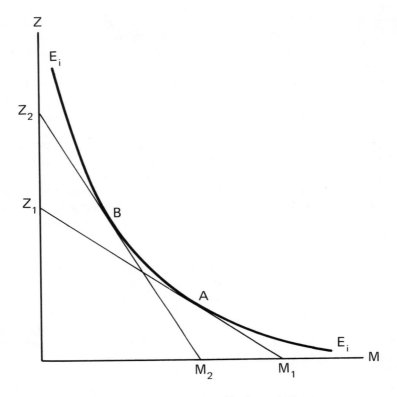

Figure 5-3. Community Choice of Firms

Second, P_z is not likely to be a linear function of u. It is more probable that P_z bears the same relation to u that the firms' rent-offer curve does, and the latter is often assumed to be exponential. Therefore, estimating $P_z(u)$ is not just a task of measuring effective distance between two points.

Given the lack of information about production of E, it is not possible to estimate elasticity of substitution of zoning for public services. However, there is evidence that some substitution does occur. A frequent observation in local expenditure studies is that municipal services vary significantly by proximity to central city or by some variable which is highly correlated with u [15,20]. The production function for E just discussed provides some explanation for these observations. In addition, the empirical work (pages 000-000) indicates that proximity to CBD is a significant variable in determining the variations in selected municipal expenditures among communities.

Introduction to Empirical Work

Evidence related to the theory developed in the previous sections is presented in the following sections. The general conclusion is that there is some evidence to support the necessary conditions and implications of the idea that property taxes from firms represent compensation for external effects. This is qualified by several econometric difficulties which will be noted and by the special nature of the sample, to be described.

There are four hypotheses to be tested. First, that there are fiscal benefits associated with commercial and industrial development. Second, that the category "commercial," which may be regarded as less deleterious to the environment, is distributed quite differently from the category "industrial," which may have more noxious neighborhood effects. Third, that there may be some substitution of municipal services for zoning in communities closer to central cities. And fourth, that existing commercial and industrial property neither raises nor lowers residential property values.

The Sample and the Data

The 54 communities in the sample were chosen from the 70 municipalities of Bergen County, New Jersey. Bergen County is in the northeastern corner of New Jersey, bounded on the east by the Hudson River and connected to Manhattan by the George Washington Bridge. Several attributes of the county make it desirable for testing the theory. (i) The existence of 70 municipalities, with a median area of about 3.5 square miles, qualifies the county as a close approximation to atomistic community structure. (ii) There is no central city, by U.S. Bureau of the Census definition, within the county, although some communities are largely commercial and industrial, and three are legally classified as cities. (iii) Each of the municipalities has a zoning ordinance [29] which is taken as evidence of some ability to control land use.

The municipalities of the sample are classified as cities, boroughs, and townships. There are differences in the governments among these legal entities, and there are also differences in government within each of these three types. However, every municipality has the same legal control over land use within its boundaries, subject to the limitations imposed by the state legislature and the judicial system, and the same sources of tax revenue, i.e., principally, but not exclusively, the property tax on land and structures.

Direct zoning data are not used because land use controls are not standard with regard to firms. Many controls on firms do not appear in zoning laws at all. More importantly, firms are more likely to be accepted on a case-by-case basis than residential housing because firms vary much more in their characteristics and because it is less controversial to apply "zoning by variance" to firms than to new residents.[x] "Zoning by variance" implies that there is an ostensibly strict zoning law which excludes all or most firms. Firms desiring entrance must apply for a variance, an exception to the zoning laws. An applicant for a variance opens the firm's plans to public review, and the residents can have their say about what they think of potential neighborhood effects. Although many city planners decry such piecemeal tactics, the practice nicely fits the present theory of land use control, inasmuch as it allows for individual objections by particular residents. The difficulty is that there are no data regarding any community's inclination to grant or refuse variances by type of firm. It must remain an assumption, then, that communities that wish to exclude certain types of firms are indeed capable of doing so.

The principal data are the distribution of taxable property ("rateables") by community.[y] Although New Jersey communities are forbidden to assess or tax any class of property at a rate different from any other class (excepting certain farm properties), they are required to report assessment by class of property. There are six classes: (1) vacant, (2) residential, (3) farm, (4) commercial, (5) industrial, and (6) apartments. Residential includes the housing stock with four or less units; apartments include buildings with more than four dwelling units. Classifications are determined by local assessors. From these data it is possible to determine the amount and proportion of all property taxes paid by each land use.

The state of New Jersey also computes an "equalization ratio" for real property in each community. This is calculated annually by averaging the ratios of assessed values to market values of all rateables sold "at arms length" (i.e., between disinterested parties) in the past year. The equalization ratio is the same for all classes of property, and all sales are counted the same. The ratio is used to compute "equalized valuation" and an "equalized tax rate" to provide accurate comparisons among communities. The terms "rateable" and "tax rate" indicate equalized valuation and equalized tax rate, respectively. Thus property values and tax rates in the following sections are based on market values, not assessed values.

There is evidence that commercial and industrial property are not assessed in the same proportion to market value as is residential property [30, p. 58]. The evidence suggests that assessments may be high for the

[x]It is less controversial in the sense that public-oriented institutions are more often critical of residential zoning than of commercial and industrial zoning. For an example, see [10].

[y]The sources of all data are listed in Appendix 5A.

former land uses, but there is no indication that it varies systematically by any community characteristic.

Even if assessments are in error in terms of proportionality to market values, they still represent the proportion of taxes that property of a given class does pay. If commercial and industrial are erroneously assessed such that they represent 50 percent of the tax base, the effective tax price of local services to residents is still one half their actual cost. Thus assessments can be used as a price variable regardless of errors in variables, though there is error involved in using them as representations of the differences in value of firms among communities.

In the statistical work that follows, the estimated reduced-form equations are not derived from a formally specified model. A more rigorous approach would specify a complete model of urban location with fiscal and zoning variables and then derive the appropriate reduced forms from the model rather than relying on ad hoc specifications.[z] This is not done here because of the difficulty in combining at least two location sectors (residents and firms) with public expenditure and zoning determination.[aa] Nonetheless, we feel that the specification of the regressions in this chapter have intuitive appeal, and that the results are at least suggestive of what one might expect from a more complete model.

The Existence of Fiscal Benefits from Firms

For the theory to have validity, it must be established that there is some fiscal benefit conferred by firms to residents. The existence of such benefits is disputed. Margolis examined communities in the San Francisco area to determine if industrial development implies that a community has lower tax rates [24,25,26]. His conclusion is that there is no discernable positive association between low taxes and industrial development, and he has criticized as "inefficient" and "irrational" the practice of local officials which tends to encourage industrial development.

The empirical approach here asks much the same question as did Margolis but uses a substantially different approach. Only suburban communities of roughly similar size are considered, rather than using every community in the metropolitan area. Multiple regression analysis is employed to correct for other factors that may affect taxes. Furthermore, the theoretical structure suggests that tax rates are not the most appropriate

---

[z]This point is elaborated in [22]. Some of the econometric problems this can cause are reviewed in Chapter 9 of [19].

[aa]A recent example of a more complete model is [4]. The authors did not, however, include location decisions in their model. A reassuring aspect of their article is that their estimates are consistent with those of [3], who did not specify a complete model.

variable. Tax rates may be very low in a community simply because its residential tax base is very large or because there is very little demand for local public services among residents. In a Tiebout world, tax rates are incidental; they are but the constraining ratio that results from decisions about consumption of housing, public services, and environment.

A better means of testing for a fiscal benefit is to determine whether firms' presence in a community causes either a significant reduction in the tax bill of a typical resident of the community, or an increase in the consumption of some local service, such as schooling, which is of interest solely to residents. There may be other services that enter residents' utility function, but schooling is by far the largest expenditure and one of the few that is unambiguous in its accrual to residents, not to firms.

The counter argument to the existence of fiscal benefits is that firms may indeed lower residential tax shares for schools, but such increments to municipal services will be required in order to achieve the same level of utility as was had originally that there will be no revenues remaining to lower residential tax payments or increase school expenditures. In such a situation, there would be no positive association of school spending with the presence of firms and no negative association of residential taxes with firms. Any fiscal surplus would be consumed by municipal expenditures necessary to maintain the previous level of environment.

In equation (5.3), below, the dependent variable, TAX, is the school and municipal (not county) tax levy times the proportion of taxes paid by residential and apartment rateables in 1970, divided by the number of households in 1970. This is the mean household tax payment.

The first independent variable is COM, commercial rateables (taxable property values) per household in 1970; the second is IND, industrial rateables per household in 1970.[bb] The first control variable, Y, is median family income in 1969, as determined by the 1970 Census. This is to account for the income elasticity of demand for public services, which results in higher tax payments.[cc] Two other control variables are listed. One is $ENROLL$, public school enrollments per household in 1970. This is to account for differences among communities in the numbers to be educated. The other control variable is $MISC$, miscellaneous revenues per household in 1970. These revenues accounted for about 19 percent of all local revenues of all Bergen County municipalities in 1970. The leading sources were taxes from public utilities (26 percent), prior year surpluses (25

[bb]The more logical representation of commercial and industrial rateables as factors affecting the price of public services would be as proportions of the local tax base. This is, however, highly correlated with rateables per household, and the latter offers a more intuitive basis for interpretation.

[cc]Residential property value is another variable which could be included as a control variable. This was not done because of the nearly perfect correlation between this and median income.

percent) and business personalty replacement taxes (16 percent). The letter C indicates a constant term in this and all other equations.

The ordinary least squares regression is equation (5.3). In this equation, as in the five that follow, the t statistics are in parentheses below the coefficients of the independent variables. The numbers in brackets beneath the t statistics are the means of the variables. The sample size is fifty-four. Sixteen of the seventy communities in the county had to be excluded for lack of data, as they were not large enough to correspond to a single census tract.[dd] The communities included are listed in Appendix 5B.

$$TAX = -\underset{(-3.52)}{347C} - \underset{(-3.10)}{0.0086COM} - \underset{(-2.93)}{0.0104IND}$$
$$[1] \qquad [4465] \qquad [3505]$$

$$+ \underset{(6.77)}{0.0607Y} + \underset{(4.60)}{414ENROLL} - \underset{(-1.64)}{0.244MISC} \qquad (5.3)$$
$$[14{,}356] \qquad [0.67] \qquad [205]$$

$R^2 = .86$
[678]

As (5.3) indicates, the presence of commercial and industrial rateables in a community does indeed have a significant, negative effect on average residential tax payments. By one perspective, the effects are not very large. A gain of $1000 per household (a 29 percent increase, at the mean) of commercial rateables tends to lower average residential tax payments by only $8.50 or 1.25 percent.

However, if we consider the coefficients of COM and IND in relation to the actual tax payments by the firms, the effects are larger. Assuming a typical local tax rate of 2.4 percent (the mean real rate of all Bergen County municipalites), an extra $1000 of commercial or industrial property could generate about $24 extra tax revenue. This potential "fiscal dividend" could be used to lower residential taxes.[ee] The coefficients in (5.3) imply that of this $24 fiscal dividend, about $8.60, or 36 percent of commercial property taxes is used to lower residents' taxes, and about $10.40, or 43 percent, is gained by residents from industrial property. The remaining parts of the fiscal dividend may either be used for increases in school expenditures or municipal services.

[dd]This lost some of the more interesting "industrial enclaves" such as Teterboro and Rockleigh. These are quite dramatic on a per capita basis but do not form a significant part of the county tax base.

[ee]Because of the tax price effect already mentioned, the size of the dividend would decrease somewhat as lower tax rates would apply to firms as well as residents. However, because commercial and industrial property comprise less than 20 percent of the tax base, the extra $1000 (30 percent increase) is less than an increase of 6 percent of the total tax base. Thus using the figure of $24 as a fiscal dividend is not too unrealistic, if not formally correct.

Other important factors in (5.3) are median family income and school enrollments per household. A thousand-dollar (7 percent) increase in Y brings forth a \$60.70 (9 percent) increase in tax payments, for an elasticity of 1.28. The elasticity of TAX to a change in $ENROLL$ is 0.41. Miscellaneous revenues have a rather small effect, with an elasticity of 0.07. The above results are similar to those obtained by Litvack and Oates for the Minneapolis-St. Paul area [22].

A remarkable observation is the high intercommunity income elasticity of average tax payments. This indicates that the wealthier communities of Bergen County pay progressively higher property taxes than poorer communities. (Recall that there are no central cities in the sample.) This does not, however, indicate that the property tax is progressive, as it will be seen that wealthier suburbs also get more local services for their taxes than poor ones, as is consistent with the Tiebout hypothesis.

Lower taxes are only one form of fiscal benefits firms may confer on residents. Another is the possibility that residents may be able to get more local services of interest to them without having to pay more taxes. This is the proposed substitution effect of lower tax prices of local services. As a proxy for resident-specific local services, the dependent variable in (5.4), below, is $SCHOOL$, school tax levy per weighted pupil in 1970.[ff] The school levy is the total amount raised by local property taxes for school purposes. School levies are used rather than expenditures because many school districts include several municipalities. Many communities do not have their own schools and send some or all of their students to other districts or to regional high schools. Cost-sharing arrangements in these districts are largely on a per pupil basis, so that the local school levy (though not the school tax rates) per pupil in municipalities of the same district are about equal. It would be better to have expenditure data, but these are not available because enrollments in school districts are not broken down by number of students from constituent municipalities. The difference between expenditures and levies is largely state aid, which is not large in New Jersey, relative to other states. In Bergen County, state aid was about 12 percent of all school revenues for the 1969-70 term, and much of this was for interdistrict transportation. (For a sample of 34 communities in which school districts coincided with municipal boundaries, the R^2 from regressing $SCHOOL$ on per pupil expenditure was 0.68.)

The independent variables in (5.4) are the same as those in (5.3). The result of the ordinary least squares regression is as follows:

$$SCHOOL = \begin{array}{ccc} 387C + & 0.0121COM + & 0.0032IND \\ (2.67) & (2.96) & (0.62) \\ [1] & [4465] & [3505] \end{array}$$

[ff]The weighting formula is 0.5 for kindergarten, 1.0 for elementary school, and 1.25 for high school. This was borrowed from [32, p. 962].

$$+ 0.0562Y - 397ENROLL - 0.3105MISC \quad (5.4)$$
$$(4.26) \quad\quad (-2.99) \quad\quad\quad (-1.42)$$
$$[14{,}346] \quad [0.67] \quad\quad\quad [205]$$

$R^2 = .45$
[929]

Variables in (5.4) behave as expected except for two terms. The Variable *IND* has only a small positive effect on school levies and it is not significantly different from zero. Commercial rateables, on the other hand, are significant in their effect. Median family income and enrollments per household had larger and more significant effects, with respective elasticities of 0.87 and −0.29. The miscellaneous revenue variable had the wrong sign, for unknown reasons.

In terms of the $24 potential fiscal dividend mentioned above, (5.4) implies that $12.10 of commercial property taxes, about half the total, would go to increased school expenditures. However, $3.20 of industrial taxes, only 13 percent of the potential dividend, would go to schools; and even this amount cannot be said to be statistically different from zero. This indicates that communities with industrial property tend to lower tax payments or increase municipal expenditures rather than raise school expenditures.

To compare the fiscal gains in (5.4) to those in (5.3), multiply the gains in (5.4) by two-thirds, the number of pupils per household, because the variable *SCHOOL* is expenditures per pupil. Thus the average household's fiscal gain from a $1000 increase in commercial rateables should lower its tax payments by about $8.60 and give it about $8.10 extra school expenditures for the $24 potential fiscal dividend. The other $7.30 is unaccounted for, and presumably goes for other municipal services that may or may not be of interest to residents. For industrial rateables, the gains are about $10.40 in reduced tax payments and only $2.15 in extra schools, leaving $11.45 unaccounted for. This suggests that the income effect of lower tax prices from industrial property is much larger than the substitution effect. For commercial property, the two effects are nearly equal.

In summary, it appears, by this very rough method of calculation, that about 70 percent of all commercial and 52 percent of all industrial property tax payments benefit residents in terms of lower taxes or more schooling. This suggests that the fiscal benefits of commercial property are larger than those of industrial property. This result is consistent with the findings in [21].

The Distribution of Commercial and Industrial Rateables

In regressions (5.3) and (5.4), *COM* and *IND* were used additively as separate variables, and it was observed that *IND* behaved differently in that it had no significant effect on school spending. This implies that commercial and industrial are different, though the theory is couched only in terms of firms. For many activities, the distinction between commercial and industrial might be clear. Establishments that process and assemble commodities are generally called industrial, while retail outlets are usually thought of as commercial. Because a large proportion of firms probably fall into such distinct categories, commercial and industrial were separated in the previous equations.

A justification of such a procedure is that the environmental effects of one might be less than those of the other. That is, commercial establishments may be thought of as having fewer undesirable externalities than industrial rateables. The category "commercial" may be thought of as including mostly "pleasant" firms and the category "industrial" may include more than its share of "noxious" firms. This section examines the factors that influence the location of commercial and industrial establishments.

The theory predicts that communities that value their environment will get fewer of both firms, since they will demand more compensation than communities that value their environment less. As a proxy for demand for *E* (and hence for effective restrictiveness of zoning), median family income, *Y*, is used. This assumes that demand for environmental quality is income elastic. However, median family income is also very closely correlated with demand for housing, so that, other things being equal, tax rates would be lower in high-income communities. It was argued earlier that the lower tax rates would make such communities more attractive to the "pleasant" firms, which may be designated as commercial rather than industrial.

It is assumed that firms prefer to locate close to a central city, so direct distance in miles from the George Washington Bridge (*GWB*) is included as an independent control variable. The *GWB* is the primary access to New York City.

It is desirable also to normalize for the possibility that externalities do not affect residents closer than a few blocks from the firms. This relaxes the assumption that *E* is uniformly distributed within the community. If a community can put its firms off in some unused corner of the municipality, downwind and downstream, it can have its fiscal benefits and a good environment, too. The communities that can do this are most likely those with a larger land area, so *AREA* in square miles is included as an additional independent variable.[gg]

[gg]*AREA* is highly correlated with vacant land in a sample of communities for which the latter data were available. A more detailed set of geographic variables, such as drainage, slope, and soil conditions, would be preferable. Gross density is inappropriate because it says nothing about the distribution of housing.

An omitted variable is the school tax rate. If commercial firms are more "pleasant" than industrial, they should go to the communities with lower tax rates, according to the theory. This cannot be tested with cross-section data, however, since firms have already located and tax rate adjustments have already taken place.

The ordinary least squares regressions on COM and IND are

$$COM = \begin{array}{cccc} -4612C + & 0.9138Y - & 700.5GWB + & 492.8AREA \\ (-1.13) & (3.02) & (-3.03) & (1.90) \\ [1] & [14,346] & [8.26] & [3.56] \end{array} \quad (5.5)$$

$R^2 = 0.22$
$\quad [4465]$

and

$$IND = \begin{array}{cccc} 15.374C - & 0.8756Y - & 230.5GWB + & 729.4AREA \\ (4.19) & (-3.21) & (-1.11) & (3.12) \\ [1] & [14,346] & [8.26] & [3.56] \end{array} \quad (5.6)$$

$R^2 = 0.29$
$\quad [3505]$

Some interesting contrasts are shown by (5.5) and (5.6). The latter suggests that an increase of $1000 (7 percent) in Y brings forth a *decrease* in industrial rateables per household of $88 (25 percent) at the mean, for a large, negative elasticity of -3.58. The former indicates that a similar increase in median family income causes an *increase* of $91 in commercial rateables per household at the mean, a large, positive elasticity of 2.94.

The variable GWB, the proxy for distance from the central city, is significant in explaining the location of COM in (5.5) but it is not significant in explaining the location of IND in (5.6). This is consistent with trends in the suburbanization of employment. Manufacturing is generally more sub-urbanized than the retailing, service, or wholesaling classification [27, p. 94] so one would expect that distance to central cities would be less important.

In (5.6), $AREA$ is significant (t ratio $= 3.12$) and relatively important (elasticity $= 0.74$) in explaining location of industrial rateables. In (5.5), with COM as the dependent variable, $AREA$ is much less significant and has an elasticity of 0.39 at the mean. Because industry is assumed to be more noxious than is commercial, it is more important to segregate the former from residents than the latter. Thus the communities with larger areas would tend to have an advantage in obtaining acceptable industrial rateables. Commercial rateables are less noxious, so $AREA$ may be less important in obtaining permission to locate in a community.

The important result here is that the wealthy communities get the commercial establishments while the poorer communities end up with the industrial firms.[hh] The modification of the PTS whereby it is assumed that firms have different external effects (ranging from "noxious" to "pleasant"), may account for this. In the modified PTS, it is logical for communities with larger residential property values (i.e., wealthy communities) to get many pleasant firms while poorer communities get a few noxious firms, assuming that demand for environment and schooling are the same. This is because the wealthier communities will have lower tax rates. This argument cannot be accepted a priori because demand for schooling is also income elastic, and it is probable that demand for E is quite income elastic, too.

To show this difficulty more clearly, consider the two equations that must be solved by a community when it attempts to create a situation in which the modified PTS (with variable external effects) is equivalent to the DPS. It must satisfy equations (5.1) and (5.2), that is

$$t(V_h + V_f) = P_s S \quad \text{and} \quad tV_f = P_e F(E_i)$$

in which $P_e F(E_i)$ is the direct payment in the DPS and $P_s S$ is school expenditure in the DPS. These reduce to

$$t = \frac{P_s S - P_e F(E_i)}{V_h}$$

If the demand for schooling, environment, and housing all have an income elasticity of unity, the higher-income communities must have higher tax rates. This is because the direct payment associated with firms goes down as demand for E rises since more firms are excluded. Thus the numerator will not keep pace with the denominator because while $P_s S$ rises with V_h, $P_e F(E_i)$ will tend to fall. Although there is evidence about income elasticity of demand for housing which suggests that it is at least unity [13], schooling demand is somewhat less income elastic, between 0.50 and 1.00 according to [4], and demand for environment is largely unknown. The income elasticity of demand for environment would have to be fairly small to obtain the lower tax rates for richer communities which would cause the commercial establishments to go there.

A factor that may shift the attractiveness of wealthier communities is the location preference of commercial firms. Commercial, as opposed to industrial firms, may taken into account the income of the community in which they locate. This is not so much to reduce commuting by employees as to increase accessibility and attractiveness to higher-income consumers.

[hh]This result may explain the difference in the income and substitution effects of lower tax prices from commercial and industrial property observed earlier. It was seen that industrial property tended to lower average household tax payments rather than increase school expenditures. If industrial property is concentrated in low-income communities, it may be that the preferences of the communities' residents account for the different tax price effects rather than differences in the types of property.

Community residents, on the other hand, may be interested in having the convenience of pleasant shopping areas within their own borders. Two assumptions are modified: (i) Firms produce only for export from the community in which it locates, and (ii) residents have no economic interest in firms which locate in their communities. It is less likely that industrial firms would be subject to the same modifications, since they usually produce for export. These modifications, combined with the possibility that wealthy communities may have lower school tax rates, especially if there are fewer children per family, enables them to have the best of both worlds: many commercial firms that are fiscally lucrative and that cause relatively little reduction to E.

The Effects of Firms on Municipal Services

An implication of the theory in the Municipal Services and Environment section is that municipal expenditures that are "environment" oriented should also increase with the amount of commercial and industrial rate-ables. A difficulty in measuring such expenditures is that there is no convenient breakdown between services which accrue directly to residents and those which are made necessary because of the physical externalities of firms. In fact, most services involve aspects of joint production of direct services to residents, environmental control, and services to firms, which is perhaps why they are in the local public sector to begin with [6, pp. 34-36]. The presence of firms has two effects on such services. It causes a shift in demand for environmental services as firms' externalities are felt, and it lowers the tax price to residents of such services. Both effects would be taken into account by rational communities in their decisions to admit firms.

A second implication of the discussion of municipal services is that distance from the central city should be a determinant of municipal expenditures. This is because firms may be willing to pay more in property taxes to communities closer to the CBD, so residents may substitute one factor of production of E, municipal services, for another factor, exclusion of firms.

A test of these implications aggregates certain categories of expenditures and uses the sum, designated $PUBLIC$, as the dependent variable. The expenditures represent services that are "environment" oriented, in a broad sense. The variable $PUBLIC$ (public safety and works per household in 1970) includes noncapital municipal expenditures under the categories police, fire, streets, sewers, garbage, environmental protection, and public buildings and grounds. Together they accounted for about 56 percent of all noncapital municipal expenditures in Bergen County municipalities in 1970.

Estimates of the effect of *COM* and *IND* and distance from the *GWB* on *PUBLIC*, are given in (5.7) with the previously defined *Y* and *MISC* as control variables.

$$
\begin{aligned}
PUBLIC = \quad & 62.24C + 0.0021COM + 0.0033IND \\
& (1.60) \quad\ (1.91) \qquad\quad (2.39) \\
& [1] \qquad\ [4465] \qquad\quad [3505] \\[6pt]
& -\ 5.70GWB + 0.0109Y + 0.145MISC \qquad (5.7) \\
& (-3.29) \qquad (3.50) \qquad (2.42) \\
& [8.26] \qquad\ \ [14,346] \quad [205]
\end{aligned}
$$

$R^2 = 0.58$
$\quad[224]$

This equation is consistent with the implications of the theory. An increase in $1000 of industrial property per household would increase the households' selected public expenditures by $3.30. A gain of $1000 in commercial rateables would increase the dependent variable by $2.10.

Industrial and commercial rateables are both significant at the 5 percent level in (5.7). Note that these figures are substantially smaller than the fiscal dividend residuals determined on page 153. Of the $24 potential fiscal dividend from $1000 of commercial property, $7.30 was unaccounted for by either lower taxes to residents or more school expenditures. Presumably, the rest should have gone to other services, but (5.7) indicates that only $2.10 appears to have gone to services which are environmentally related. The disparity for industrial rateables is even greater, as the residual is $11.45, while the coefficient in (5.7) indicates $3.30 went to additional public safety and health expenditures. If these estimates are valid, the rest must have gone for municipal services that are not broadly related to controlling external effects. It could also be that the average tax rate of 2.4 percent used for a $1000 increment in the tax base is too large, considering the possible tax rate reductions that could be made. (See note 31 above.)

An interesting result in (5.7) is the distance from central city variable, *GWB*, which has a relatively large elasticity of −0.21, and which is significant. This suggests that proximity to central city is an important determinant of basic public expenditures. This may be caused by the substitution of municipal services for zoning by communities near the central city. However, there are other reasons why *GWB* might behave as it does, such as scale economies in more densely populated areas, or relatively lower costs of some services, such as sewage disposal in areas adjoining the Hudson River and its tributaries. The current result is at least consistent with the theory however.

Capitalization of Commercial and Industrial Rateables

The final empirical test deals with the possibility of capitalization of lower effective tax prices in the value of residential housing. For heuristic purposes, consider three hypotheses about capitalization of commercial and/or industrial property. The first is called the "environmentalist" hypothesis. This argues that commercial and industrial rateables, particularly the latter, will tend to reduce the value of homes in the communities in which they locate. This position maintains that the fiscal benefits are insufficient to compensate residents for the neighborhood external effects of firms, and thus residential values would tend to fall. The second position, that of the "fiscalists," would argue the opposite, that the process of zoning and regulation causes firms to have only minimal external effects or at least isolates them from existing housing. The lower effective tax prices which firms bring with them should make housing there more valuable since home owners can get more schooling and/or lower tax shares by locating there.

The third hypothesis, the theory supported here, predicts that there should be no capitalization, positive or negative, of commercial or industrial property itself in any community in equilibrium. Economic theory causes one to be skeptical of capitalization of any reproducible asset in a competitive situation. Capitalization is the discounted value of economic rent, and rents accrue only to nonreproducible assets, such as land a certain distance from a given point. Firms are reproducible and mobile, and there are many communities in which they may locate. Competition among communities and mobility of firms tend to insure that no firm pays more than the minimum amount communities demand in compensation for neighborhood effects, and community zoning practices tend to ensure that at least that amount is paid. Lower effective tax prices are a direct exchange for loss in environmental quality. The exchange mechanism works through the property tax, but that is only an institutional peculiarity. It could as well work through direct payments or other tax bases.

The foregoing argument does not imply that no community has any competitive advantages over any other in attracting firms. It was suggested earlier that communities closer to central cities would be in a better position to attract firms. Such communities might succeed in getting lower tax shares for their residents than other communities, but this is due to location itself, not to the firms. Thus the distance from the central city would be capitalized, as economic theory generally predicts, but not the tax shares that result from this distance.

The procedure used to test the capitalization hypothesis was to run a regression attempting to explain variations in the median value of single-unit, owner-occupied dwellings. In this regression, proportion of all taxes paid by commercial and industrial rateables (*not* per household) was entered in addition to several other variables that would normally be expected to cause variations in housing value.

The appropriate data for the regressions were available only for urban places of 10,000 population or more, so only 30 communities from the previous sample were available. In order to obtain more degrees of freedom, twenty additional communities from three neighboring counties were included. The list of communities is in Appendix 5C. The selection criteria were incorporated urban places with populations between 10,000 and 50,000.

In his study of capitalization of fiscal variables, Oates [32] concluded that intercommunity differentials in tax rates are capitalized in housing values in his sample, and he noted, as is confirmed by (5.3), that commercial and industrial rateables are a significant determinant of local taxes rates.[ii] The present hypothesis is not necessarily inconsistent with Oates' results. There may be a scarcity of communities of particular mixes of services which accounts for the capitalization of differences in taxes and expenditures, while at the same time all residents regard one particular cause of such differentials, commercial and industrial rateables, as a direct exchange for environmental quality. Therefore, even using a specification and sample quite similar to Oates', there is no reason to expect commercial and industrial property to be capitalized.

The dependent variable in (5.8) is *VALUE*, median value of owner-occupied, detached dwellings in 1970. The independent variables are as follows: *ROOMS*, median number of rooms in owner-occupied houses; *LCBD*, the natural logarithm of air-line distance from Pennsylvania Station in New York City; *NEW*, a weighting for decade in which houses were built;[jj] *PRENT*, proportion of dwelling units that are renter occupied; and *COM(P)* and *IND(P)*, proportion of rateables designated as commercial or industrial.

$$VALUE = -64,485C + 8576ROOMS - 27,571LCBD + 64,674NEW$$
$$(-3.47) \quad (6.84) \quad\quad (-2.55) \quad\quad (3.99)$$
$$[1] \quad\quad [6.13] \quad\quad [0.4805] \quad\quad [0.81]$$

$$+ 7829PRENT - 4643COM(P) - 1608IND(P) \quad\quad (5.8)$$
$$(1.81) \quad\quad (-0.60) \quad\quad (-0.26)$$
$$[0.379] \quad\quad [0.1138] \quad\quad [0.0828]$$

$R^2 = 0.67$
[29,590]

[ii]Twenty-four of Oates' sample of fifty-three communities are also in the present sample.
[jj]The weighting was determined by the following formula: 1 for houses built since 1960; 0.9 for those built from 1950 through 1959; 0.8 for those built from 1940 through 1949; and 0.7 for those built before 1940.

Each of the independent variables in (5.8) behaves as expected except *PRENT*, had been expected to have a negative sign. The very low *t* statistics in both *COM(P)* and *IND(P)* are taken as evidence that they are not capitalized. This is an ambiguous test, since there are three hypotheses advanced: The "environmentalists" would argue for negative capitalization, the "fiscalists" would claim positive capitalization, and the present theory predicts no capitalization. Simply to note that both the environmentalist and fiscalist positions are not proven does not establish the third position, however. All that can be said is that the very low *t* statistics in this regression certainly do not lead to rejection of the null hypothesis that the true coefficients on *COM(P)* and *IND(P)* are zero.

In addition to problems of criteria for rejecting hypotheses, there are two major objections to the form of the equation. The first is that it is a reduced-form equation, not formally derived from any model. Thus it is quite difficult to decide what any of the coefficients mean, since there may be complicated terms derived from other variables. In addition, some important variables may have been omitted, which could affect the distribution of the error terms.

The second problem is the exact form of the capitalization equation, even when all relevant variables are included. Hamilton [16] has shown that a measure of capitalization consistent with economic theory is a form that cannot be linearized. Whether this is true or not, it is clear that the capitalization regression is not derived from economic theory, other than some ad hoc notions about which variables are important.

Summary of Empirical Work

Bearing in mind the econometric qualifications and crude data, the regressions shown in equations (5.3), (5.4), and (5.8) provide evidence to support some of the necessary conditions and implications of the theory in this chapter.

A necessary condition of the theory that fiscal benefits of firms represent a payment for environmental costs by those firms is that there actually be some fiscal benefits. From the regressions in (5.3) and (5.4), it appears that there are some benefits from firms which accrue to residents of suburban communities in the form of lower tax payments or larger school expenditures. The benefits do not seem large relative to other determinants of taxes and expenditures, which is consistent with the hypothesis that competition among communities and the institutional constraints of the property tax system tend to keep them low. It also appears that the benefits from industrial rateables are not as great as those from commercial rateables, at least by the standard of local school spending.

An implication of the theory is that communities that value their environment highly should not have many noxious firms. Equations (5.5) and (5.6) show that commercial rateables are positively associated with median family income in a community, but industrial rateables have a negative association. If we assume that demand for environment is income elastic and that industrial firms are more noxious than commercial establishments, then these results confirm the theory. Previous studies have seldom made any distinctions between these two categories, but their different distribution among communities is among the stronger results of the statistical work.

One of the theory's corollaries, discussed under Services and Environment, implies that certain municipal services may be used as substitutes for zoning by communities to maintain desirable levels of environment. Because of the greater fiscal benefits forgone, communities closer to central cities choose to use more of these services than do communities farther away, thus allowing more firms to enter. The regression in equation (5.7) provides evidence that both the existence of commercial and industrial property in a community and proximity to the central city increase per capita expenditures on public services related to safety and health. However, the former effect is not large and can not account for all of the potential revenues that firms could provide the community.

The final test, equation (5.8), sought to determine the effects of commercial and industrial property on the value of housing in a community. The theory predicts that there is none because the noxious effects of firms would be offset by the fiscal benefits they confer on residents. The test for capitalization of commercial and industrial rateables indicates neither positive nor negative effects on value of housing. Coupled with the relatively small fiscal benefits, this indicates that current commercial or industrial development is not very offensive to residents in the sample. This result does not indicate that *any* potential industrial or commercial development would not affect residential values, however, because zoning may well have excluded the more noxious firms altogether.

Several other empirical observations could confirm our theory. More detailed geographic data should indicate that the more noxious firms are located away from residential centers or near the borders of the community. A more detailed breakdown of municipal budgets might indicate that the fiscal benefits to residents are greater than those indicated by using schooling as the measure of resident-specific local services. If one could classify firms by their neighborhood effects, it should be observed that suburban communities are fairly homogeneous with respect to the type of firms which locate in them. More detailed institutional data could be used to establish the effectiveness of zoning and other restrictive devices. Accurate time series data would enable us to judge the effect of fiscal variables on the location of firms, and to get some idea of how mobile various firms are. Time series data would also enable us to determine the importance of population size or density in obtaining firms and to determine whether the proposed dynamics of suburban population growth are valid.

Local Property Taxes and Metropolitan Government

The basic premise here has been that the property tax provides the means of exchange between firms and residents of suburban communities. Residents voluntarily surrender some of their community environment by granting permission to firms to locate there in return for fiscal benefits from the firms. Any proposal that threatens to limit this exchange will be opposed by the parties that benefit from the system.

One proposal that would limit this exchange is the sharing of commercial and industrial tax bases of each community with other communities throughout the metropolitan area. This has been the essence of many proposals favoring metropolitan government. Communities with substantial parts of their tax bases composed of firms would oppose this because they would get only negligible fiscal gains from a firm in their community while still sacrificing the same amount of environment. Such communities would not be able to exploit the value of their asset, environment, and their residents' real income would decline. Many firms would also oppose this because they would become pariahs in their search for new locations. Unless firms could find another method of compensating communities, they would be unwelcome in any residential suburb, unless community residents had compelling nonfiscal interests in the firm.

The same situation would arise if the state or federal government were to provide most of the services, particularly schools, presently financed by local governments. Even if the local property tax still existed for a limited number of services, the opportunity cost of excluding a firm would be greatly reduced, and many fewer firms would be permitted to locate in a given community.

There have been some experiments in which metropolitan areas share part of the tax base of commercial and industrial firms [33, p. 236]. The evidence offered here suggests that such an arrangement might be progressive in its effects with respect to commercial rateables, but regressive with respect to industrial rateables. This is because the wealthier communities tend to get commercial establishments while the poorer ones get the industrial firms. Because the sample included only suburban communities, this cannot be confidently asserted for an entire metropolitan area, but rateable sharing schemes should be examined to see if they prevent poor communities from exploiting their assets.

If the property tax system does provide an efficient exchange mechanism, then metropolitan zoning policies should deal only with inter-municipal spillovers. Except for these, the theory suggests that community residents get just as good an environment as they are willing to pay for in fiscal benefits forgone. The theory is not reality, and the dynamics may be quite inefficient, but its implications suggest that decentralized zoning and property taxation may not be the worst of all possible worlds, as they are frequently asserted to be.

References

[1] Babcock, Richard F., *The Zoning Game* (Madison: University of Wisconsin Press, 1966).

[2] Bailey, Anthony, "Worried about Being Xeroxed," *New York Times Magazine,* November 18, 1973, pp. 42 ff.

[3] Bergstrom, Theodore C., and Robert P. Goodman, "Private Demands for Public Goods," *American Economic Review* 63 (June 1973): 280-296.

[4] Borcherding, Thomas E., and Robert T. Deacon, "The Demand for the Services of Non-Federal Governments: An Econometric Approach to Collective Choice," *American Economic Review* 62 (December 1972): 891-901.

[5] Bradford, David F., Richard A. Malt, and Wallace E. Oates, "The Rising Costs of Local Public Services: Some Evidence and Reflections," *National Tax Journal* 22 (June 1969): 185-202.

[6] Buchanan, James M., *The Demand and Supply of Public Goods* (Chicago: Rand McNally, 1968).

[7] Buchanan, James M., "Principles of Urban Fiscal Strategy," *Public Choice* 11 (Fall 1971): 1-16.

[8] Buchanan, James M., and Charles J. Goetz, "Efficiency Limits of Fiscal Mobility: An Assessment of the Tiebout Model," *Journal of Public Economics* 1 (Spring 1972): 25-43.

[9] Crecine, J. B., O. A. Davis, and J. E. Jackson, "Urban Property Markets: Some Empirical Results and Their Implications for Municipal Zoning," *Journal of Law and Economics* 10 (October 1967): 79-99.

[10] Davidoff, Linda, Paul Davidoff, and Neil Gold, "The Suburbs Have to Open Their Gates," *New York Times Magazine,* December 7, 1971, pp. 40 ff.

[11] Davis, Otto A., "Economic Elements in Municipal Zoning Decisions," *Land Economics* 29 (November 1963): 375-386.

[12] Delafons, John, *Land Use Controls in the United States,* 2nd. ed. (Cambridge: The MIT Press, 1969).

[13] DeLeeuw, Frank, "The Demand for Housing: A Review of Cross Section Evidence," *Review of Economics and Statistics* 53 (February 1971): 1-10.

[14] Due, John F., "Studies of State and Local Tax Influences on Location of Industry," *National Tax Journal* 14 (June 1961): 163-173.

[15] Fisher, Glen W., "Determinants of State and Local Expenditures," *National Tax Journal* 14 (December 1961): 349-355.

[16] Hamilton, Bruce M., "Capitalization of Intra-Jurisdictional Differences in Local Tax Prices" (Washington: The Urban Institute, 1973), (draft copy).

[17] Hamilton, Bruce M., "Zoning and Property Taxation in a System of Local Government," *Urban Studies* (forthcoming).

[18] Johnson, Eric G., Jr., "Is Population Growth Good for Boulder Citizens?" (Boulder, Colorado: Boulder Zero Population Growth, 1971), (mimeographed, 2nd ed.).

[19] Johnston, J., *Econometric Methods* (New York: McGraw-Hill, 1963).

[20] Kurnow, Ernest, "Determinants of State and Local Expenditures Re-examined," *National Tax Journal* 16 (September 1963): 252-255.

[21] Ladd, Helen F., "Local Public Expenditures and the Composition of the Property Tax Base," (Ph.D. Dissertation, Harvard University, 1974).

[22] Litvack, James, and Wallace E. Oates, "The Impact of Commercial-Industrial Property on the Fiscal Position of Local Governments in the Minneapolis-St. Paul Metropolitan Area," (Master's thesis, Princeton University, 1972).

[23] Mace, Ruth L., *Industry and City Government* (Chapel Hill: University of North Carolina Institute of Government, 1963).

[24] Margolis, Julius, "Municipal Fiscal Structure in a Metropolitan Region," *Journal of Political Economy* 64 (June 1957): 226-236.

[25] Margolis, Julius, "On Municipal Land Policy for Fiscal Gains," *National Tax Journal* 9 (September 1956): 247-257.

[26] Margolis, Julius, "The Variation of Property Tax Rates within a Metropolitan Region," *National Tax Journal* 9 (December 1956): 326-330.

[27] Mills, Edwin S., *Urban Economics* (Glenview, Ill.: Scott, Foresman, 1972).

[28] Morgan, William E., "Taxes and the Location of Industry," *University of Colorado Studies,* Series in Economics No. 4 (Boulder: University of Colorado Press, 1967).

[29] New Jersey Division of State and Regional Planning, *Zoning in New Jersey, 1967* (Trenton: 1968).

[30] New Jersey Tax Policy Committee, *Report of the New Jersey Tax Policy Committee, Part 2, The Property Tax* (Trenton: New Jersey State Library, 1972).

[31] Oates, Wallace E., *Fiscal Federalism* (New York: Harcourt Brace Jovanovich, 1972).

[32] Oates, Wallace E., "The Effects of Property Taxes and Local Public Spending on Property Values: An Empirical Study of Tax Capitalization and the Tiebout Hypothesis," *Journal of Political Economy* 77 (November/December 1969).

[33] Reilly, William K., ed., *The Use of Land: A Citizens Guide to Urban Growth* (New York: Thomas Crowell, 1973).

[34] Rinehart, James R., and William E. Laird, "Community Inducements to Industry and the Zero-Sum Game," *Scottish Journal of Political Economy* 19 (February 1972): 73-90.

[35] *San Antonio Independent School District* vs. *Rodriquiz,* 411 U.S. 1, 41 L.W. (U.S.) 4407 (1973).

[36] Struyk, R. J., "Evidence on the Locational Activity of Manufacturing Industries in Metropolitan Areas," *Land Economics* 48 (November 1972): 377-383.

[37] Tidemann, T. Nicolas, "Three Approaches to Improving Urban Land Use" (Ph.D. Dissertation, University of Chicago, 1969).

[38] Tiebout, Charles M., "A Pure Theory of Local Expenditures," *Journal of Political Economy* 64 (October 1956): 416-424.

[39] U.S. Bureau of the Census, *Census of Governments: 1962, Vol. 1, Government Organization* (Washington: U.S. Government Printing Office, 1963).

[40] White, Michelle J., "A Study of Suburban Zoning in Fragmented Metropolitan Areas" (Ph.D. Dissertation, Princeton University, 1973).

Appendix 5A
Data Sources

The following sources were used in calculating variables for equations (5.3) through (5.8). The alphabetical listing of the variables provides the particular sources of the calculations by reference number. Several of the communities in the sample were not listed under some of the census aggregations, so data had to be constructed from census tracts.

1. Hagstrom Company, *Bergen County New Jersey,* (New York: Hagstrom Company, 1971?), map.
2. New Jersey Department of Community Affairs, Division of Local Finance, *Thirty-Third Annual Report of the Division of Local Finance* (Trenton: 1970).
3. U.S. Bureau of the Census, *Census of Housing: 1970, Detailed Housing Characteristics.* Final Report HC(1)-B32 New Jersey (Washington: U.S. Government Printing Office, 1972).
4. U.S. Bureau of the Census, *Census of Population: 1970, General Social and Economic Characteristics.* Final Report PC(1)-C32 New Jersey (Washington: U.S. Government Printing Office, 1972).
5. U.S. Bureau of the Census, *Census of Population and Housing: 1970 Census Tracts.* Final Report PHC(1)-145 Paterson-Clifton-Passaic, New Jersey, SMSA (Washington: U.S. Government Printing Office, 1972).

    AREA: Area in square miles (2).

    COM: Commercial rateables (2) per household (4,5).

  COM(P): Proportion of tax base that is commercial (2).

 ENROLL: Public school enrollments (4,5) per household.

    GWB: Air-line distance in miles from geographic center to the George Washington Bridge in Fort Lee, New Jersey (1).

    IND: Industrial rateables (2) per household (3,5).

  IND(P): Proportion of tax base that is industrial (2).

  LCBD: The natural logarithm of air-line distance from geographic center to Penn Station in New York City (1).

  MISC: Total municipal revenues minus all property taxes collections (2) per household (3,5).

NEW: Weighting for age of housing (3) constructed during: 1960, 1.0; 1950-1959, 0.9; 1940-1949, 0.8; before 1940, 0.7.

PRENT: Proportion of occupied units that are rented (3).

PUBLIC: Current municipal expenditures in categories of police, fire, streets, sewers, garbage, environmental protection, and public buildings and grounds (2) per household (3,5).

ROOMS: Median number of rooms in owner-occupied houses (3).

SCHOOL: School tax levy (2) per weighted (kindergarten, 0.5; elementary 1.0; high school 1.25) pupil (4,5).

TAX: Residential, noncounty property tax payments (2) per household (3,5).

VALUE: Median value of owner-occupied homes (3).

Y: Median family income (4,5).

Appendix 5B
Sample of Fifty-Four New Jersey Municipalities for Equations (5.3) through (5.7)

Bergen County

Allendale, Bergenfield, Bogota, Carlstadt, Cliffside Park, Closter, Cress-kill, Dumont, East Paterson, East Rutherford, Edgewater, Emerson, En-glewood, Englewood Cliffs, Fair Lawn, Fairview, Fort Lee, Franklin Lakes, Garfield, Glen Rock, Hackensack, Hasbrouck Heights, Hillsdale, Hohokus, Leonia, Little Ferry, Lodi, Lyndhurst, Mahwah, Maywood, Midland Park, New Milford, North Arlington, Oakland, Oradell, Paramus, Park Ridge, Ramsey, Ridgefield, Ridgefield Park, Ridgewood, River Edge, River Vale, Rochelle Park, Rutherford, Saddle Brook, Teaneck, Tenafly, Waldwick, Wallington, Washington, Westwood, Wood-Ridge, and Wyck-off.

Appendix 5C
Sample of Fifty New Jersey Municipalities for Equation (5.8)

Bergen County (30)

Bergenfield, Cliffside Park, Dumont, East Paterson, Englewood, Fair Lawn, Fairview, Fort Lee, Garfield, Glen Rock, Hackensack, Hasbrouck Heights, Hillsdale, Lodi, Maywood, New Milford, North Arlington, Oakland, Palisades Park, Paramus, Ramsey, Ridgefield, Ridgefield Park, Ridgewood, River Edge, Rutherford, Tenafly, Waldwick, Wallington, and Westwood.

Essex County (7)

Belleville, Nutley, Orange, South Orange, Verona, West Caldwell, and West Orange.

Passaic County (5)

Hawthorne, Pomptom Lakes, Ringwood, Totowa, and West Paterson.

Union County (8)

Linden, New Providence, Plainfield, Rahway, Roselle, Roselle Park, Summit, and Westfield.

6

Firm Location in a Zoned Metropolitan Area

Michelle J. White

In this chapter, a Tiebout model of local services provision is applied to a metropolitan area in which independent local communities include firms as well as residents. We will show that the introduction of firms into residential communities does not necessarily destroy the efficiency properties of the Tiebout system.

Under the Tiebout system [3] as reformulated by Hamilton in Chapter 2 of this volume, communities raise revenue via a local property tax. They allow new residents to enter if they pay taxes equal to the cost of the local public services they consume. Free riders are excluded by a zoning ordinance which requires (perhaps indirectly) that all housing in the community have at least a specified minimum value. If many communities with different characteristics exist in the metropolitan area, then all residents choosing to locate in a particular community tend to have the same demand for housing and local services. No loss of efficiency occurs as a result of providing local public services through the public sector.

The Tiebout-Hamilton system, which will be referred to as "neutral zoning," is a model of residential location choice only. The view in the literature is that the entry of firms into a residential community is inconsistent with the model and must introduce biases into local decision making. Barlow [1] argues that voters perceive tax revenues from firms as a reduction in the tax price of a given improvement in the quality of local services. He therefore concludes that the entry of firms into a community causes the output of local services in a community to rise. We will show, however, that this is not necessarily the case, since firms, like residents, are free to choose locations in which their tax payments equal the community's expenditure in providing them with local services. If the community decides to raise its tax rate, the firm can relocate.

This chapter demonstrates that the neutral-zoning concept can be extended to include mixed residential-industrial communities, while retaining its efficiency properties. Consideration of this problem includes the development of some results concerning the location pattern of firms of various types within a metropolitan area, as well as development of a zoning model for the case in which firms produce adverse externalities. In this latter case, zoning under certain assumptions can result in Pareto-optimum pricing of firm-caused externalities.

In order to discuss firm location, it is necessary to make several sim-

175

plifying assumptions. First, except where noted it is assumed that all firms are in perfectly competitive industries. Second, it is assumed that communities compete with each other for firms. In Chapter 3, this author has shown that communities may have monopoly power as suppliers of housing sites to new residents. This argument assumes that consumers generally wish to locate near their workplaces and that they prefer communities whose residents have the same income level as themselves. But it seems logical to assume that firms are freer than households in choosing locations and that they consider many more communities' sites to be substitutable. Firms can be supplied with the local public services they need in many locations. Another assumption is that firms are not constrained in their locations by the dwelling places of their employees. Therefore their location is limited only by willingness to pay for various sites, since firms cannot locate where the cost of land is so high that they would incur a loss. No community is assumed to have any monopoly power as a supplier of firm sites.

Third, it is also assumed that communities do not have any special attributes that could reduce production costs for firms. The fourth assumption is that a community's property tax rate is determined by its residents, by factors such as per household property consumption and demand for local services such as schools. This tax rate is exogenous for firms considering entering the community.[a] It might be objected that this assumption ignores the effect that firms might have in changing the community's tax rate. It is shown, however, that when firms are competitive and produce no externalities, the entry of firms into a previously residential community does not change its tax rate. Fifth, firms' output is assumed to be exported from the metropolitan area or sold generally within the area. No firm can increase its sales by varying its location within the metropolitan area. Finally, a large number of communities is assumed to exist.

All firms in an industry are assumed to require a particular mix of local public services. The services required may vary among industries but are the same for all firms in one industry. All communities are assumed able to provide these services, which are produced with constant returns to scale. Locally supplied services that affect firm location are those that enter directly into a firm's production function and for which demand changes as the firm's output changes. The most obvious examples are firms' use of community-provided water and sewer services. Police and fire services have less effect on firm location, since demand for them does not increase as the firm increases its output level. Another example is firms' use of community roads and parking places for transport of employees, inputs, and outputs.

---

[a]Property tax rates for firms and residences are assumed to be the same since it is unlawful for any community to levy discriminatory tax rates.

A community may be forced to provide other services to firms. Recent lawsuits have cast doubt on the right of a community to admit firms but to bar their workers from living near the firms by its residential zoning. If a community expected to lose this right then it would want to charge many new public service costs to the firm. The costs of school expansion, the possible fiscal transfers from existing residents to new residents of lower income who work for the firms and the negative external effects of a population increase—all would be charged to entering firms.

The first three sections of this chapter explore the effects of firms' demands for local public services on firm location, under the assumption that firms produce no undesirable externalities that would downgrade a community's environment. Locational patterns are considered both when communities are located in a diffuse metropolitan region with no appreciable land rent gradient and when communities are located in a centralized metropolitan area. We will then consider the effect of firms' demand for local public services when firms cause negative externalities and communities demand compensation for these externalities. Two systems of pollution zoning are discussed and their resource allocation results within the metropolitan area are developed.

Neutral Zoning in Mixed Residential-Industrial Communities

The simplest case of firm location under zoning is one in which a set of neutrally zoned communities exists in a noncentrally defined setting. The price of land is assumed to be constant. The communities initially are entirely residential. All households in any particular community consume the same value housing (V_i) and demand the same quality local public services (S_i). The community raises uniform revenues per household via a property tax rate, $t_i = S_i/V_i$. Revenues equal the per household cost of providing local services.

Suppose firms wish to locate in the communities. Firms are assumed to belong to one of J industries, and all firms within an industry are alike. They produce at the same scale, using the same capital and land input levels. For industry j, the cost of local services per firm is C_j. This cost is assumed to be constant regardless of where the firm locates.

For a firm to enter a community without destroying its neutral-zoning characteristics, property tax payments by the firm to the community must equal the costs incurred by the community in supplying local services to the firm. If the community is to raise revenues equal to C_j through a property tax at the predetermined rate t_i, firms must have taxable property, including land and capital, of value F_{ij} where

$$F_{ij} = \frac{C_j}{t_i} \tag{6.1}$$

Thus F_{ij} is a set of minimum property-use levels which community i must require of firms in industry j in order to prevent cross-subsidization between firms and households. If each community determines a set of F_{ij} levels in this manner, then, in equilibrium, firms entering each community must use property of value F_{ij}, not more nor less. If a firm with property use less than F_{ij} were to enter the community, it would pay property taxes less than C_j and the community would incur a deficit in supplying local services to the firm. This would force it to increase its tax rate, which would cause residents to leave. Therefore it is assumed that all communities, through zoning, exclude firms that use less property than F_{ij}.

Conversely, a firm would not want to enter a community if its desired property-use level were greater than F_{ij}. Suppose this level is F_{ij}^*, where $F_{ij}^* > F_{ij}$. If the firm entered community i, it would pay taxes of $t_i F_{ij}^*$, more than the cost of its local services. Since perfect competition prevails within each industry, the firm cannot afford to enter community i. Other firms in industry j pay C_j for local services. Therefore one firm cannot pay more than C_j without incurring a loss and going out of business.

Suppose however that some community attempts to collect more than C_j from firms in industry j. It sets property requirements $100\tau_j$ percent above F_{ij}, or $\hat{F}_{ij}$, where

$$\hat{F}_{ij} = (1 + \tau_j)F_{ij} \quad (\tau_j > 0) \tag{6.2}$$

If firms entered this community, they would generate a resource transfer to the community's residents. Suppose firms in some industry have a desired property-use level $F_{ij}^* \geq \hat{F}_{ij}$. Under the assumptions made above, firms in industry j could not enter the community. If they did, other firms would gain a competitive advantage by locating in communities whose property-use level F_{ij} equals F_{ij}^*. In such communities the tax rate would be lower since firms would not be overcharged for local services. Therefore they could undercut the firm located in the fiscal-squeeze community and drive it out of business.

This zoning strategy is called fiscal-squeeze zoning. It is clear that under perfect competition among firms, communities cannot fiscally squeeze firms by forcing them to use more than their desired property levels. Communities therefore have a choice of setting property requirements for firms that yield revenues equal to costs or setting higher property requirements and thereby excluding all firms. Since (by assumption) firms have no external effects, communities should be indifferent between these two strategies. The outcome is that neutral zoning prevails in both residential and mixed communities.

It can be shown that the same result holds when communities set land use rather than property use requirements, because of legal constraints. If communities know the function relating land to capital use, $K_j = K_j(L_{ij})$, then they can determine land use requirements L_{ij} such that entering firms must use property equal to the target level, F_{ij}. Thus,

$$L_{ij} = \frac{C_j}{t_i} - \frac{K_j(L_{ij}) \cdot P_k}{P_L(L_{ij})}$$

In this case, communities might attempt to extract a fiscal-squeeze transfer from firms by raising either t_i or L_{ij}. It can be shown that raising t_i accomplishes a transfer from landowners to the community, but does not affect firms that rent their land. Similarly, raising L_{ij} does not accomplish a transfer from firms to the community since the higher required land use either causes the price of land to fall, thus offsetting the intended effect, or forces competitive firms to leave the community. Thus communities using land-use zoning cannot exact subsidies over the cost of local services from perfectly competitive firms.

Firm Location in a Noncentral Metropolitan Region

This section considers the way in which firms in various industries distribute themselves among communities pursuing neutral-zoning strategies. Communities are assumed to be located in a spread-out metropolitan region where no appreciable land value differences exist between communities. Thus, all communities might be considered suburban. None is close enough to the center of the metropolitan area to have higher land value by virtue of accessibility to the center. This assumption is relaxed in the next section.

Suppose each of the J industries located in the metropolitan area has a Cobb-Douglas production function with constant returns to scale. There are three factors of production: land (L), capital (K) and public services (E).[b] The production function for industry j takes the form,

$$Q_j = L^{\alpha j} E^{\beta j} K^x \qquad (x = 1 - \alpha_j - \beta_j) \tag{6.3}$$

Firms' desired level of property use relative to public services use is determined by a cost minimization procedure. The firm minimizes the Lagrangian,

$$P_L L + P_K K + P_E E - \lambda(L^{\alpha j} E^{\beta j} K^x - Q_j) \qquad (x = 1 - \alpha_j - \beta_j) \tag{6.4}$$

where P_E is a cost price for public services and P_L and P_K are yearly rental

[b]Labor is left out of the production function on the assumption that the amount of labor used in production does not vary with firm location. However the production function could be expanded to include labor without changing any of the results developed in the paper.

rates for land and capital. The first-order conditions for this expression show that relative expenditures on each factor of production should be in proportion to their exponents in the production function. Total yearly expenditure should therefore be equal to

$$P_L L + P_K K + P_E E = P_E E \left(1 + \frac{\alpha_j}{\beta_j} + \frac{1 - \alpha_j - \beta_j}{\beta_j} \right)$$

$$= P_E E \left(\frac{1}{\beta_j} \right) \tag{6.5}$$

The cost of public services, C_j is equal to $P_E E$. The value of property used by the firm is equal to the capitalized value of its yearly (perhaps implicit) expenditures on land and capital, or

$$F_{ij} = \frac{P_L L + P_K K}{r} \tag{6.6}$$

The interest rate, r, is assumed to be the same for all firms.

Substituting these definitions into (6.5) results in an expression for the firm's desired ratio of local service costs to property use.

$$\left(\frac{C_j}{F_{ij}} \right)^* = \frac{\beta_j r}{1 - \beta_j} \tag{6.7}$$

The ratio of public services use to property use required by each community is $C_j/F_{ij} = t_i$, from (6.1).[c] It was established previously that a firm in a perfectly competitive industry would not locate in a community if the firm's desired property use level, F_{ij}^*, were greater than or less than the community's required level, F_{ij}. Therefore the condition for firms in industry j to enter community i is

$$t_i = \frac{\beta_j r}{1 - \beta_j} \tag{6.8}$$

If communities could bargain individually with each firm, they could agree on a total tax payment equal to C_j to be paid via a special property tax rate separately determined for each firm entering each community. Under these circumstances any firm could enter any community, regardless of its desired property-use level. However we wish to explore the more realistic case in which tax rates are not variable, but are exogenous for the marginal firm entering a community. Then not all industries can enter any one community. Rather, only firms in an industry demanding the proper level of

---

[c]If firms in an industry produce with constant returns to scale, then the community can set a variable property consumption requirement $F_{ij}(Q_j) = C_j(Q_j)/t_i$. The ratio $C_j(Q_j)/F_{ij}(Q_j)$ is constant as long as public services are produced by the community also with constant returns to scale.

public services relative to total expenditures can enter a given community. It is possible that zero, one, or more industries might have the proper β_j level, but in general firms from only one industry rather than a heterogeneous mix of firms would enter any particular community.

Suppose industries and communities are separately ranked on the basis of their β_j and t_i levels, from lowest to highest. The ranking of communities is by residential tax rates, since under neutral zoning the entry of firms does not affect these tax rates. Communities having the lowest tax rate might be those with the highest levels of residential property per household or those with a high fraction of households without children. Industries having the lowest β_j levels might be office- and research-oriented sellers of services, while heavy manufacturing firms would place at the high end of the β_j scale.[d]

Since t_i and β_j are positively related in (6.8), firms with low public service demands tend to locate in low tax communities, while firms with high public service demands locate in high tax communities. Firms have no way of paying for local services other than through property taxes. Therefore firms that are heavy consumers of local services can only pay for what they consume by moving to communities which—for other reasons—have high tax rates. They are zoned out of low tax communities.

As an example, suppose in a metropolitan area there are 100 communities with 100 different tax rates, but only 25 different industries. Suppose also that the relative variation in tax rates is wider than the variation over values of β_j, so that

$$t_i > \frac{\beta_j r}{1 - \beta_j} \qquad \text{and} \qquad t_i < \frac{\beta_j r}{1 - \beta_j}$$

for the maximum and the minimum values, respectively, of t_i and β_j. Then communities with the highest and lowest tax rates have no firms, due to choice of the firms at the high end and zoning by the communities at the low end. In the middle part of the range, there is a tendency for all firms within a single industry to cluster in one community, since a single community has the best tax rate for each industry. This community's tax rate may be greater than or equal to $\beta_j r/(1 - \beta_j)$, but cannot be less. If it is less, the community does not allow firms in that industry to enter. If it is greater, the industry pays slightly more than the cost of local services. But all firms in that industry have at least as great a cost disadvantage. Therefore unless firms located outside the metropolitan area can undercut the local firms, they stay in business.

But suppose the favored community is too small or does not wish to

---

[d]The ranking of firms of a β_j scale is complicated by the fact that some services that are provided by the local government in one community may be provided by the firm itself in another.

allow an entire industry to enter. Then some firms are displaced to the community with the next higher tax rate, where they operate at a cost disadvantage. Given constant returns to scale, firms in the lower-tax community can undercut them and supply the entire market. However if U-shaped cost curves prevail, firms in the higher-tax community can survive. They just break even while their competitors make a profit. The low-tax community cannot appropriate any of this rent directly, because its tax rate is fixed. However, the rent should be capitalized into a high F_{ij} value for these firms. The community then can tax the increment in property value.

Finally, if there are more industries than communities, we would expect that whole industries would tend to locate in single communities, with more than one industry per community. If the relative variation in β_j levels at the high end were wider than the variation over t_i levels—that is, $(\beta_j > t_i/(r + t_i)$ for the highest values β_j and t_i—then some industries might not be able to locate in the metropolitan area at all, assuming all land in the area is zoned. These industries' demands for local services are so high that no community exists with a high enough tax rate to enable firms to pay for the local services they would consume.

Thus when perfectly competitive firms allocate themselves to noncentral, neutrally zoned communities, a stratification effect by industry occurs. In general, firms of only one or a few industries, not a heterogeneous mix of firms, locate in any one community. The property use zoning system enables communities to prevent cross-subsidization of firms by residents. It thus enables firms to enter previously residential communities without causing any changes in the property tax rates of those communities.

It should be noted that this result can be generalized from the closed Cobb-Douglas case assumed in (6.3). Suppose instead that firms produce according to an open Cobb-Douglas production function,

$$Q_j = L^{\alpha_j} E^{\beta_j} K^{\delta_j} \tag{6.9}$$

In this case firms would locate in communities according to the condition.

$$\frac{C_j}{F_{ij}} = t_i = \frac{\beta_j r}{\alpha_j + \delta_j} \tag{6.10}$$

Here firms would locate in communities according to their expenditure on local services relative to their expenditures on capital and land. As in the previous case, firms with high relative use of local services in production would locate in high-tax communities while firms with low relative use of local services would locate in low-tax communities.

If all firms have decreasing returns to scale in production ($\alpha_j + \beta_j + \delta_j < 1$), then the outcome in this case should be similar to the outcome in the closed Cobb-Douglas case. However if increasing returns to scale exist in some industries ($\alpha_j + \beta_j + \delta_j > 1$ for some j), then perfect competition cannot exist in these industries and the locational results would change.

Firm Location in a Centrally Defined Metropolitan Area

It is assumed here that firms are located in a centrally defined urban area, where land values are determined by distance from the center. Firms are assumed to produce goods which are exported from the city via a terminal located at the center.

We wish to examine the effect of zoning on firm location in the centrally defined setting. In the previous case of a noncentrally defined urban region, firms selected communities where the firms' own desired level of property use, F_{ij}^*, equalled the communities' required level of property use, F_{ij}. Here, however, firms have a twofold objective. They wish to select a community that requires the correct level of property use. In addition they wish to select a community where land values are such that the firm can operate at minimum cost.

Firms in each industry determine an optimum location from the viewpoint of the capital-land substitution by maximizing the profit function:

$$\pi = (P_j - c_j u) \cdot Q_j(L, E, K) - P_K K(u) - P_L(u) \cdot L(u) - P_E E(u) \qquad (6.11)$$

$Q_j(L, E, K)$ is a general production function. $(P_j - c_j u)$ is the net price received by the firm for its output, where P_j is the constant price of a unit of output at the central terminal and $c_j u$ is the per unit cost of transportation to the terminal. Since firms in each industry compete in a wider market than the metropolitan area, all receive the same price for output delivered to the terminal. In (6.11), it is assumed that firms are able to buy local services at a cost price, P_E, that does not vary with distance. (The assumption is discussed further below.) The price of capital, P_K, is also assumed not to vary with distance, but the price of land depends on distance, $P_L(u)$.

Equation (6.11) is maximized with respect to L, E, K, and u. Substituting the expressions for $\partial\pi/\partial L$, $\partial\pi/\partial E$, and $\partial\pi/\partial K$ into the expression for $\partial\pi/\partial u$ and solving, we get

$$\frac{\partial P_L(u)}{\partial u} = -\frac{c_j Q_j}{L_j(u)} \qquad (6.12)$$

Equation (6.12) gives the amount that firms in industry j can offer for land at various distances from the center while making a constant profit level at all locations. Given the possibility of factor substitution, (6.12) must decline faster than linearly with distance for all industries. However its intercept and slope clearly depend on the cost of transporting each industry's output $(c_j Q_j)$ and the industry's land demand at each distance

(L_j). A different equation of the form of (6.12) exists for each industry and is called its "price of land offer curve."

The set of j price-of-land-offer curves might look as in Figure 6-1. Industries able to operate with the highest capital-land ratios offer the most for land at the center of the metropolitan area; industries needing large amounts of land are outbid for central-area land but can outbid other industries for suburban sites. If landlords are profit maximizers, then they should sell or rent land at each distance to the highest bidder. In that case, an industry must outbid all other industries at some u in order to locate in the metropolitan area. The actual land price function for the metropolitan area is the heavy envelope curve in Figure 6-1.

Figure 6-1 suggests that the capital-land substitution effect should cause firms in different industries to locate in concentric rings around the center of the metropolitan area. Firms in industries that can operate in high-rise buildings or lofts should be observed at the center, while firms using land-intensive production processes should locate in the suburbs.

Residents also have a price-of-land-offer curve, derived by a procedure analogous to (6.12)[e]. They must outbid firms for land at some distance in order to obtain housing sites in the metropolitan area. However, observation suggests that households tend to be intermixed with firms at almost all locations in metropolitan areas, except in the central business district. Thus we might surmise that residents have a price-of-land-offer curve similar in shape and intercept to the envelope curve in Figure 6-1.

Thus the capital-land substitution effect suggests that firms in each industry should prefer to locate in a ring around the center of the city at a particular distance range. Firms stratify themselves by type due to their tradeoff of transportation costs against land prices at various distances. But there is still a second stratification effect. That is the process described at the beginning of the chapter, whereby firms search out communities with the desired property use zoning requirements.

By (6.1), communities' property use requirements are inversely related to their tax rates, or $t_i = C_j/F_{ij}$. Therefore firms in industry j can buy local services at a cost price only if communities with the desired tax rate exist in the ring preferred by these firms. If such communities exist, firms would choose to locate only in the particular communities in their respective rings which have the correct tax rates. All other communities would remain entirely residential. Firms with high local services demand need to locate in high-tax-rate communities and vice versa. Thus we need to know, first, the relation between firms' local service demand levels and their locations, $\beta_j(u)$, and second, the relation between communities' tax rates and their locations, $t_i(u)$. If β_j and t_i both increase with distance, then firms can locate optimally with respect to the capital-land tradeoff and still buy local ser-

[e]See [2, ch. 4] for a fuller discussion of both firms' and residents' price-of-land-offer curves.

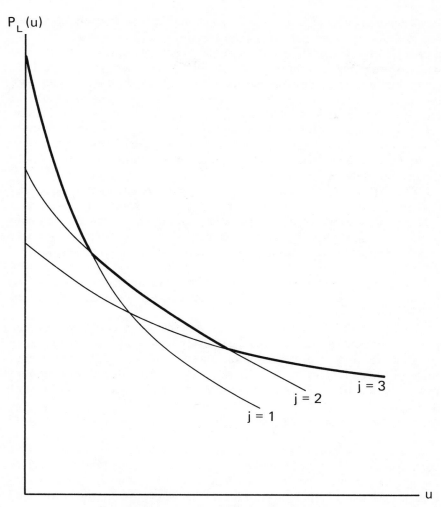

Figure 6-1. Price-of-Land Offer Curves

vices at minimum prices. The same outcome would hold if β_j and t_i both fell with distance or if both were random. However if one relation increased with distance and the other decreased, then firms would have to locate suboptimally with respect to either the capital-land substitution effect or the purchase of local services.

In fact, neither the $\beta_j(u)$ nor the $t_i(u)$ relationships are easy to predict. The slope of $\beta_j(u)$ depends on whether firms with high or low capital-land ratios tend to use more local services in production. We know of no empirical studies of this relationship. The slope of $t_i(u)$ is somewhat easier.

It is a generally accepted result in urban economics that households spending more on housing generally take advantage of lower land prices by locating in the suburbs.[f] Thus property tax payments rise with income and with distance from the center. But demand for local services, particularly education, also rises with income and distance from the center. Therefore the slope of $t_i(u)$ could be either positive or negative. It depends on the size of the income elasticity of demand for housing relative to the income elasticity of demand for local services. In a sample of 64 suburban communities in the New Jersey suburbs of the New York metropolitan area in 1970, the simple correlation of property tax rates and distance from Times Square is −0.09 and insignificant.[g]

Thus if firms' β_j values were also unrelated to distance, we could predict that firms could locate according to their desired capital-land ratios and still find communities with the proper zoning requirements within the optimum ring. This would require that many communities with different tax rates exist in the metropolitan area. Firms in each industry would then concentrate on one or a few communities having the correct location and the correct zoning requirement. Firms would be even more concentrated in a few communities than in the diffuse metropolitan area case discussed earlier.

Finally, it should be noted that the type of tax-rate-distance relation prevailing in a metropolitan area depends on what type of zoning strategy communities pursue. If communities pursue neutral zoning, the entry of firms or residents leaves their tax rates unchanged. But, if communities were able to collect a markup over local service costs from either firms or new residences, the surplus could be used to lower tax rates. In this case non-nuetral zoning would distort the simple tax-rate-distance relation postulated by the model.

Another complication might arise if firms in some industries have objectionable external effects. Under neutral zoning, communities derive no net benefit from the entry of firms. Thus objectionable firms are excluded. These firms then have to locate elsewhere—either in an unzoned central city or outside the metropolitan area entirely. But firms do locate in suburban communities. Thus it is likely that some non-neutral zoning scheme serves as a vehicle by which firms bribe communities to compensate their residents for the firm's external effects.

This complication may further distort the tax-rate-distance relation. First, if communities use fiscal-squeeze zoning with respect to firms, then tax rates may fall. Second, different communities have different degrees of

---

[f]See [2].

[g]Tax rates are significantly related to distance in this and other samples when the influence of other factors is allowed for. But it is the uncorrected relation which would be relevant to firm location choice.

aversion to the entry of firms. Therefore the tax-rate-distance relation is affected by higher-income communities' tendency to exclude firms, since the offered fiscal-squeeze transfer does not compensate them for their environmental loss. If firms entered, then these communities' tax rates would fall. Therefore excluding them pushes the tax-rate-distance relation upward for high-income communities and downward for low-income communities.

In the next sections, we will drop the assumption that firms create no externalities and examine the problem of firm location in a context of fiscal zoning.

Zoning with Firm Externalities

Here, and in the following sections it is assumed that firms adversely affect their surroundings and that communities demand payment in compensation for these effects. The mechanism by which payments are made for externalities is similar to that by which communities might fiscally squeeze firms—property tax payments are demanded over and above the cost to the community of supplying public services to the firms. However the implications for community behavior are somewhat different. A community that tries to maximize total fiscal-squeeze transfers from firms can succeed only if it has monopoly power over the supply of firm sites or if its sites have some production cost advantage over other sites. But a community that demands ''pollution compensating transfers'' in return for firms' adverse external effects could reasonably be operating in a context of competition among communities. It is likely that all communities would demand to be compensated for the external effects of firms. Thus if competition among communities caused the pollution transfer level to be bid down toward zero, the supply of firm sites would also become very small, since most communities would prefer a high quality environment to pollution without compensation. However, if pollution transfer levels were high enough, communities would be induced to allow firms to enter.

This policy is called ''pollution zoning.'' All communities are assumed to inhabit a metropolitan region with a flat price-of-land-distance function.

Figure 6-2 shows community i's social welfare function, which is determined by some mysterious process of aggregating over individual residents' utility function.[h] The indifference curves trade off two ''goods''—environment (ENV_i) and pollution transfers (PT_i). The horizontal axis shows a higher quality environment from left to right. It is assumed that the community can achieve a higher quality environment only by

[h]This diagram and the specification of the community utility function are due to Fischel (see Chapter 5).

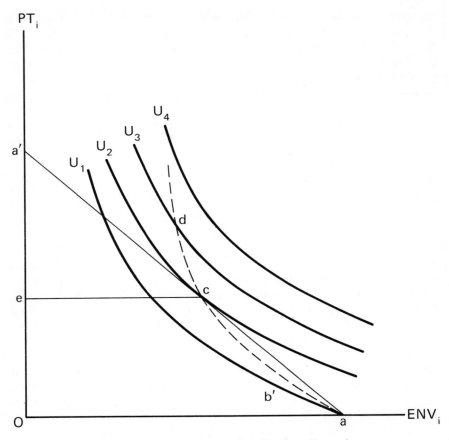

Figure 6-2. Community Social Welfare Function

excluding firms. The pollution transfer is the excess of tax payments over local service costs for all firms located in the community. Thus the total transfer level is

$$PT_i = \sum_j N_{ij} \cdot PT_{ij}$$

where N_{ij} is the number of firms in industry j located in community i and

$$PT_{ij} = t_i(P_K K + P_L L) - C_j$$

for a firm in industry j entering community i. The community can increase its total pollution transfers only by admitting more firms.

Point a is the outcome that would prevail under neutral zoning if the entry of firms downgraded a community's environment. Communities would receive no compensation for their lower-quality environments, therefore they would exclude all firms. This would put them at utility level U_1 with the highest possible environmental quality. Under neutral zoning, firms would only be allowed to enter communities if they had no adverse external effects.

The assumption of previous sections that a community's tax rate is exogenously determined is retained here. Therefore equation (6.1) relating tax rates, costs of local services, and required property use still holds, although the cost of local services now includes a pollution transfer. Equation (6.1) now becomes

$$F'_{ij} = \frac{C_j + PT_{ij}}{t_i} \qquad (6.13)$$

Since communities still cannot negotiate a special tax rate for firms in each industry, they must set new required property use levels for each industry, F'_{ij}.

Suppose all firms in any industry are the same size. Then entry of a firm in any industry is assumed to have the same downgrading effect on the environment regardless of which community it enters, ΔENV_j. This means that environmental effects are additive rather than multiplicative—the entry of a particular type of factory has the same deleterious effect whether the community is a high-quality residential town or an already polluted city. All communities are assumed to know the set of values ΔENV_j for all j; they are published by an environmental protection agency. From knowledge of the ΔENV_j values, and of its own utility function, the community decides on required pollution transfers from firms in each industry that wish to enter the community.

Suppose a community is considering whether to allow firms to enter and at what price. Firms initially offer zero pollution compensating transfers, so the $PT_i - ENV_i$ budget line runs along the horizontal axis. The community then chooses point a in Figure 6-2 where it allows no firms to enter. Since some firms need sites, they offer a positive PT level, thus raising the budget line to some level such as aa'. The community is willing to allow firms to enter if their entry raises community welfare. Thus at various budget lines it determines an offer curve (acd in Figure 6-2) consisting of the locus of tangency points between rising $PT_i - ENV_i$ budget lines and higher community indifference curves. To induce the community to allow more firms to enter, firms must offer higher pollution transfers. At budget line aa', the community moves to point c, where a lower-quality environment and pollution transfers equal to Oe move it to a higher indifference curve. Given the construction of Figure 6-2, the locus of possible outcomes must have a negative slope. A positively sloped locus would imply a better environment and higher transfers simultaneously. But this is a contradiction as these two objectives are achieved respectively by excluding and admitting firms.

The offer curve in Figure 6-2 can be mapped into an upward sloping community supply curve of "environmental quality loss" or pollution, as shown in Figure 6-3. On the vertical axis, property consumption requirements are derived from the pollution transfer levels of Figure 6-2 using (6.13). On the horizontal axis, the supply of "environmental loss" can be translated into a supply curve of firm sites for various types of firms using the technical constants that give the amount of pollution produced by a standard firm in each industry. The community is indifferent among industries at any given pollution level.[i]

Each industry has a demand for sites which can be translated into a demand for "environmental loss" in community i. Given this common denominator, industry demand curves can be aggregated horizontally to give a total demand curve. This is shown in Figure 6-3, where bb is the sum of two demand curves, b_1b_1 and b_2b_2. The overall intersection of supply and demand gives the equilibrium pollution transfer that the community will charge per unit of pollution and the amount of pollution it will accept, P^*. This overall pollution level is allocated among the industries as shown so that $P_1^* + P_2^* = P^*$. Using the technical constants, P_1^* and P_2^* translate into a certain number of sites for standard firms in each industry.

The community does not actually publish a whole supply curve, it only chooses a point on the supply curve. It then sets a schedule of required property consumption levels for firms in each industry, F'_{ij}, and offers to supply sites to as many firms as wish to enter at these levels. The community can however, quickly change its F'_{ij} levels if it perceives demand for sites to be higher or lower than expected at the prevailing transfer levels. Of all the points on the supply curve in Figure 6-3, only one represents an equilibrium where the community has as many entering firms as it wants, given the prevailing pollution transfer levels. A rational community varies its prices until it finds the equilibrium. At equilibrium it enforces some set of property consumption requirements F'_{ij}. Its total pollution transfer from all entering firms is

$$PT_i = \sum_j PT_{ij} \cdot Q_j \quad (PT_{ij} = t_i F'_{ij} - C_j) \quad (6.14)$$

At equilibrium this set of PT_{ij} and F'_{ij} values determines the community's marginal trade-off between pollution transfers and environmental quality.

$$\frac{dPT_i}{dENV_i} = \frac{PT_{ij}}{\Delta ENV_j} \quad (6.15)$$

The PT_{ij} values are determined by the search process, while the environ-

[i]The supply curve could be backward-bending at some level where the community is so wealthy that no amount of pollution transfer would make it indifferent to incurring more pollution. At this level, the income effect would outweigh the substitution effect.

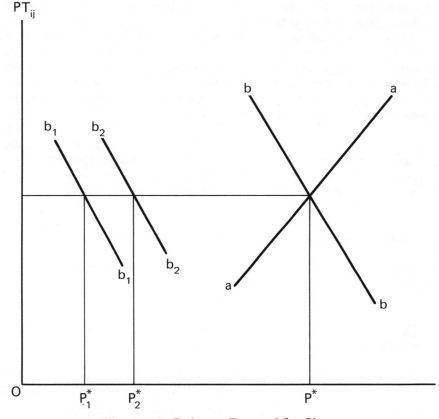

Figure 6-3. Industry Demand for Sites

mental impact of a single firm in each industry, ΔENV_j, is known in advance. Since communities are assumed to be indifferent among firms in each industry given the degree of environmental downgrading, the quantity of $dPT_i/dENV_i$ is the same for all industries. However it varies among communities. Wealthier communities probably value a high quality environment more than poor communities. They demand a higher price for a given degree of extra pollution.

There are many ways that a community might determine the pollution transfers it demands from firms in each industry. It might decide on a transfer of some fixed dollar amount from firms in each industry. This method might be effective if most pollution were unrelated to firms' use of local public services. Alternately the community might base its pollution requirements on firms' use of local public services. For example, if most firm-caused externalities were in the form of water pollution, then firm use of community water or sewer facilities would provide an index on which pollution transfers could be based.

These two systems are discussed separately in the next two sections. It is assumed that all communities in the region shift simultaneously from neutral to pollution zoning, with a resulting relocation of firms among communities. Communities' property tax rates are again assumed to be determined in their residential sectors and are exogenous to the entering firms. However since firms pay pollution transfers to communities, the tax rate could be affected by the entry of firms, depending on how the transfers are used. It is also assumed that communities are able to distribute the transfers to residents successfully without leakage back to the firms. They could do this by spending the transfers on education, but not by lowering their tax rates, since this would benefit firms as well as residents.

Location of Firms under Fixed Dollar Transfers

Suppose a particular community shifting to pollution zoning determines that it will require pollution transfers equal to

$$PT_{ij} = \gamma_{ij} \tag{6.16}$$

where γ_{ij} is a dollar amount. The community's tax rate remains constant at t_i so its property use requirement must rise to

$$F'_{ij} = F_{ij} + \frac{\gamma_{ij}}{t_i} = \frac{C_j + \gamma_{ij}}{t_i} \tag{6.17}$$

The firm must increase its output price enough to raise a transfer payment equal to $\gamma_{ij}/P_j Q_j$ percent of its total revenues. It must also increase its property use level from F_{ij} to F'_{ij}. Factor prices to the firm remain unchanged.

The firm could meet the transfer payment merely by increasing its output price, without changing its production method or its use of any input. Thus if the pollution transfer were extracted simply as a bribe, there would be no incentive for the firm to relocate. However the community also requires the firm to increase its use of capital and land to meet the high property use requirement. The firm's previous method of production is most efficient given the unchanged set of input prices. Therefore it has an incentive to move to another community with a different tax rate, where the property requirement under pollution zoning is not a binding constraint on the firm's choice of production method.

Figure 6-4 shows the firm's original production method at a on isoquant Q_1. Local services are on the vertical axis and other factors of production, capital and land, on the horizontal axis. To stay in the original community,

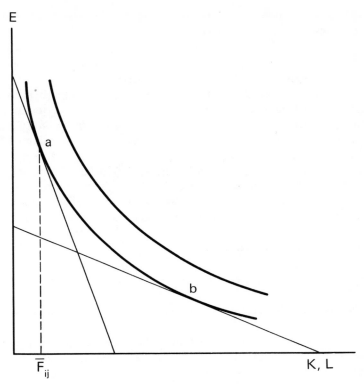

Figure 6-4. Firm Isoquants

the firm must move down the isoquant to some point like *b*, where it uses more capital and land and less local services. Since no change in input prices has occurred, such a shift is not efficient. The firm is better off relocating to another community where it can continue to produce at point *a*.

To find this new community, the firm searches for communities where the property use requirement under pollution zoning is equal to the firm's property use level under neutral zoning. This amount is referred to as $\bar{F}_{ij}$. Since the firm still consumes C_j of local services, the new community must have a higher tax rate than t_i, as the tax rate must raise enough revenue to cover the community's public service expenditures on the firm plus its pollution transfer.

Different communities with the specified property requirement, $\bar{F}_{ij}$, demand different pollution transfers depending on their assessments of the desirability of a good environment relative to extra transfer income from firms. Suppose communities in the $\bar{F}_{ij}$ class set different pollution transfer requirements. All communities' local service expenditures on a firm in industry j are identical and equal to C_j. This implies that the communities have tax rates

$$t_i = \frac{C_j}{\bar{F}_{ij}} + \frac{\gamma_{ij}}{\bar{F}_{ij}} \tag{6.17}$$

Any community with property requirement $\bar{F}_{ij}$ permits the firm to operate efficiently. Therefore the firm chooses among these communities by searching for the one with the lowest required pollution transfer. This community has the lowest tax rate of those in the $\bar{F}_{ij}$ class. All other firms in the industry do the same thing.

Suppose this community has a pollution transfer requirement $\bar{\gamma}_{ij}$ and the minimum tax rate $\bar{t}_i$. This new community's tax rate is higher than the tax rate of the community where the firm was previously located. If both demand an equal pollution transfer, then the new community's tax rate is given by (6.18), while the old community's tax rate is the same as the one it levied under neutral zoning,

$$t_i = \frac{C_j + \gamma_{ij}}{F_{ij}} = \frac{C_j}{\bar{F}_{ij}} \tag{6.19}$$

The tax rate in (6.19) is clearly lower, since γ_{ij} and C_j are the same for both communities and $F_{ij} > \bar{F}_{ij}$.

Thus a firm faced by pollution zoning finds that its optimum response is to search over all communities whose property requirements under pollution zoning are equal to the firm's desired level of property use. It should locate in the community in this class which has the lowest tax rate.

Given that all communities in the metropolitan area employ pollution zoning, this is the best the firm can do. But at best the firm must raise its output price by γ_{ij}/Q_j, since its expenditures are higher while output remains the same. If the industry is perfectly competitive and has a national market, then firms in the industry may not survive in the metropolitan area. Firms in other metropolitan areas may face less stringent zoning and be able to undercut the local firms. (This requires that residents of other areas have a higher tolerance for a polluted environment). However, if the firm produces in a perfectly competitive industry with a metropolitan area market only, then it can survive in a pollution-zoned community. In that case, the best its competitors can do is move to the same community. Firms in the industry that move to this community raise their prices by the smallest possible amount, $\bar{\gamma}_{ij}/Q_j$.

Thus under pollution zoning a concentrated locational allocation of firms again emerges. Suppose at the beginning of the relocation process that firms in each industry all try to crowd into one community. There is excess demand for sites in these communities, which are unwilling to allow all firms to enter at the posted $\bar{F}_{ij}$ level. A realignment of property use requirements takes place, with the minimum tax rate community raising its property requirement somewhat. Other communities with the same tax rate, $\bar{t}_i$, but slightly higher F_{ij} levels have not been considered as possible sites by firms in the industry and have had fewer firms entering than expected. These communities lower their property requirements to $\bar{F}_{ij}$ to induce more firms to enter. Firms in the industry might also enter communities in the $\bar{F}_{ij}$ class that have tax rates slightly higher than t_i. The long-run competitive outcome should be for several communities with tax rates in a narrow range around $\bar{t}_i$ and property requirements in a narrow range around $\bar{F}_{ij}$ to provide enough firm sites for the entire industry to locate in these communities.

Under these assumptions the locational pattern of firms in a pollution-zoned metropolitan area is somewhat different from that of firms in a neutrally zoned metropolitan area. In long-run equilibrium, firms tend to locate in communities with higher tax rates under pollution zoning. Under both regimes, as long-run equilibrium is approached, firms tend increasingly to locate in communities according to their tax rates. However in the pollution-zoning case, firms in a given industry concentrate in only a few communities in the relevant tax class. Other relevant communities may decide they value a high quality environment more than they value pollution compensating transfers at the level offered by the firms. They remain residential. Therefore as long as some communities have a taste for a high quality environment, firms concentrate in fewer communities in the pollution-zoning case than under neutral zoning.

Location of Firms under Local Services-Related Transfers

Suppose communities require pollution transfers proportionate to firms' expenditures on public services,

$$PT_{ij} = \theta_i(P_E E_j) \qquad (6.20)$$

The proportionality factor, θ_i, is different for each community but the same for all industries in a given community. Since tax rates are exogenous, the community raises its property use requirements from F_{ij} to $F_{ij}(1 + \theta_i)$ since

$$t_i = \frac{P_E E_j + PT_{ij}}{F_{ij}(1 + \theta_i)} = \frac{P_E E_j(1 + \theta_i)}{F_{ij}(1 + \theta_i)} \qquad (6.21)$$

The community's shift from neutral to pollution zoning makes local services more expensive and requires firms to use more property. A firm's optimum response is to move down its production isoquant to a position in which it uses less local services but more capital and land. This is shown in Figure 6-4 as a movement from point a to point b. At b, the firm uses less public services but pays a higher unit price for them. The difference in price is the pollution transfer, equal to $\theta_i(P_E E_j)$. At some point such as b, the firm uses enough land and capital to meet the community's property requirement.

The closed Cobb-Douglas production function constrains local services expenditures including the pollution transfer to a constant proportion of total expenditures at any point on the isoquant. Thus local services expenditures plus transfers at point b are still equal to β_j percent of total expenditures by the firm. This means that the firm under pollution zoning should locate in a community with the same tax rate that it chose under neutral zoning, or $t_i = \beta_j r/(1 - \beta_j)$. However the firm may not wish to remain in the same community. It can produce efficiently in any community with tax rate t_i. But its total expenditures must increase from their neutral zoning level to a higher level under pollution zoning. The new expenditure level must be determined.

Suppose land and capital in the production function are combined into one composite factor, G. The production function becomes

$$Q = E^{\beta_j} G^{1-\beta_j} \tag{6.22}$$

Then the relation holds,

$$\frac{G}{E} = \frac{1 - \beta_j}{\beta_j} \frac{P_E}{P_G} \tag{6.23}$$

Substituting for E from (6.22) and solving for G/Q, we get

$$\frac{G}{Q} = \left[\frac{P_E}{P_G} \frac{1 - \beta_j}{\beta_j} \right]^{\beta_j} \tag{6.24}$$

The imposition of pollution zoning raises the price of public services from P_E to $P'_E = P_E(1 + \theta_i)$. Substituting into (6.24), we get

$$\frac{G'}{Q} = \frac{G}{Q} (1 + \theta_i)^{\beta_j} \tag{6.25}$$

Since $(1 + \theta_i)^{\beta_j}$ is greater than one, utilization of the capital-land factor, G, increases under pollution zoning.

By an analogous procedure it can be shown that

$$\frac{E'}{Q} = \frac{E}{Q} (1 + \theta_i)^{\beta_j - 1} \tag{6.26}$$

$(1 + \theta_i)^{\beta_j - 1}$ is less than one, therefore under pollution zoning the firm uses less local services. These shifts in production method enable the firm to meet zoning requirements at a minimum increase in costs.

The firm's total expenditure under pollution zoning is

$$P'(Q) = P_G G + P_E(1 + \theta_i)E' = P_G G(1 + \theta_i)^{\beta_j} + P_E E(1 + \theta_i)^{\beta_j}$$
$$(6.27)$$

Therefore the firm's total expenditure under pollution zoning is $PQ(1 + \theta_i)^{\beta_j}$. Since its output level is unchanged, its breakeven price is

$$P' = P(1 + \theta_i)^{\beta_j} \qquad (6.28)$$

The firm can minimize this price increase by searching over the class of communities with tax rate $t_i = \beta_j r / 1 - \beta_j$ and locating in the one with the lowest pollution transfer proportion, $\overline{\theta}_i$. The community with the proper tax rate and the minimum property level, $\overline{F}_{ij}$, also has the minimum pollution transfer proportion, $\overline{\theta}_i$, since

$$t_i = \frac{P_E E_j(1 + \theta_i)}{\overline{F}_{ij}} \qquad \text{where} \qquad \overline{F}_{ij} = F_{ij}(1 + \overline{\theta}_i) \qquad (6.29)$$

This is the optimum response by all firms in the industry to the imposition of pollution zoning. All firms in the industry try to locate in the community with tax rate t_i and minimum property requirement $\overline{F}_{ij}$. Initially, all firms in the industry try to crowd into the same community, causing excess demand for its sites. The community is not willing to provide sites to all firms in the industry at the posted price $\overline{F}_{ij}$ and increases its property requirement. Other communities with the same tax rate but slightly higher property requirements have fewer entering firms than expected and lower their requirements slightly. At equilibrium, enough sites to accommodate the entire industry are provided by communities that require some uniform property use level slightly above $\overline{F}_{ij}$. The industry concentrates in these communities. Other communities with the same tax rate but higher property requirements remain entirely residential. At the equilibrium pollution transfer level, these communities prefer a high-quality environment. As under fixed dollar transfers, perfectly competitive industries under pollution zoning survive or not in the metropolitan area depending on the size of their market areas and on the tolerance of other metropolitan-area residents for pollution.

Resource Allocation Results of Pollution Zoning

Suppose all industries in the metropolitan area are perfectly competitive and sell their products only within the metropolitan area. All communities follow pollution zoning strategies and collect pollution transfers from firms. In this situation, no firms make positive profits but no industries disappear entirely under pollution zoning. Zoning causes the prices of all goods to rise according to their pollution-creating characteristics. Firms, however, do not retain any portion of the higher prices. These are transferred directly to the community. The incidence of a community's pollution transfer thus falls on households that buy the output of its firms, while the incidence of its property tax falls on resident households in the community. These are two very separate groups.

Pollution zoning as a tax has interesting allocation effects. It is an attempt by communities to charge firms for externalities those firms impose on community residents. The system causes the prices of goods to rise directly in proportion with the pollution-causing characteristics of production processes and inversely with the efficiency of production in each industry. The higher prices of highly polluting, inefficiently produced goods should induce consumers to substitute away from them, and, consequently, less of these goods will be produced. Zoning has the effect of causing the market to value properly the externalities caused by production of each good.

In addition, competition among communities should cause firms to locate in communities where residents' utility loss due to firms' external effects is minimized. Residents of these communities are fully compensated for incurring pollution and the total of pollution transfers paid is minimized. Thus the "full prices" of all goods (including pollution transfers) are minimized.

However, the efficiency of pollution zoning is limited by two factors which may be ignored by rational communities acting in their self-interest. First, communities have an incentive to ignore any firm-caused pollution that spills over their own boundaries and affects the residents of neighboring communities. By ignoring these effects, the community holds down its pollution transfer requirements and gains a competitive advantage vis-a-vis its neighbors. A frequent practice is for communities to zone an area on their borders for firms in order to maximize spillover effects.[j] If the neighboring communities do not retaliate, then the original communities may gain extra pollution transfers for externalities not incurred by their own residents.

Second, pollution zoning does not properly price one set of goods, the local public goods and services produced by the communities themselves. In the absence of special tax levies on these services, they will be underpriced relative to private goods and too much of them will be produced.

Pollution taxes fall on households according to the level and composition of their consumption. But households that reside in communities with firms get back the pollution taxes paid in their community when the community spends them on projects that benefit its residents. Residents of some communities get back more than they pay in taxes and residents of other communities get back less. Generally, residents of poorer com-

[j]This was pointed out to the author by Fischel.

munities should admit more firms than residents of richer communities, assuming that demand for a clean environment rises more than proportionately with income. In this case, zoning acts as a progressive tax. In either case, zoning causes a resource transfer from residents of no-firm communities to residents of communities that do have firms. Residents enjoying high-quality environments are made to pay for them while residents of communities with firms are compensated for the firms' externalities with a transfer that they have voluntarily accepted as full compensation.

Thus a system of pollution transfers can in theory properly price firm-caused externalities. But the systems of fixed dollar transfers and local services-related transfers have different incentive effects. Fixed dollar transfers give firms an incentive to use cleaner production processes. Each firm searches out a community with the optimum property use requirement $\bar{F}_{ij}$ and the minimum tax rate $\bar{t}_i = (C_j + \gamma_{ij})/\bar{F}_{ij}$. Since C_j is constant, the cleaner a firm's production, the lower the pollution transfer that communities demand and the lower the property taxes the firm has to pay. Thus if the firm produces cleanly, it can get into a lower-tax community.

The local services-related pollution transfer system, in contrast, causes firms to move away from use of public services. But if public services are relatively clean to produce and if their pollution is properly priced, then this may be inefficient. The firm that uses more land and capital causes other types of pollution which may not be properly priced. Thus firms may substitute for properly priced water pollution improperly priced air pollution (via use of more capital) or "land pollution" (via extensive and ugly use of land). Effluent charges on all types of pollution would be the obvious solution to this dilemma.

The fixed dollar pollution transfer system provides an interesting illustration in which the classical free-rider problem of public finance does not hold and actors are forced by competition to reveal their preferences. Suppose competition among communities drives down the pollution transfer level. As the level falls, communities drop out of the competition for firms each at the point where its social marginal disutility from extra pollution is equal to its social marginal utility from extra pollution transfers. Below this point, a community excludes all firms, preferring a high-quality environment. It excludes firms by setting a high pollution transfer level. Firms locate in communities that require the minimum pollution transfer level. In these communities, the utility loss due to firms' external effects is at a minimum.

This situation is analogous to the Tiebout model of residential zoning in which consumers reveal their preferences for local public services by choosing to locate in a community with the most preferred public service provision level and tax rate. The Tiebout model applied directly to firm location does not work unless firms have zero external effects. Otherwise communities exclude firms because they would incur pollution without receiving compensation. However, the pollution-zoning case described here provides a Tiebout-type model which applies to the location of firms that do produce externalities. Like the Tiebout residential model, this model is efficient, assuming that firm-caused externalities fall entirely on residents of the community in which the firm locates.

One final source of slippage in this efficient system is the presence in the metropolitan area of a central city which by assumption has no property use requirements. The production costs of goods and services produced in the central city are lower than in the zoned suburbs. There are two possible results from this situation. If the central city provides enough sites for an entire industry to locate there, then the price of that industry's output would not reflect its pollution. This good would have too low a price and too much of it would be produced. The other possibility is that the central city cannot provide enough sites to any industry, so all industries locate either partly or completely in the suburbs. Then the prices of all goods would reflect the suburban pollution taxes, but firms located in the central city would make a positive profit. This profit represents the pollution tax which other firms in the industry must pay, but which the central city does not levy. The central city can recover part of the pollution charge, since it is capitalized into the value of firm sites and can be taxed. To the extent that the city's marginal property tax rate on firms is less than 100 percent, however, central-city residents suffer an income loss relative to suburb residents since they pay pollution transfers on the goods they purchase but do not receive any transfers back. Thus under the system of pollution transfers, central-city residents have too little income and suburb residents too much.

Finally, these results depend on the assumption that the property tax rate in each community is the same for all residents and firms. However, if tax rates could vary, the location equations derived here can be reinterpreted as determining the particular tax rate a community must charge an entering firm to compensate it for incurring the firm's externalities. If separate tax rates could be set for each firm, then firms would not be restricted as to location by their demand for public services. However, there would still be a process of movement by firms toward communities that required the lowest pollution transfers. And some communities would still value their environments enough to bar all firms.

References

[1] Robin Barlow, ''Efficiency Aspects of Local School Finance,'' *Journal of Political Economy* 78 (September 1970): 1028-1041.

[2] Edwin S. Mills, *Urban Economics* (Glenview, Ill.: Scott, Foresman, 1972).

[3] Charles Tiebout, "A Pure Theory of Local Expenditures," *Journal of Political Economy* 64 (October 1956): 416-424.

Index

Agglomeration economies, 140
Ann Arbor, Mich., 106n
Apartment building, 34, 82-84, 88-89, 90
Architectural controls, 34
Assessment, 98, 131, 134, 151-52
Atlanta Ga., 106n

Babcock, Richard, 142n
Barlow, Robin, 175
Bell, John C., 35
Bergen County, N.J., 149, 154
Binghamton, N.Y., 106n
Blacks, 9, 10, 117, 118
Boston, 56n
Buchanan, James, 3, 13, 134n, 142
Building codes, 39n, 120n
Busing, 35

California Supreme Court, 35
Capital gains, 97
Capitalization, 25, 27-28, 42, 85-86, 97-98,
    161-63
Census data, 105-106
Central city, 9, 18-19, 57n, 59-62, 63, 87, 98,
    112, 134n, 200; housing prices, 25-27,
    37, 65, 96; incomes, 112-13; and sub-
    urbs, 108-109; unemployment, 10;
    zoning, 98-99, 134n
Chicago, 56n
Coase, R.H., 32
Cobb-Douglas functions, 52-53, 55, 147, 179,
    196
Coleman Report, 7
Commuting, 10, 62, 123; costs, 58, 93, 103
Congestion costs, 1n, 3, 103
Construction rates, 77-80
Consumer surplus, 64-66, 67, 68, 71
Crime rates, 7, 10
Cumulative districting, 33

Deadweight losses, 17, 61, 64, 66, 99; and
    property taxes, 4, 15, 24, 67; and zon-
    ing, 64
Decatur, Ill., 21-22
Decentralization, 2
DeLeeuw, Frank, 84
Denver, 106n
Derived demand theory, 83
Developments, 43-44, 73, 82; environmental
    costs, 39-41, 48-50
Distance from central city, 21, 22-23, 58-59,
    104, 118, 144, 157, 164; and land

prices, 61, 62; and property tax,
    186-87

Economies of scale, 3, 103, 104, 123
Education, 38-39, 107-108, 112, 186. *See also*
    Schools
Environment, 8, 40, 126; and developments,
    39-41, 48-50; and firms, 38, 121-22,
    123, 142, 188-91; price, 39-41, 48-50,
    127-29, 144, 159-61
Environmental impact study, 120n
Equal protection clause. *See* U.S. Constitu-
    tion, Fourteenth Amendment
Equalization ratios, 150
Euclid v. *Ambler*, 34n
Excise tax, 19, 24, 28
Exclusive districts, 34-35
Externalities, xiii; of industry, 32-33, 121-22,
    136-41, 143, 156, 158, 159, 176; inter-
    community, 4n; and zoning, 32, 34,
    73-74, 187-92

Factories, 81
Farmers, 43, 150
Fifth Avenue Association, 33
Fire service, 7, 145, 159, 176
Firms: location decisions, 8, 119-66, 175-200;
    in metropolitan areas, 8, 175-200. *See
    also* Industry
Fiscal zoning, 6-7, 8, 32; history, 32-36; and
    land values, 80-83
Fiscal-squeeze zoning, 31-32, 38, 40, 43,
    44-48, 55-56, 58, 63-64, 70-71, 72, 75,
    79, 93-94, 98-99, 178-79
Fischel, William A., 8, 198n

Gini coefficients, 18n, 105-106, 108
Goetz, C.J., 13, 142
Greenwich, Conn., 140n

Hamilton, Bruce, 4, 22n, 36-38, 68, 70-71, 96,
    102, 114, 125, 128
Head tax, 5, 17, 18, 101
Health and welfare zoning, 33, 34
Hettich, Walter, 38
High-income households, 46, 48, 87, 96; and
    suburbs, 9-10, 59, 108, 187
Honolulu, 21-22
Households, 87; consumption, 16-17; loca-
    tion choice, 10-11, 15-16, 36, 56-73,
    99; size, 11, 15-16
Housing: central city, 19, 37, 64; consump-

203

Editors' Note

We dedicate this book to our former friend and colleague, Neil David Sosnow, who died tragically in an accident in Princeton in 1973. We regard these essays as an appropriate, if inadequate, memorial to Neil, who was himself greatly concerned with and active in the analysis of public policy. Shortly before his death, Neil completed a provocative study of the principles of income redistribution, "Optimal Policies for Income Redistribution," which appeared posthumously in the May 1974 issue of the *Journal of Public Economics.*

Born in New York City, Neil was an outstanding product of the public elementary schools and Francis Lewis High School in the borough of Queens. He attended Queens College of the City University of New York, from which at the age of 20 he graduated *cum laude* and with departmental honors in economics. Following two years of teaching in an elementary school in Brooklyn, he began his graduate studies at Princeton in 1970. During his three years at Princeton, Neil was the recipient of a number of awards, including a Proctor Honorific Fellowship, a competitive graduate school award given only to the most outstanding graduate students irrespective of department. In addition, he taught an undergraduate class in urban labor markets.

We have felt deeply the loss of Neil's simulating mind and warm friendship and hope this book, along with the Neil Sosnow Memorial Library for graduate study in economics at Princeton, will keep alive our memory of him and his dedication to the cure of the social and economic ills of our times.

About the Editors and Contributors

Edwin S. Mills received the Ph.D. in economics from the University of Birmingham, England, in 1956. He is professor of economics at Princeton University. His professional interests are urban and environmental economics.

Wallace E. Oates received the Ph.D. in economics from Stanford University in 1965. He is associate professor of economics at Princeton University. His professional interests are environmental economics and public finance.

William Fischel received the Ph.D. in economics from Princeton University in 1973. He is assistant professor of economics at Dartmouth College. His professional interests are metropolitan government consolidation, industrial location patterns and land use controls.

Bruce Hamilton received the Ph.D. in economics from Princeton University in 1972. He is assistant professor of economics at Johns Hopkins University. His professional interests are local public finance and urban economics.

David Puryear received the Ph.D. in economics from Princeton University in 1974. He is assistant professor of economics at Syracuse University. His professional interests are public finance and urban economics.

Michelle White received the Ph.D. in economics from Princeton University in 1973. She is assistant professor of economics at the University of Pennsylvania. Her professional interests are urban economics and public finance.